Zimbabwe's Lost Decade

By the same Author

The One-Party State and Democracy
The Zimbabwe Debate
(co-edited with I. Mandaza, 1991, Harare: Sapes)

Democracy, Civil Society and the State
(1995, Harare: Sapes)

Labour Markets and Migration Policy in Southern Africa
(1997, Harare: Sapes)

Labour Regimes and Liberalization
The restructuring of state–society relations in Africa
(co-edited with B. Beckman, 2001, Harare: UZ Press)

Striking Back
The Labour movement and the Post-colonial State 1980–2000
(co-edited with B. Raftopoulos, 2001, Harare: Weaver Press)

Consolidating Democratic Governance in Southern Africa
The Case of Zimbabwe
(with S. Chawatama, C. Mangongera, N. Musekiwa and C. Ndoro, 2007, Johannesburg: EISA)

Trade Unions and Party Politics
Labour Movements in Africa
(co-edited with B. Beckman and S. Buhlungu, 2010, Cape Town: HRSC)
Winner of the Book of the Year Award of 2010 of the International Labour History Association

When a State turns on its Citizens
Political culture and institutionalized violence
(2011, Johannesburg: Jacana Media)

Zimbabwe's Lost Decade

Politics, Development & Society

Lloyd Sachikonye

Weaver Press
PO Box A1922
Avondale
Harare
Zimbabwe
www.weaverpresszimbabwe.com

Cover: Danes Design, Harare
Typeset by forzalibro designs
Printed by Mazongororo Paper Converters, Harare

The author and publishers would like to express their gratitude
to the Open Society Initiative for Southern Africa for the support
they have given to Weaver Press in the development of this title.

ISBN 978-1-77922-171-1

for John, my father,
and Anna, my wife,
for their love and generosity over the years

List of Acronyms

ACHPR   African Council for Human and People's Rights
ACPD   African Community Publishing & Development
ANC   African National Congress
ANC   African National Council
AIPPA   Access to Information and Protection of Privacy Act
AU   African Union
BACOSSI   Basic Commodities Supply Side Intervention
BSAC   British South African Company
BIPPA   Bilateral Investment Promotion and Protection Agreement
CCJPZ   Catholic Commission for Justice and Peace in Zimbabwe
CSVR   Centre for the Study of Violence and Reconciliation
CIO   Central Intelligence Organisation
CSOs   Civil Society Organisations
CHRA   Combined Harare Residents Association
CFU   Commercial Farmers Union
COMESA   Common Market for Eastern and Southern Africa
CAZ   Conservative Alliance of Zimbabwe
COPAC   Constitutional Parliamentary Committee
CSU   Counselling Services Unit
CZC   Crisis Zimbabwe Coalition
DP   Democratic Party
DRC   Democratic Republic of Congo
DFID   Department for International Development
EDF   European Development Fund
EISA   Electoral Institute for Sustainable Democracy in Africa
EMCOZ   Employers' Confederation of Zimbabwe
ESAP   Economic Structural Adjustment Programme
ESC   Electoral Supervisory Commission
EU   European Union
FCTZ   Farm Community Trust of Zimbabwe
FTLR   Fast Track Land Reform
FPTP   First Past the Post
FAO   Food and Agricultural Organisation

FROLIZI	Front for the Liberation of Zimbabwe
GAPWUZ	General Agricultural and Plantation Workers Union of Zimbabwe
GPA	Global Political Agreement
GNU	Government of National Unity
GDP	Gross Domestic Product
IFIs	International Financial Institutions
IMF	International Monetary Fund
JAG	Justice for Agriculture
JOC	Joint Operations Council
LRF	Legal Resources Foundation
MDC	Movement for Democratic Change
MDC-T	Movement for Democratic Change-Tsvangirai
MDC-M	Movement for Democratic Change-Mutambara
MPOI	Mass Public Opinion Institute
Misa-Zimbabwe	Media Institute of Southern Africa–Zimbabwe
NAGG	National Alliance of Good Governance
NCA	National Constitutional Assembly
NDP	National Democratic Party
NANGO	National Association of Non-Governmental Organisations
NUST	National University of Science and Technology
ODA	Overseas Development Administration
OM	Operation Murambatsvina
ONRHI	Organ of National Reconciliation, Healing and Integration
PCC	People's Caretaker Council
PF	Patriotic Front
PF ZAPU	Patriotic Front Zimbabwe African Peoples Union
PR	Proportional Representation
POSA	Public Order and Security Act
RBZ	Reserve Bank of Zimbabwe
RENAMO	Mozambique Resistance Movement
SADCC	Southern African Development Coordination Conference
SADC	Southern Africa Development Community
SADC RHDR	SADC Regional Human Development Report
SALO	Southern Africa Liaison Office
SPT	Solidarity Peace Trust
SRANC	Southern Rhodesia African National Congress
TNDP	Transitional National Development Plan
UANC	United African National Council

UDI	Unilateral Declaration of Independence
UNDP	United Nations Development Programme
UNECA	United Nations Economic Commission for Africa
UNICEF	United Nations Children's Fund
USD	United States Dollar
UZ	University of Zimbabwe
WFP	World Food Programme
WOZA	Women of Zimbabwe Arise
ZANLA	Zimbabwe African National Liberation Army
ZANU	Zimbabwe African National Union
ZANU-PF	Zimbabwe African National Union-Patriotic Front
ZAPU	Zimbabwe African People's Union
ZCTU	Zimbabwe Congress of Trade Unions
ZEC	Zimbabwe Electoral Commission
ZESN	Zimbabwe Election Support Network
ZFTU	Zimbabwe Federation of Trade Unions
ZHDR	Zimbabwe Human Development Report
ZHR NGO Forum	Zimbabwe Human Rights NGO Forum
ZIDERA	Zimbabwe Democracy and Economic Recovery Act
ZLHR	Zimbabwe Lawyers for Human Rights
ZIMPREST	Zimbabwe Programme for Economic and Social Transformation
ZINASU	Zimbabwe National Students Union
ZIPRA	Zimbabwe People's Revolutionary Army
ZNA	Zimbabwe National Army
ZNLWVA	Zimbabwe National Liberation War Veterans Association
ZPP	Zimbabwe Peace Project
ZUD	Zimbabwe Union of Democrats
ZUM	Zimbabwe Unity Movement
ZWD	Zimbabwe Dollar

List of Tables & Boxes

Preface & Acknowledgements

Zimbabwe occupies a special place in African politics and international relations. Its politics and socio-economic policies have been subjects of intense national introspection as well as international debate over the years. One sign of the preoccupation was the outpouring of theses and publications in the form of books, polemical tracts, reports and journal articles over the past quarter century. It was scarcely surprising that the country hogged the headlines for many years. Zimbabwe was a major ideological issue for those who believed that it valiantly stood against imperialism and neo-colonialism, and those that pointed out that it trampled basic civil rights and values through repression of its people.

Its octogenarian leader for more than 30 years, the articulate and combative Robert Mugabe symbolised the fortunes and misfortunes, the rise and decline, of a country that was described as a 'jewel' when it attained independence in 1980. Here was a rare African leader who stood up against the powerful countries of the West, reminded them of their colonial past and railed against their imperialist machinations. But here was also a leader who plunged his country into economic decline and poverty, violence and widespread trauma. It would be fashionable but simplistic to explain the rise and decline of Zimbabwe solely in terms of the leadership and role of Robert Mugabe. Historical, structural and systemic factors should loom large in any explanation. But it would be naïve to ignore the strong imprint of Mugabe's policies, decisions and personality on the direction and fortunes of the country.

There were initially high hopes for the potential and future of Zimbabwe at independence in 1980. With one of the best infrastructures as well as impressive literacy and education levels, the country was the second most industrialised country on the continent. Endowed with a strong agrarian base and a relatively skilled and educated population, the prospects for the country's development were much better than elsewhere in Africa. There were even hopes for a possible Zimbabwean model of transition to industrialised development. Furthermore, there was a belief that Zimbabwe would learn from governance and development mistakes made by its neighbours and peers in Africa. It did not.

In less than two decades, Zimbabwe became mired in deep political and economic crises. Towards the end of the third decade of independence, the economy has collapsed, transforming the country into a basket case. Between 2000 and 2008, Zimbabwe effectively developed into a repressive authoritarian state in which state-sanctioned violence was a major instrument of containing dissent and manipulating the electoral system.

How can we explain the country's decline during these 'lost decades'? Less endowed countries, including its neighbours, have managed their politics, economics and societies better while Zimbabwe stagnated or declined. To the west, Botswana experienced one of the longest sustained booms while to the north, Zambia steered a largely democratic transition involving changes of government. How should Zimbabwe's 'exceptionalism' be explained? It is clearly not sufficient to carve some 'conspiracy theory' in which the West and sanctions play a dominant role in Zimbabwe's slide into authoritarianism and underdevelopment.

This book seeks to explore the factors that contributed to the entrenchment of authoritarianism, underdevelopment and poverty during the lost decades. It attempts a sustained critique of the post-colonial state and its leadership but does not spare the white colonial state which laid the conditions for a fundamentalist version of African nationalism in the 1960s. It is argued that Zimbabwe's lost decades date from the 1950s when opportunities for moderate African nationalism and peaceful transfer of power were squandered. As is argued elsewhere in relation to the culture of political violence, the roots of narrow and exclusive nationalism underpinned by intolerance of diversity and opposition were laid during that period. While independence provided opportunities for notable progress in the social sector (chiefly in education and health), mismanagement in later decades made such progress unsustainable. Due to lack of coherence in policies, there was a large mismatch between education and opportunities for employment. Developments in human capital formation were cancelled out by large-scale migration in which a quarter of the country's population participation departed. Zimbabwe became a training ground for teachers, nurses, doctors, engineers, accountants and technicians for other countries including those in the West. Capacity in public and private sectors shrank. During these lost decades, Zimbabwe declined from middle- to low-income status.

Drawing from a broad political economy framework, this book explores the interplay between politics and socioeconomic policies, and wider changes in society. The first part of the book analyses the various dimensions of the national question (Chapter 1) and the composition and tendencies of the inherited state (Chapter 2) before assessing the role of political parties (Chapter 3).The pivotal position of the electoral and constitutional frameworks is then assessed (Chapter 4) while observing how their defectiveness largely contributed to the longevity of authoritarianism and dictatorship.

The second part of the book explores the effects of political decisions and management, with specific reference to the economy (Chapter 5), and its agrarian base (Chapter 6). The steep decline during the period between 2000 and 2008 is assessed in considerable detail, and explains the slow recovery in the post-2008 period. Profound developments in state–civil society relations (as surveyed in Chapter 7) reflected authoritarian politics as well as pressure for democratic reform. Values and norms in the wider Zimbabwean society could not remain unaffected by these conditions of authoritarianism and decline, corruption and violence as captured in Chapter 8. Against this broad background of mediocrity and decline, international ostracism and regional anxiety, the country's foreign policy weakened rather than strengthened, as we argue in Chapter 9.

Zimbabwe's lost decades relates to opportunities wasted during the period under review. Other countries used their opportunities wisely or prudently and have since forged ahead in their development and democratization. It will take a candid re-assessment and self-criticism for Zimbabwe to identify where it made mistakes. It will take brave and inspired leadership as well as collective renewal and action to seize opportunities to build sustainable development and democracy. This will necessarily entail a paradigm shift as the conclusion to the book indicates.

The essays constituting the present chapters were written over a period of a quarter century. They were largely based on individual research but in several instances on collective work as appropriately acknowledged in the respective part of the text. The thread that links the various chapters relates to a commitment to values and aspirations for democracy, development and peace in my country. This commitment and hope animate our critique of policies and measures designed and implemented during the lost decades. Zimbabwe will recover from the lost decades. Another Zimbabwe,one that enjoys prosperity, peace and democracy, is possible.

In a book whose component parts were written over several decades, it is almost impossible to acknowledge those to whom I am indebted. My intellectual and institutional pedigree should be acknowledged. My intellectual formation owes to early education in Zimbabwe, university education at Ahmadu Bello University in northern Nigeria in 1975–1981, and doctoral research at Leeds University in northern England in 1985–1989. Many of the friendships and intellectual interests nurtured during those years have endured a lifetime. Since 1983, my institutional home has been the Institute of Development Studies, formerly the Zimbabwe Institute of Development Studies. Many colleagues have directly and indirectly shaped my thinking on development and democracy. I am profoundly grateful to the following for their help, encouragement and solidarity over the decades:

Godfrey Kanyenze, Sakhela Buhlungu, Bjorn Beckman, Brian Raftopoulos, Godfrey Magaramombe, Steve Kibble, Peter Gibbon, Adebayo Olukoshi, Yusuf Bangura, Jibrin Ibrahim, Hashim Yahaya, Gunilla Andrae, Ibbo Mandaza, Sarah Bracking, Andries Rukobo, Eldred Masunungure, Khabele Matlosa, Said Adejumobi, Abdala Bujra, Karen Colvard, Tawana Kupe, Tony Reeler, David Moore, Lionel Cliffe, Davie Malungisa, Donald Chimanikire, Elinor Sisulu, Ray Bush and Jan Burgess.

Finally, I am sincerely thankful to the Open Society Initiative for Southern Africa (OSISA) and to the publishers, Weaver Press, for their support and editorial inputs respectively.

LMS
April 2012

Part I

1

Colonialism, Nationalism & the National Question

Introduction

This volume wrestles with the question of why and how Zimbabwe 'lost' five decades of development and democracy. This was not a conscious decision on the part of either the settler colonial or post-colonial political elites. The wasted decades were an unintended outcome of policies and measures formulated and implemented between 1958 and 2008. These years signify the demise of a liberal colonial regime under Garfield Todd which gave way to a series of white supremacist regimes from 1958 to 1979. Significantly, the conjuncture of the late 1950s also marked a strong shift to radical African nationalism whose tendencies included dependence on violence for political mobilisation.

The struggle between settler colonialism and African nationalism reverberated well beyond 1980, its consequences including the violent land reform of 2000-03 and the deepening of state authoritarianism up to 2008. In order to develop a deeper understanding of political and social processes after Independence, their roots in colonialism and formative nationalism should be identified and their importance assessed. This is why an understanding of the significance of colonialism is indispensable. Colonialism conditioned the form and orientation of African nationalism which mobilised the mass force for independence. We therefore need to explore how and why colonialism triggered this massive social and political movement.

The Legacy of Settler Colonialism

The fashionable approach to colonialism has been to denounce it as unjust, exploitative and incorrigible. Like apartheid, it has few, if any, defenders in the contemporary world. A system imposed by imperial powers in the nineteenth and twentieth centuries, colonialism came under universal condemnation especially after the Second World War. The condemnation of colonialism in general and in pre-independence Zimbabwe in particular was not shared by its ideologists and practitioners. The ideologists, some would say apologists, of colonialism trumpeted it as a progressive force for modernisation in backward, underdeveloped societies.

Consider the benefits of colonialism as enunciated by one of the eminent settler colonial leaders:

> *Blacks were happy to have and, for the first time in their lives, earn money which enabled them to join in the excitement of this new adventure of purchasing and selling – something they had not previously known. Land was plentiful, so there was no problem over crop growing, which again provided an opportunity to earn money. Moreover, because of the primitive agricultural implements used by black people, which were wooden as opposed to the iron used by the white man, they were concentrated on light sandy or loam soils, which they found easier to work. The white man, on the other hand, preferred the heavier soils. (Smith 1997:2)*

The rationale for colonisation was that it introduced a transformation in production processes and relations of exchange, in short, capitalist relations, that involved trade and wage-labour from which Africans began to benefit on an extensive scale. The mission of colonialism was further elaborated upon in glowing terms:

> *Britain, a small island … this mighty atom which had spread its western Christian civilisation over half the globe, introducing proper standards of freedom, of justice, and the basics of education, health and hygiene. And right now, here in the centre of southern Africa, the dark continent, men of British stock were once more carrying the torch on one of the few frontiers yet to be civilised. (Ibid.:3)*

Colonialism was a 'civilising' mission, according to this perception. It was also a 'development' mission for backward societies. The views of Ian Smith are as candid, blunt and unvarnished as you can get.

Other related perspectives from the colonial school are a little more sophisticated. One such a perspective on the first 60 years of colonialism was that whites had achieved a 'pretty good record':

> *economic development was extraordinarily widespread, and achieved without any cost to the British taxpayer or any free handouts from anyone else. Public administration was efficient and entirely incorrupt. African education and rural development were more advanced than in other, non-self-governing colonies. The whites' attitude of racial superiority was no doubt arrogant, but there was respect for justice and the rule of law, and no great cruelty. (Holderness 1985:5)*

Although they differed on political strategy toward African nationalism, both writers cited above shared a broad belief in the colonial 'civilising' and 'development' mission. To some extent, their claims about investment in development were borne out by the facts. At independence in 1980, Zimbabwe was the second most industrialised country in Africa, and had some of the best infrastructure in the form of roads, dams and hydro-electric plants. Literacy levels were amongst the highest in Africa; education and health services were also relatively advanced. Nevertheless, this model of colonial development hid within it various injustices and inequalities which included skewed access to natural resources and social services.

Despite its seeming advances in the social and economic fields, nothing quite succeeded in erasing the view that colonialism was an imposed domination from outside. Memories of conquest in 1893, and the crushing of uprisings (*zvimurengas*) in Matabeleland and Mashonaland in 1896 remained fresh. The grabbing of land and the looting of livestock were festering sores of injustice. The implementation of racial discrimination, although not as systematic and rigid as apartheid in South Africa, caused a great deal of humiliation and resentment. The combination of these factors sowed the seeds of a backlash in the form of a nationalist movement for independence; initially, this was small and moderate, but it transformed into a massive and radical force from the late 1950s, as we explain below.

However, before concluding our discussion on its significance and legacy, we need to stress that colonialism in Rhodesia was of a special variety. Unlike most colonies in Africa, Rhodesia was not under direct British tutelage. Indeed between 1890 and 1923, it was under the rule of the British South Africa Company (BSAC), originally founded by Cecil Rhodes. White settlers were in direct charge of political and economic affairs between 1923 (when Britain granted them Responsible Government status) and 1980. The detachedness of Britain was a prominent feature of the relationship with the Colony. Misunderstandings and mutual recriminations marked the relationship in the 1960s over a new constitution and the demand for independence by the settler government:

> *British power and influence over the Colony was very limited, as became clearer in the 1960s and 1970s. The option of sanctions was pursued following UDI in 1965, but the use of force to quell the rebellion was not. In sum, however, although the expectations of the settlers and nationalists regarding*

the British role were different, both sides were disappointed. Both saw Britain's limited involvement as an abdication of responsibility, a theme which resonated strongly over the land question, especially after Independence.

The turning point for settler colonialism was the late 1950s, with the decisive shift to white supremacist ideology and practice under Edgar Whitehead. This was consolidated under the tenure of the Rhodesia Front during the leadership of Winston Field and Ian Smith, and found expression in exclusive white nationalism. But white nationalism resorted to increased state repression in the form of widespread detention of African nationalists and the successive banning of their parties – the Southern Rhodesia African National Congress (SRANC), National Democratic Party (NDP), Zimbabwe African Peoples' Union (ZAPU), Zimbabwe African National Union (ZANU) and the People's Caretaker Council (PCC). This repression had the consequence of radicalising African nationalists, and convincing them of the need to take up arms. White extremism begat black extremism. Yet this eventuality was neither inevitable nor unavoidable:

> *the general election of 1958 put an end to the possibility of new measures being implemented ... and thus an end to a unique opportunity which white Rhodesians had possessed as a sort of gift from history. Improbably, that small group of people had held in their hands a key to the peaceful evolution of politics in Africa, and at this point they had thrown it away. (Holderness 1985:6)*

As we argue below, it was not only white liberals who lost out to white extremists. Moderate African nationalists and democrats were sidelined by radical leaders who had no compunction about using violence (Scarnecchia 2008; Sachikonye 2011). The contest between the two nationalisms and extremisms would lead to more than 20,000 deaths in the liberation war between 1966 and 1979. The two main protagonists were only able to reach an agreement under a British umpire at Lancaster House in 1979, but the social contract did not last long. It collapsed in 1982 with the descent into a civil war in Matabeleland and into authoritarianism in 2000 with large-scale land reappropriation and state violence against the political opposition.

The Legacy of African Nationalism

For a society that had experienced the trauma of conquest, land expropriation and racial discrimination, nationalism provided a necessary

4

counter-response and the possibility of self-determination. It was a powerful force that swept through colonies from India to Indonesia, from Algeria to Mozambique, from Guyana to Jamaica. Anti-colonialism found strong expression in nationalism, which was a multi-class force for self-determination. While specific national experiences followed different trajectories, the ideology and idiom of nationalism shared basic similarities. The Zimbabwean nationalist ideology and trajectory was no exception.

As we explain below, there was a progression from the moderate nationalism of the 1930s to the early 1950s. The late 1950s witnessed a qualitative change due to both external and domestic factors. The granting of independence to Ghana and the leading role that its leader, Kwame Nkrumah, played in propagating pan-Africanism and supporting nationalist movements were significant developments. Domestically, white intransigence sparked a drift to radical nationalism.

Let us briefly trace the evolution of African nationalist thought before we reflect on the vicissitudes that the Zimbabwean nationalist movement experienced in the 1960s and 1970s. A major exponent of African nationalism was Ndabaningi Sithole, who argued that:

> African nationalism is directed against European domination, and not against the white man .... What the African wants is not to drive away the white man, but to have his full independence .... The physical presence of the white man in Africa is welcome, but his domination is unwelcome. (Sithole 1958:25)

Sithole went further:

> the basic ingredients that go to make up African nationalism may be enumerated as the African's desire to participate fully in the central government of the country, his desire for economic justice that recognises fully the principle of 'equal pay for equal work' regardless of the colour of his skin, his desire to have full political rights in his country, his dislike of being treated as a means for the white man's end and his dislike for the laws of the country which prescribe for him a permanent position of inferiority as a human being...The present African nationalism is, paradoxically, the child of white supremacy, the product of an exclusive policy. (Ibid.)

Nationalism was thus the antithesis of white supremacy and colonialism.

There is remarkable consistency in nationalist thought and prescriptions during the late 1950s and early 1960s. For instance, the SRANC, which was prominent in the 1950s before the emergence of the NDP,

ZAPU and ZANU, emphasised that it was opposed to tribalism and racism in its imagination of an integrated nation founded on 'true partnership regardless of race, colour and creed'. The NDP stressed the attainment of freedom through the granting of 'one man, one vote' for all inhabitants of the country. ZAPU was the first party to use 'Zimbabwe' in its name and emphasised 'one man, one vote' as the foundation of democratic govern-ance and 'majority rule' in the country.

In a new addition to the discourse on nationalism, ZANU – which split from ZAPU in 1963 – proclaimed that it would establish 'a nationalist, democratic, socialist and pan-Africanist republic'. Within a period of ten years, one could observe how nationalist thought had mutated from a mildly moderate to a broader and more radical version.

But to what extent did the African nationalist parties practice what they preached? We examine this issue in relation to the question of national unity and democracy largely because these issues carried resonance in the following 50 years. National unity and democracy would prove elu-sive for many years. In other words, a major legacy of African nationalism has been its limitation in forging sustainable national unity as well as authentic democracy.

The first test was whether the nationalist movement itself would remain united during the struggle for independence. It failed the test. As we have observed elsewhere, not only did divisions in the movement weaken the nationalists but violence between them dissipated their energies (Sachikonye 1996, 2011). For example, the ZAPU-ZANU split had reverberations in the labour movement and other sectors of society. This split in 1963 preceded later splits and fragmentation such as those that led to the formation of the Front for the Liberation of Zimbabwe (FROLIZI) and the United African National Council (UANC). Such fragmentation had 'a very negative impact on the crystallisation and formation of a cohesive national identity called "Zimbabwe"' (Ndlovu-Gatsheni 2010).

Nationalist leaders themselves conceded that the inter-party conflicts gave advantage to the colonial authorities who were not averse to stok-ing the fires to the conflicts (Nyagumbo 1980; Nkomo 2001; Tekere 2007). The causes of the conflicts included ethnicity, regionalism and political ambition. National unity suffered, with disastrous consequences. This is not to suggest that attempts were not made to address the disunity. The formation of the Patriotic Front (PF) in 1976 and the setting up of a Government of National Unity in 1980 were such attempts, but they both collapsed amidst mutual recriminations between ZANU-PF and PF-ZAPU. The 1987 Unity Accord between the two parties provided a platform for unity, which lasted until Dumiso Dabengwa broke away in 2008 to form a rump of ZAPU.

Nor has the opposition movement been spared internal conflicts. For instance, in 2005 the MDC split into two parties, a split which in retrospect cost it the 2008 election. Once again, ethnicity and personal power struggles featured strongly. Even ZANU-PF itself has suffered a split (that of Tekere in 1989) as well an uneasy co-existence of several factions since 2004. To observe that unity has been elusive to parties and to nationalism is not, however, to argue against diversity of parties and different strands of political expression and representation. Diversity can be a source of strength in the construction of a nation and state.

It is when diversity is repressed that authoritarianism comes into play. There is a strong tradition of authoritarianism in nationalist and liberation movements (Raftopoulos 1999); those members who did not toe the party line were often ostracised; those who dared criticise the party were labelled as 'sell-outs', 'stooges' or 'Tshombes'. This style of denigration grew in the late 1950s:

> as the Southern African region became part of a larger revolutionary epoch, nationalist leaders had a new vocabulary to use in their claims to the nation. Younger leaders used this rhetoric as ammunition against the older generation or those of their same age with more experience in trade union and political organisations, mobilising support against the 'sell-out' or, by the early 1960s, the 'imperialist stooge'. (Scarnecchia 2008:8)

Furthermore, from the 1950s on, the public sphere became less about competing visions of a political future and more about immediate confrontations between a more consciously 'authentic' nationalism and those politicians who still held out – at least until 1962 – for a possibility of a peaceful negotiated transfer of power to majority rule (Ibid.).

The trajectory of nationalism from the early 1960s had long-term repercussions on intra-party democracy, inter-party relations and more broadly on political values. A tendency toward intolerance and a propensity for violence against opponents became defining features of nationalism. Unlike the earlier variety of nationalism and activism associated with figures such as Charles Mzingeli and Reuben Jamela, the later variety was less tolerant and inclusive. To this intolerance was added a proclivity towards personality cults, around such leaders as Joshua Nkomo and Robert Mugabe. Instead of a nationalism imbued with broad democratic values and practice, an authoritarian variety took its place, a variety that has proved resilient half a century later. In summarising this trajectory of nationalism, it has been argued that:

> by 1960, as the stakes became higher, nationalist politics became less about expanding ideas of reciprocal nationalism and more about defending a core leadership against state repression and against rival leadership factions and their followers. In what was to be a short span of time, the nationalist visions held by many of a more democratic and progressive political future gave way to a siege mentality, in which the disciplining of supporters and attacks against non-members became the overarching concern. In the process, the concept of the nation and of citizenship changed from earlier community-based visions to a nationalist struggle where rights to state power were more important than the rights of individuals. (Scarnecchia 2008:158)

Subsequent political culture reflected this drift towards intolerance, exclusivity, authoritarianism and violence. Half a century later, it is a culture that is also reflected in the deep political polarisation that is embedded into Zimbabwean society.

This perspective is broadly shared in studies in the 1990s on the link between nationalism, human rights and democracy. There is posited the observation, which obviously draws from hindsight, that:

> perhaps there was something inherent in nationalism itself, even before the (liberation) war and the adoption of socialism, which gave rise to authoritarianism. Maybe nationalism's emphasis on unity at all costs – its subordination of trade unions and churches and all other African organisations to its imperatives – gave rise to an intolerance of pluralism. Maybe nationalism's commitment gave rise to a post-colonial cult of personality. Maybe nationalism's commitment to modernisation, whether socialist or not, inevitably implied a 'commandist' state. (Ranger 2003:2)

The Legacy of the Liberation Struggle

No discussion of the legacies of colonialism and nationalism would be complete without assessing the legacy of the liberation war. Fought between 1966 and 1979, the war was ferocious, and left deep scars on society apart from shaping the content and orientation of nationalism.

The main protagonists were the settler colonial state, ZAPU and its military wing, ZIPRA, and ZANU and its military wing, ZANLA. Towards the end of the struggle in 1978-79, internal political leaders – Abel Muzorewa and Ndabaningi Sithole – had their own militias as well. These forces subscribed to different ideologies: ZAPU to a Soviet-type socialism (it received most of its material support from the USSR), ZANU to a Maoist variety (it was supported by China), and the settler colonial state to a fierce variety of anti-communism drawing its material and moral support from apartheid South Africa and the West.

All of the protagonists used violence as an instrument of mobilisation. Violence against civilians in the war zones featured heavily (CIIR 1975), and coercion against civilians by state forces and guerrilla armies was widespread (Kriger 2003; Nyarota 2005). Although participation in the armed struggle was voluntary, there were also instances of coercion and retributive violence. The numbers of civilians killed, wounded, tortured and dispossessed during the struggle was considerable (CIIR/CCJP 1975). The scars from these excesses have not been officially acknowledged or addressed; indeed, there has been repeated use of violence as an instrument of mobilisation in the post-independence period, particularly between 2000 and 2008, and especially at election time.

A final enduring legacy has been the impunity enjoyed by those who perpetrated excesses during the struggle. An indemnity law absolved those who carried out torture and killings during the struggle, and presidential pardons were later given to state security personnel and ZANU-PF members involved in violence against political opponents. Political violence between 2000 and 2008 was a major strategy of the incumbent regime to cripple the opposition movement. Although this failed, the trauma of violence on society is still deep and widespread, as various studies have shown (ZHR NGO Forum 2009, 2010; CSVR 2008). The role of the military, police and intelligence services in the administration of this violence has been central to the authoritarian practices of the post-colonial state.

The Nation-State Project and the National Question

The post-independence state, like most other states in developing societies, has placed a great deal of emphasis on the concept of national unity, recognising that other forms of consciousness and identity continued to co-exist, albeit in modified forms, alongside the nationalist one. While the existence of other forms of consciousness may not, by itself, constitute a problem, it becomes one when their existence contradicts or obstructs the implementation of the nation-state project. The post-independence government views the inculcation of national consciousness and the dilution of ethnic or regional particularism as a major challenge in its project of nation-building.

The new post-independence government acceded to power amidst the constraints of the Lancaster House Constitution and the geopolitical/military threat from the then apartheid regime in South Africa. Its room for manoeuvre was generally limited. Further, ZANU-PF, having won 57 out of 100 parliamentary seats, was short of the two-thirds majority necessary for major constitutional amendments. This was the immediate context within which the imperative of national unity was enunciated. As the architect of the post-independence government explained:

> by its multi-faceted character and effect, national political unity not only enhances the national spirit, but in so doing creates a conducive atmosphere for the reconciliation of divergent and sometimes antagonistic political and social outlooks and philosophies. By its ennobling and elevating effect, national unity destroys petty and divisive loyalties based upon tribe, region, race, sex and religions and in their place creates and nurtures a national ethos. It has the capacity and power to sublimate these inferior and divisive energies into a superior and transcendent spirit. (Mugabe 1989:356)

In the first year of independence, there was, therefore, a conscious attempt to create an atmosphere of national unity and stability. It was a policy hailed for its pragmatism, and one outcome was the pre-empting of a white exodus such as had occurred in neighbouring Mozambique. The economy and the machinery of the government did not, therefore, collapse.

Writing at the end of the first decade of independence, some analysts interpreted the policy of reconciliation as a bargain with the 100,000 or so whites who stayed on after 1980. The bargain, according to Herbst, was that:

> the whites can stay, continue to operate their businesses and farms, and lead the 'colonial life style' that they are accustomed to for the rest of their lives. However, their children are discouraged from staying ... The racial bargain implies that Zimbabwe will not have to Africanise the economy by force because in a generation or so the white population will have dwindled into insignificance. (Herbst 1990:222)

However, as Herbst himself acknowledged, the policy rested on a fragile basis at the best of times. There had been 'a reconciliation of interests' but not of attitudes: the significant electoral victory in 1985 of Ian Smith's party (which won 15 of 20 seats specially reserved for whites) over a more liberal-minded group of white candidates demonstrated this embarrassingly to the Mugabe government.

It is questionable whether it is helpful to view the reconciliation policy as one which achieved 'a reconciliation of interests', especially in view of the growing antagonism among blacks towards the policy in the 1990s. But this is not to assert that in those first few years of independence, the policy did not enhance the credibility and international respectability of the Mugabe government. It is difficult to think of what an alternative policy towards the whites should have been in the aftermath of the liberation struggle and in the context of the belligerent destabilisation strategy of South Africa. In our view, in spite of its obvious limitations, the reconciliation policy was a component of the 'national unity' project as defined by Mugabe and the ruling ZANU-PF. The 'racial bargain', for what it was worth, has since come unstuck, but while it lasted, racial tolerance was an important feature of the stability which prevailed in the post-independence period.

Of course, the most important component of the project related to internal unity within the nationalist movement. We have already observed that such a unitary project as conceived by the nationalist movement was neither coherent nor cohesive. Power struggles had resulted in the formation of those fractions which drew their support from ethnic bases in Mashonaland and Matabeleland. The Patriotic Front, formed in 1976, and prior to it, the African National Council, represented attempts to unify competing tendencies within the nationalist movement. As it was candidly admitted:

> The tribal character of both ZANU and ZAPU could be explained only in terms of loyalties emanating from old feudal social formations, which revolved around the authority of the tribal king. The fact that the leader of ZANU was Shona and that of ZAPU was Ndebele, played into these feudal loyalties with the result that the Shonas tended to drift to ZANU while the Ndebele tended to drift to ZAPU. (Mugabe 1989:338)

The unitary project was tenuous even after the formation of the Patriotic Front. It was so weak in concept and practice that the two fractions fought the independence elections separately. Subsequent attempts to establish a government of national unity initially succeeded (but only partially) with the appointment of several ZAPU ministers in that government. ZAPU's leader, Joshua Nkomo, refused the constitutional Presidency, preferring a cabinet position in which he could wield real power. Tensions, exacerbated by the discovery of arms caches on ZAPU-owned properties, provided the immediate context for the collapse of that fragile unity in 1982. In the next section we will explore the consequences of that collapse and the subsequent gradual movement towards a compromise between ZANU-PF and PF-ZAPU.

There were other elements in the amorphous unitary project pursued by the Mugabe government. The pursuit of state constitutionalism in mediating conflicts between various social interests was one method used to enhance the new government's credibility. At least for the period 1980-87, the Lancaster House constitutional provisions concerning property relations and minority interests were not tampered with. While this provided a semblance of stability, it also blocked opportunities for reform, especially that of land ownership. Only a third of the projected 160,000 families had been allocated land by 1990. Although popular but disorganised pressure existed for substantial agrarian reform, the stalling by government was viewed in some quarters as reflecting the ruling elite's acquiescence with the existing structure of property relations. Revelations in 1994 about the predominance of this elite (politicians, senior bureaucrats, military officers, and others) in the ownership both of state tenant farms and private farms confirmed some suspicions regarding the government's weak commitment to substantive agrarian reform.

Finally, the unitary project was often conceptualised in somewhat narrow terms from a party political perspective. At the heart of the project was the ascendancy of the ZANU-PF vis-à-vis other political groups. One expression of this desire was the stated goal, from the mid-1980s onwards, to establish a one-party state. The one-party state would represent the fruition of the unitary project. It was forcefully argued that:

> *Zimbabweans realised that there would never be permanent peace, development, democracy and social justice in Zimbabwe for as long as there existed two political parties based upon regional or tribal consideration. What was needed was one political party to which everybody would owe allegiance and be a member, irrespective of tribe, religion or race. (Mugabe 1989:344)*

While there may be some basis for the assertion that regionalism and 'tribalism' can, in certain circumstances, militate against stability, it does not follow that the existence of only one party can guarantee such stability. Yet, increasingly, this line was articulated by ZANU-PF. There were references to a 'one-party participatory democracy' which it would be ZANU-PF's vocation to construct. There were scathing pronouncements about the role of opposition parties:

> National unity under ZANU-PF discourages the formation of opposition parties by exposing their bankruptcy in political and ideological direction. Indeed, against the background of the existence of a united, mass democratic, socialist-oriented national party, what political programme and ideological direction can an opposition party give to the people as an alternative? (Mugabe 1989:357)

Clearly, as the 1980s wore on, the project of national unity was reduced by ZANU-PF to the issue of single-party rule. This was hardly original: much of Africa in the 1980s was still wedded to such an orthodoxy.

The Collapse of the Unitary Project and its Resuscitation: 1982–1987

Although it was a powerful force in the struggle against colonialism, the nationalist movement itself was riven with divisions. Those divisions, compounded as they were by ethnic tendencies, were not capable of displacing the overall objective of the movement to dislodge the settler regime and seize state power. Squabbles between the petit bourgeois leadership of the two nationalist fractions did not extend to disputes over the territorial integrity of the existing state. There were no threats of secession. However, the collapse of the government of national unity in 1982 did create a much more volatile atmosphere. Not only were PF-ZAPU cabinet ministers sacked, but a low-intensity civil war erupted in Matabeleland and raged intermittently until 1987.

Thousands of casualties resulted from armed clashes between the military and the so-called 'dissidents' or 'bandits' (ex-combatants from PF-ZAPU's liberation army). Civilians constituted the majority of the casualties as the military sought to flush out the 'dissidents', who were basically engaged in a guerrilla war. Property worth millions of dollars was destroyed, and by 1984 about 500,000 acres of commercial farmland had been abandoned in Matabeleland (Ncube 1991). Clearly, there existed amongst the Ndebele peasantry some disaffection over access to land and this would have been thoroughly exploited by the 'dissidents' who depended on them for succour and security intelligence.

The economic and human cost of that civil conflict has still not been fully evaluated. It was certainly enormous. The size of the 'dissident' army may have run into several hundreds; it included both ex-combatants and deserters from the newly constituted Zimbabwe National Army (ZNA), and was never short of arms. However, as the conflict spread to Midlands Province, there were allegations of collusion between the 'dissidents' and South African agents. A group of 'dissidents' calling itself 'Super ZAPU' was reportedly receiving assistance from the South African military as part of that country's regional destabilisation strategy.

This presumed support provided the Mugabe government with another pretext for intensifying military operations in Matabeleland and inflicting punishment on the civilian population. Curfews such as had been enforced during the liberation struggle were imposed, and food was used as a method of coercion against civilians during the drought years of 1981–83. As one observer recalled:

> The suffering of the people arising from the security situation was exacerbated by a drought, which had resulted in an almost total crop failure. In May 1982, Government instituted a drought relief programme for the region. The delivery of relief supplies, however, was very inconsistent. The food situation was further exacerbated by the fact that store owners were unable to transport goods to their stores during this period, and as no buses were running; neither the people nor food commodities could be transported between rural and urban centres. (Auret 1992:150)

The deployment of a North Korean-trained army brigade to the affected provinces raised the level of reported brutalities as well as the alienation of the civilian population from the army and government.

This account of the conflict is not meant merely to describe the disastrous consequences of the collapse of the nationalist coalition in 1982. It also suggests an all-too familiar scenario in Africa: a nation-state gradually but inexorably sliding into a bloody conflict which, over time, becomes more complex and difficult to resolve. Similar conflicts, but on a grander scale, were under way in neighbouring Angola and Mozambique. However, the Zimbabwean conflict was more unjustified precisely because it was primarily the outcome not of inherent ethnically based differences, but of power struggles within the leadership of the nationalist coalition. The conflicts in Angola and Mozambique were, of course, fuelled by the more explicit and aggressive intervention of South Africa, but if they represented negative lessons for the new Zimbabwe government, the lessons were not thoroughly digested. The 'iron-fist' policy employed against the 'bandits' – similar nomenclature was used in Mozambique – had been expected to quell the dissident problem once and for all, and marginalise PF-ZAPU politically. It failed woefully between 1982 and 1987. PF-ZAPU won handsomely in general and local elections in 1985. At the same time, the ethnic bitterness generated by the conflict became more hardened.

The limitations of the military approach to the 'dissident' problem were to become quite clear as the fighting dragged on, but the repercussions were far-reaching:

> Many lives were lost, property robbed or burnt and thousands fled their homes. Development programmes came to a near standstill. Going side by side with this, there were accusations and counter-accusations traded between ZANU-PF and PF-ZAPU with each party blaming the other for the state of terror in western Zimbabwe. While there was little or no development in Matabeleland and part of the Midlands, development went ahead in the provinces of Mashonaland, Manicaland and most parts of Masvingo and the Midlands. The country was thus divided into two parts of unequal development. The government's policy of regional equity in development had been compromised. (Mugabe 1989:344)

This candour was possible with the benefit of hindsight, but the outcome was inevitable given that coercive rather than political means were employed in tackling the crisis. We shall return to the long-term effects of the civil conflict, especially in relation to the heightening of ethnic consciousness, in the next section.

Protracted negotiations for unity between PF-ZAPU and ZANU-PF began in earnest in 1985. The pressure for reconciliation increased because of the economic, human and political cost of the conflict. Neither fraction was reaping political dividends from it, nor were either of them fully in control of their forces or supporters on the ground. In its proposals, PF-ZAPU suggested the merger of the two parties with Mugabe serving as the president, and two vice-presidents, one from each party. It also proposed that the name of the new party should be 'ZANU-ZAPU'. ZANU-PF countered by urging PF-ZAPU negotiators to drop the name of their party, disband and join ZANU-PF (Chiwewe 1989).

The haggling involved six meetings of the Unity Committee (drawn from the two parties) and nine meetings between Robert Mugabe and Joshua Nkomo. Intensive discussions centred on the sharing of positions in the merged party, and of portfolios in the cabinet. The terms of the subsequent Unity Accord, signed in December 1987, were underpinned by a conscious realisation that 'the two parties jointly command the overwhelming majority of the people of Zimbabwe as evidenced by the general election results of 1980 and 1985' (Chiwewe 1989:282). At the same time, the leadership of PF-ZAPU pledged 'to take immediate vigorous steps to eliminate and end the insecurity and violence prevalent in Matabeleland'. More disconcertingly, the agreement also stipulated the establishment of a one-party state. From ZANU-PF's perspective, with the PF-ZAPU's agreement to merge, no credible opposition existed any longer. What was surprising was PF-ZAPU's acquiescence to this clause in the agreement.

Between 1982 and 1987, then, ZANU-PF's hegemonic project was under serious strain. Although PF-ZAPU did not proclaim any intention to separate the Matabeleland provinces from the rest of the country, it had generated a great deal of ethnic support during the civil conflict. These sentiments sharpened as casualties mounted and development lagged, and would continue to simmer after the 1987 Unity Accord. Following the Accord, there was a restructuring of the two parties with the merging of their cell, branch, district, provincial and national executive structures. At the formal level at least, this fusion signified a new political era, the symbolism of which was reflected in the spectacle of the erstwhile 'warring parties' mobilising jointly and their top leaders addressing rallies in Ndebele and Shona heartlands.

Following the fratricidal 'trial of strength' between ZANU-PF and PF-ZAPU, there were substantial interests at stake to ensure that the Accord was given a chance to succeed. For the PF-ZAPU elite in particular, some of whose assets had been expropriated at the height of the dissident campaign, the Accord provided a basis for the resumption of their participation in the capitalist accumulation process, an attitude that many in the democratic and human rights movement were to find both disappointing and dispiriting.

Several sets of pressures beset the project of national unity and threatened to undermine ZANU-PF's efforts. The first related to the switch to orthodox, market-based economic liberalisation following indecisive attempts at socialist-oriented redistribution and at implementing a Leadership Code to curb the more rapacious forms of accumulation by the political leadership. Economic liberalisation was effected through a structural adjustment programme (SAP) whose first phase ran from 1990 to 1995. Its chief objectives were the opening up of the economy to market forces through trade and monetary policy liberalisation, the deregulation of industrial relations, the reduction of the budget deficit, the withdrawal of subsidies, and the promotion of an outward orientation in a hitherto inward-looking economy. The terms of the programme were contested by certain sectors of the business community, labour unions, and consumer associations, which had been marginalised in its original design. The introduction of the austerity package, which included considerable cuts in social sector spending, slashed the earnings of middle and lower income groups, and removed subsidies on basic commodities (especially food) and services, created the basis for popular alienation, especially among the working poor.

While the adjustment programme drew financial and political support from the World Bank and the International Monetary Fund and from the leading Western donor countries, it underscored an explicit ideological shift from populist to capitalist development. In the process, the fragile 'social contract' between an initially weak labour movement and the state collapsed. In the 1990 elections, the bulk of the opposition vote was drawn from the urban-based working-class. Thus, although the adjustment programme had not, by itself, provided the full conditions for the crystallisation of a stronger opposition, it did stimulate widespread discontent, especially amongst low-income groups and consumer associations.

The adoption of adjustment measures suggested that the government had become increasingly distant from its erstwhile grassroots constituency and closer to the wealthier sections of society and the international financial institutions (IFIs). Although the tensions generated by these pressures did not appear to threaten national unity directly or immediately, they chipped away at the hegemony and legitimacy of the ruling party. Of wider significance were the stresses created by limiting of resources, especially public resources, available to the regions and 'party clients'; this caused particular dissension within ZAPU-PF.

In spite of the triumphalism that attended the Unity Accord in 1987 and the subsequent party congresses, fault-lines also existed in the edifice of ZANU-PF itself. One of the most critical was the renewed power struggles at the provincial level.

The tendency for these barons with their local base to compete with each other at the national level posed several kinds of difficulties within the party. First, the sustaining of their local base and the furthering of their national standing determined their tactical calculations rather than the furtherance of any coherent strategy. They had to be opportunist and acquisitive to gain the spoils – to be able to pass them on, and there were thus in-built tendencies, apart from their own personal interests, to corruption and to nepotism (Cliffe and Stoneman 1989:85).

Provincial level competition among the party elite stirred factionalism with ethnic connotations even within the groups which constitute the Shona. The power struggles in the Masvingo and Harare provinces in the 1990s reflected some of these tendencies. First, there were clashes of interest between the top party leadership and the provincial leadership over how the power structure at the provincial level should be constructed in the run-up to the 1995 elections. In Masvingo, the contest was between the Eddison Zvobgo and Vice-President Simon Muzenda, both of whom backed surrogates – Stan Mudenge and Dzikamai Mavhaire respectively – for the provincial chairmanship. It was characterised by bitter recriminations, and degenerated to the level of Zvobgo publicly questioning the nationalist and liberation credentials of his opponents. The cohesion of the provincial party structures was threatened, and it required the mediation of the party's Vice-President Nkomo, National Chairman Msika and Political Commissar Mahachi for calm to be restored. Even the Speaker of Parliament was moved to denounce the factionalism:

> Such malicious manipulations by some unscrupulous individuals to further their own political agendas should be condemned in the strongest of terms …. Politicians should expend their energies towards accountability and transparency, and more importantly towards the development of the economy. (Speaker Makombe, as quoted in the Daily Gazette, 14 May 1994)

There was no ideological dimension to these struggles, nor to the acrimony between the party's national and provincial leadership in Harare. The latter dispute concerned the authority to select candidates to stand in local by-elections, with the provincial leadership under the mercurial Herbert Ushewokunze seeking to assert its autonomy and safeguard its base of patronage. Although less critical than the struggles in Masvingo, it illustrated the tenuousness of the relationship between the party's centre and its provinces. The provincial dimension incorporates ethnic sentiments which can feed on feelings of popular alienation and grassroots revulsion against the top party leadership and government policies. This became explicit in the Matabeleland provinces in 1992-94. The context of the verbal flare-up between Ndebele leaders and ZANU-PF was the SAP-related cutbacks in government spending, but this was reinforced by the general perception in Matabeleland that development funds were being directed to other provinces.

The resources in question ranged from public investment to student quotas at tertiary institutions of learning (including teachers' colleges). In the opinion of Ndebele leaders, their region was being discriminated against:

> Such prominent politicians as Maben (a provincial governor), Lesage (a former government minister), Malinga (the former mayor of Bulawayo) and Malaga (the late respected parliamentarian) ruefully observed that Matabeleland was not being allocated a fair proportion of those resources. To worsen matters, Shona students from outside the region allegedly dominated enrolment in colleges. The census figures (of 1992) for the province's population had been allegedly 'doctored' to show only a marginal increase, so as to limit the amount of resources which Matabeleland deserved, it was further argued. (Sachikonye 1996:149)

A criticism often laid at the door of Ndebele politicians (by grassroots constituents and opposition spokesmen) was that they had not pursued the development of their province as vigorously as other politicians. According to this critique, the Unity Accord might have conferred benefits on individual PF-ZAPU elites, but these had not trickled down to the Ndebele people. Thus regional discrimination becomes a popular explanation for social and economic difficulties. In 2011, a debate on uneven development and de-industrialisation in Bulawayo erupted, pitting Vice President John Nkomo against opposition and civil society groups in Matabeleland. Further, a festering sore still remains: the government's refusal to award compensation to the civilian victims of the 1982–87 civil conflict, or to provide assistance to the widows and children of these victims. Add the procrastination of the government in resolving the water question in this drought-prone region, and we have a checklist of grievances on which ethnic sentiments can be easily focused and have increasingly been focused in spite of the Unity Accord.

The use of these grievances to play the ethnic card has been termed 'cheap politicking' not only by the top ZANU-PF leadership, but also by the press:

> The problem [of tribalism] remains one which is fuelled by small-minded politicians. The Shona and Ndebele have not fought each other since the 'kneeless' ones invaded the country. What we have had are attempts by diverse politicians to set them at each other's throats again. (Daily Gazette, 13 December 1994)

In the 1990s, what prevented the situation from getting out of hand and unravelling the unitary project was the commitment of the leadership of the former PF-ZAPU (principally Joshua Nkomo, Cephas Msika and Dumiso Dabengwa) to the Unity Accord. That would change a decade later when Dabengwa and others pulled out to resuscitate ZAPU in 2008.

To that extent, the twenty-year-old compromise symbolised by the Accord acted as a brake on potentially more militant demands for the re-negotiation of the terms on which the present nation-state was constituted. As we observed, in the mid-1990s, post-Nkomo, Msika, and Dabengwa, it was not unlikely that the Accord would come under some strain unless concerted and credible attempts were made to address the concerns of the Ndebele people.

Finally, let us consider how the factor of race impinged on the unitary project. In the 1990s, but particularly after 2000, it became much more explosive than at any other time since independence. While the policy of reconciliation might have worked, at least for a while, in promoting stability, blacks have increasingly viewed it as an obstruction to their economic advancement. Black (or 'indigenous' as they often prefer to call themselves) business groups have become exasperated over the snail-like pace at which their advancement is occurring. Increasingly, they blame the institutions of the relatively wealthy white community for blocking that advancement through restrictive lending practices (by the largely white-owned financial institutions), unfair competition (through the activities of the mainly white-controlled monopolies), and insensitive treatment of indebted businessmen (through the repossession of their residential property).

There has also been a groundswell of opposition to what have been perceived as the continued racial privileges and superior advantages in the economy enjoyed by the white minority. Ironically, economic liberalisation unleashed a burst of black entrepreneurship but also involved stringent conditions and high interest rates. A notable number of black-owned small and medium-sized enterprises have gone bankrupt. Such groups as the Indigenous Business Development Centre (IBDC) and the Zimbabwe National Chambers of Commerce (ZNCC) complained bitterly about the effects of adjustment on the borrowing or debt-servicing capacity of the business interests they represent. They view the financial sector – commercial banks, building societies, insurance companies and pension funds – as being ranged against them. Further, the challenge to state powers of land acquisition by the white-dominated Commercial Farmers Union (CFU) has been interpreted in racial terms. Whites are seen as monopolising the 'ill-gotten' fruits of 'colonial conquest' while being utterly oblivious of the pressures being generated within the peasantry for land redistribution.

The sense of anger among black business interests towards the 'privileged' white sector was given vent in statements by certain political figures, notably Joshua Nkomo (who had considerable business interests himself), by the business groups themselves, but also by the student leadership and sections of the press. Demonstrations were organised in 1994 and 1995 specifically against 'white racism' and 'privileges' by university students, the IBDC, the bank workers' union and other interest groups. These have been mounted to act as a mobilising vehicle and a source of public pressure on the Mugabe government to institute financial reforms more favourable to black business groups.

Conclusion

This chapter has surveyed the legacies of colonialism and nationalism for the national project of building an independent and unified state. The unitary project was as elusive under colonialism as under nationalism. Rivalry between nationalist organisations in the 1960s degenerated into inter-party violence and the formation of separate liberation armies, and the creation in mid-1970s of a Patriotic Front did not last beyond the signing of the Lancaster House agreement.

The unifying potential of the reconciliation policy and a constitutionalist approach to reform was not sufficient to mitigate the slide into a civil conflict in 1982–87. As it became more obvious that the 'trial of strength' between the two fractions would be costly in political and human terms, the stage was set for a Unity Accord in 1987.

Such a compromise created a stronger basis for national unity, but pressures for regional equity and democratisation continued to accumulate, and the legacy of racial polarisation further complicated the terms on which that unitary project could proceed.

However, aspects of the national question such as reconciliation, equitable distribution of resources and sustainable access to social services were not addressed successfully. By the end of the 1990s, the unitary project was under considerable pressure from social forces that sought to pursue their own interests regardless of the overall implications for society. The economic debacle that resulted from demands by war veterans and labour in the late 1990s, and the political fall-out from authoritarian violence mounted against the newly founded opposition movement by the state and ruling party tore the unitary project asunder. An increasingly paranoid state labelled the opposition movement and civil society as 'stooges' and 'sell-outs'; they were dismissed as 'totem-less'. The nation-state had become exclusive instead of inclusive. The race card was widely used in expropriation from white farmers of the land and property that they owned. The national project was therefore in crisis throughout the first decade of the twenty-first century.

2

The State & its Institutions

Introduction

A great deal of the explanation of Zimbabwe's 'lost decades' lies in the nature and orientation of the state and its institutions that emerged at Independence. To what extent was the post-independence state really a *new* or *different* state? The same question can be asked in relation to institutions of the post-colonial state: the public service, judiciary, security apparatus, parliament and parastatals. These institutional components should be scrutinised because they are the foundations and bedrock of the state. Their content, structure, capacity and orientation have a direct bearing on the performance and efficiency of the state. They determine whether it becomes a 'developmental state' which prioritises economic and social development or a 'predatory state' which consumes the surpluses of the economy as government offices become income-generating sinecures. In short, the capacity and orientation of institutions which constitute the state determine to a great extent whether or not conditions for development are generated and sustained. These are the considerations that bear on our assessment of the record of the Zimbabwe state in stalling development during the past 30 years. We observe that its performance in managing development has been lacklustre and, on the whole, below average in comparison to its neighbours in southern Africa.

The Nature of the Post-Colonial State

In this chapter, we explore *why* and *how* the post-colonial state has had a poor record in stimulating and managing economic and social development during the 'lost decades'. A large portion of the new state was inherited, for better or worse. This inheritance could have been used to its advantage but it could also have been to its disadvantage.

The nature and orientation of this state cannot be understood without knowledge of the structure and tendencies of the one that preceded it, and much analytical writing acknowledges and explores this (Mandaza

1986; Cliffe and Stoneman 1989). Despite their pronouncements during the liberation struggle, the new rulers did not 'smash' the old state, partly due to its resilience but partly due to strictures imposed by the Lancaster House agreement and the 1979 Constitution (Weitzer 1984). Advancing the same perspective, another analyst observed that:

> in 1980, Zanu-PF did not gain control over a weak colonial state that had been hurriedly improved for Independence and on which they could quickly put their imprimatur (the typical scenario for countries that gained their Independence in the 1960s). Nor did the guerrillas win an outright victory as Frelimo had done in Mozambique, where the old state collapsed creating a vacuum into which new government structures and practices could be placed. Instead, the black government took over a bruised but not defeated settler state. (Herbst 1990:30)

By African standards, that state had invested in impressive infrastructure in the form of roads, railways, electricity and dams. The economic base was relatively strong with an industrial sector and sophisticated commercial agriculture that were second only to South Africa. The mineral and services sectors were also relatively advanced. Although the initial vision for the construction of this economic base was for settler interests, the potential for expanding it to include the black majority in an enlarged domestic market was huge. In addition, the provision of basic education had been reasonably extensive and ensured that the proportion of university and technical college graduates at independence was higher than it had been in most other African countries.

A major inheritance related to the expansion of the size of the state itself, which, even in the first decades of the colony, reflected the settlers' determination to develop a strong local institutional presence. By 1923, the settler government employed 2,000 whites in six administrative offices, even though only 33,000 settlers lived in the entire colony. Given that there were only 1,500 administrators at the height of colonial rule in Nigeria, the size of the early state was impressive. Similarly, the number of parastatals created to engage in economic activities was relatively large. On the eve of Independence, there were about 40 such parastatals in most sectors of the economy including agriculture, mining, transport, energy and utilities. Thus there was a strong propensity on the part of the state to take a prominent role in production and services sectors.

Another major inheritance was a relatively large public service. At independence, there were about 40,000 public servants of whom approximately 29,000 were black (mainly concentrated in teaching and nursing as well as clerical roles). Significantly, of the 10,570 established officers, about 3,360 were blacks, with none of them above the position of 'senior administrative officer' level. Consequently, in the new state, the governing elite constituted a thin veneer atop a largely untransformed state apparatus (Bratton 1981:452).

The state security apparatus was another untransformed institution at Independence. It would take several years for the three armies of Rhodesian forces, ZANLA and ZIPRA to be fully integrated. The Central Intelligence Organisation (CIO) had most of its structure, operational procedures and culture 'inherited' by the new state. The inheritance of the military and intelligence apparatuses proved problematic:

> despite some changes in military, certain sections of it adopted some of the most horrendous tactics of Rhodesian security forces …. Given the reproduction of the repressive institutions of the settler state, it is no accident that Zimbabwe's security system mirrors so closely its forerunner in its reaction to perceived threats. In the security sphere, the structure of the executive has been carried over into the new order unchanged in its essentials. (Weitzer 1984:115).

This inheritance conferred certain advantages in constructing a post-colonial authoritarian state because the foundations and related structures for that purpose already existed. But this would constitute a major obstacle to democratic and developmental transformation. The inheritance of the state was a compromise in itself; it depended on the goodwill of elements of the old state in its attempt to build new structures (Mandaza 1986). The challenge of reconciling the old and new into the new state would persist for a long time. Let us explore this aspect as we look at key institutions that provided the basis of the post-colonial state and the roles that they played in promoting or retarding development.

Public Service

In any modern state, the public service occupies a strategic role. It often designs state policies and programmes, and implements and evaluates them. On the whole, the record of the Zimbabwean public service has been poor. This is both surprising and disappointing in view of earlier optimistic prognoses, which were based on the availability of relatively highly educated black graduates and technicians. A national manpower survey which sought to gauge the manpower requirements for the country claimed that it had blown the myth of the indispensability of white skills (Government of Zimbabwe 1981). To some extent, this was reflected in the number of white officers dropping from 7,200 to 4,490 while the number of black officers increased from 3,360 to 17,690 between 1980 and 1983. It was claimed that 'black personnel operated in the state structures as competently as their white counterparts' (Mandaza 1986). This was not an isolated belief or assumption:

> *unlike neighbouring Mozambique and Angola, there were thousands of Zimbabweans who had received higher education in exile and other qualified and experienced Zimbabweans at home who had been denied preferment. Fairly rapid Africanisation of the civil service was thus possible as well as a policy goal. (Cliffe and Stoneman 1989:41)*

By any standards, there was a rapid Africanisation of the public service. However, there have been comparatively few studies on whether this produced the best outcome in terms of efficiency and effectiveness. Few analysts bothered about the issue of quality of performance and outcomes of the rapidly expanded civil service. Although this has not been systematically explored, the quality of development planning and implementation did not improve. It could be argued that at best, it was mediocre; at worst, it was reflected in stagnation of growth in the 1980s and 1990s, and then decline thereafter.

Parliament

Although the new parliament had a majority of black legislators, it functioned more or less like the previous white legislature. The Rhodesian parliament had not been a serious arena of political struggle over proposed policies; it was more of a publicity forum through which the public learned of government proposals (Weitzer 1984:90). As it behaved under ZANU-PF rule during the next several decades, 'Parliament failed to impose constraints on executive power because of the composition of its membership and because of the progressive elimination of intra-organ checks on the ruling party' (Ibid.).

Part of the explanation for the subservience of parliament to the executive is found in the dominance of the ruling party. Not only did ZANU-PF command an absolute majority for a decade, but it had a two-thirds majority between 1990 and 2000 as well as between 2005 and 2008, which gave it carte blanche to pass the legislation it proposed, often at the behest of the executive. The majority also enabled it to appoint a speaker and deputy speaker as well as the chairpersons of key portfolio committees. During much of the post-independence period, parliament rubber-stamped decisions of ZANU-PF's Central Committee and Politburo, as was noted by the then leader of PF-ZAPU:

> I once asked Mugabe directly the question 'what is the supreme organ in Zimbabwe?' He answered, 'the supreme body in Zimbabwe is the Central Committee of ZANU-PF'. (Nkomo 2001:3)

Part of the explanation resides in the almost untrammelled powers that the president wields in law-making. For example, the president has unilateral legislative powers provided for under the 1996 Presidential Powers (Temporary Measures) Act to deal with situations that require urgent attention. In the interests of defence, public safety, public order, public morality and public health, the president can suspend any other rights for the general public interest.

Our main observation on the role of parliament is not simply that it was under the dominance of the ruling party and therefore passed laws that reflected its agenda. It is that the post-colonial parliament abdicated its traditional function of oversight on legislation and also on the executive. It failed to provide checks and balances in the new state. In a deeper sense, parliament failed to reflect the popular will of the voters who elected it. The weakness of parliament affected the quality of democracy and governance. Innovations such as the establishment of specialist portfolio committees after 2000 were an admission that parliament had not been strong in its oversight role. However, the committees had a limited impact, and clearly were not a substitute for a robust legislature. The success of the legislature in addressing corruption, authoritarianism and development challenges during the three decades after Independence has on the whole been poor to mediocre.

The Judiciary

A credible and independent judiciary is indispensable for an effective state and a democratic society. It is the branch of the state with the mandate and capacity to limit abuses of state power. Like parliament and the public service, the Zimbabwean judiciary has undergone vicissitudes largely stemming from interference by the executive. However, this is not to ignore the fact that under the last phase of colonialism it was also under considerable pressure:

> *An executive-legislative alliance eroded judicial discretion and collapsed its sphere of jurisdiction. These trends rendered the judiciary structurally incapable of seriously mitigating repression. (Weitzer 1984:94)*

Indeed, the Rhodesian judiciary, especially in the 1970s, imposed increasingly harsh punishments on those convicted of political crimes, notably nationalists and guerrillas. The judiciary failed to resist successive encroachments in its jurisdictional field.

Lack of confidence in the judiciary by the executive persisted after Independence, when ministerial powers impeded the monopoly of courts over genuine judicial functions and the acquittal of individuals accused of security breaches provoked government attacks:

> *The manner in which our law courts dispense justice is gravely frustrating and undermining the work of law enforcement agencies like the police. The security of state is sacrificed on the altar of individual liberties. People who are engaged in activities designed to threaten the welfare and security of the state are either freed by the courts or go off very lightly .... Recalcitrant and reactionary members of the so-called Bench still remain masquerading under our hard-won independence as dispensers of justice. (Minister of Home Affairs, 13 July 1982; quoted in Weitzer 1984:97)*

The flashpoints in relations between the judiciary and the executive related to cases of freedom of the press and expropriation of white commercial farms. The executive was extremely unhappy with judgements on press freedom and property rights that went against it during this period. To illustrate this point: in 1999, the army detained the editor of *The Standard*, after the paper had reported that 23 army officers had been arrested for inciting an overthrow of the Mugabe government. The High Court held that the editor had been illegally detained and issued three court orders ordering his release, none of which were complied with. The permanent secretary in the Ministry of Defence then issued a statement that 'the judge cannot direct us, we will move at our pace'. In that particular case, the army was not entitled to arrest civilians and this was a clear violation of the journalist's right to free expression. Chief Justice Gubbay and Judge Ebrahim then wrote to the president expressing the view that the army was operating with impunity in breach of the law. The response from the executive was revealing. Calling upon judges to resign, Mugabe charged that 'the judiciary has no constitutional right whatsoever to give instructions to the President on any matter …. It is an outrageous and deliberate act of impudence' (quoted in Meredith 2002:153).

The second issue that proved very contentious was the land reform. The history of litigation began in March 2000 when the High Court issued an order for occupiers of land to vacate, and for the Commissioner of Police to execute the order. Following procrastination, and an attempt by the Commissioner to have the order set aside, the matter ended up in the Supreme Court, which upheld the High Court decision. However:

> *thereafter the matters were taken into the political arena and out of the courts, with the President declaring that the courts could do as they please, as the government would no longer be defending itself before them. (Goredema 2004:107)*

The judiciary and the executive were set upon a collision course. The rule of law was discarded by the government in relation to land reform. Thousands of commercial farms were expropriated without compensation and due process. Some judges, including Chief Justice Gubbay, were forced to resign.

The strained relations adversely affected the law and justice system and the governance system. As a legal expert observed:

> *the ZANU-PF government's record regarding respect for court rulings clearly demonstrates that it considers itself to be superior to the judiciary and to have the licence to pick and choose which decisions to comply with and which to ignore. Government is aware that in disrespecting court prescriptions it acts extra-legally or illegally, but since this does not attract any penalties, it adopts this course anyway. (Ibid.: 107)*

The impunity of the executive contributed to the deterioration of governance between 1999 and 2008. The weakening of the powers of the judiciary has repercussions on political culture and the governance framework which will take many years to repair.

The Executive

The executive consists of the presidency, cabinet and the public service. The Lancaster House Constitution provided for a largely ceremonial presidency with most of the executive powers concentrated in the prime minister. Subsequently, in 1987, an executive presidency was established on the basis of a constitutional amendment. The president became Head of State and Head of Government as well as Commander-in-Chief of the Armed Forces, and had the power to appoint a cabinet. The intelligence service is also under the President's Office. Over the decades, the president has amassed immense powers in making laws, appointing key state officials and in dispensing patronage. Major appointments made by the president include those of provincial governors, ambassadors and 33 members of the senate.

The cabinet consists of the president, the vice-presidents and such ministers as the president may appoint from time to time. Until the advent of the Inclusive Government in 2008, cabinet ministers held office at the discretion of the president. Subsequently, the MDC prime minister had the authority to fire and hire ministers in posts which his party had been allocated under the Global Political Agreement (GPA). In practice, cabinet members are collectively responsible for cabinet decisions. The president acts on the advice of cabinet except in cases where the constitution stipulates otherwise. This is done to restrain the powers of the president, but such restraint is rarely effective.

The promulgation of most Constitutional Amendments before 2008 was basically aimed at increasing the powers of the presidency (Makumbe and Compagnon 2000). These included powers of appointment and veto throughout the public service and state enterprises, including a veto on the appointment of judges (UNDP 2008).

The appointment of no fewer than eight ministers of state within the presidency also illustrated the shift of power from the legislature to the executive. The adverse consequences of this shift included the over-extended size of the executive and poor policy measures. In 2007, the ZANU-PF government had a total of 64 ministers who included 21 deputy ministers and eight ministers of state in the President's Office and ten provincial governors. In the agricultural ministries alone, there were five ministers. Under the Inclusive Government the number of ministers and governors increased further, to over 70. As one study argued:

Although the government had 18 core functions represented at ministerial level, this was arguably too large for a country of the size of Zimbabwe, particularly one with a shrinking GDP. Not only does this translate into heavy demands on both the fiscus and the country's constrained human resources base, but it gives rise to duplication, complicating the co-ordination of service delivery and accountability. (UNDP 2008:213)

A bloated state is expensive to run.

Another consequence of centralisation was poor economic policy measures stemming from over-centralisation and duplication. The president unilaterally transferred a wide range of decision-making powers from ministries, including the finance ministry, to the Reserve Bank of Zimbabwe (RBZ). Crucial economic policy decisions, including those outside the remit of a central bank were taken by the RBZ Governor. These included quasi-fiscal spending programmes, tax changes, and the provision of subsidies for agriculture, manufacturing, construction and other sectors. The expenditures proved unsustainable, and the RBZ was indebted by over US$1bn in 2010.

Local State Authorities

In the first three decades of independence, local state structures such as city and town councils, rural district councils and traditional leadership structures were largely staffed by ZANU-PF officials. Conflicts in governance flared when city or town council elections were won by the MDC, and the mayors were elected on an MDC ticket. It was an unprecedented situation: one party exercising control over central state institutions, a different party running the local ones. Conflicts of interest and purpose were inevitable.

For instance, the Minister of Local Government invoked the Urban Councils Act to suspend three MDC mayors in Harare (2003), Mutare (2004) and Chitungwiza (2005). Councillors in Harare and Mutare then resigned *en masse* when threatened with suspensions by the minister. The suspension of mayors was a major reversal of local democracy (Musekiwa 2006). Residents in the affected cities protested, arguing that government had no reasonable excuse to unilaterally dismiss popularly elected representatives without any reference to the electorate. The state's action in this respect has been a major drawback to local democracy, as local citizens have had to deal with appointed commissioners (who are accountable to the minister who appointed them in the first place) rather than an elected council.

Thus local democracy was a major casualty during Zimbabwe's lost decades. Conflicts with central authorities occurred against the background of economic crisis. The financial situation of local authorities was further jeopardised by defaulting ratepayers, government ministries and departments as well as parastatals, with councils having to beg the latter to honour their obligations.

Political parties have had a definite influence on local elections and the political organisation of local authorities. The election of council members into office is usually along party lines, with the majority of candidates being sponsored by their parties. It is a common practice that members of a council who belong to the same party can caucus to predetermine how to debate and vote on major issues to be discussed in councils. Sanctions can be imposed on members who renege on an agreed party position. It is when a ruling party pushes for the implementation of its policies by an opposition-controlled council that challenges arise. The latter insists that they have a mandate to generate and implement policy at that level for as long as it is not against national policy.

Traditional leadership structures play a significant role both in local governance and also during elections when they mobilise and deliver the vote for the ruling party. In particular, Chiefs have been relied upon by ZANU-PF to deliver the vote during elections; this was particularly visible during the 2008 run-off presidential election. The President and Minister of Local Government are responsible for appointing, cautioning, reprimanding and removing a chief or headman from office. Thus central government can caution and discipline traditional leaders and order a reduction of their salary and allowances. It is not coincidental that in period between 2000 and 2008, the salaries and perks of chiefs were significantly increased by a ZANU-PF government intent on drawing on their capacity to mobilise the rural vote.

Finally, the Traditional Leaders Act requires that every village or ward assembly needs to ensure adequate representation of women, youth and any other interest group on the village and ward development committees. Due to the dominance of ZANU-PF in most rural areas, the quotas for women and youth tended to be filled by chairpersons of respective party leagues and not through election. In theory, the assemblies and committees are inclusive and participatory but in practice traditional leaders make most decisions as few of the former are operational. Thus Zimbabwe has reaped little gain from local

institutions and processes which were originally expected to be conduits of development and democracy.

The Military–Security Complex and the State

With the deepening of authoritarianism, an important branch of the state that emerged from the late 1990s was the military–security complex, for lack of a more precise term. The complex has become deeply enmeshed in state administration and party politics as well as in business. Constituting this complex are the uniformed services (police, army, air-force and the prison service) as well as the intelligence service. The military–security complex played a leading role in buttressing Mugabe in elections held in 2000, 2002 and 2008, when his political fortunes were decidedly shaky. It was not an accident that this complex played a direct role in the electoral process to ensure that Mugabe was re-elected into power.

What explains the novel involvement of this complex which in modern democracies does not engage in politics and state administration? One important study traces the roots of the activist role of the complex to the history of the liberation struggle; it observed that since the 1970s, the party-military nexus had always been strong in ZANU-PF and PF-ZAPU, with military leaders always having a significant input into party politics (Zimbabwe Institute 2008). Most senior levels of the military have strongly supported the ruling party. Significantly also, command posts from the position of colonel upwards have been political appointments directly approved by the president (Ibid.). In some quarters, the party–military nexus helped to stabilise the situation while in others it was viewed as an authoritarian block to democracy. According to the latter position, Mugabe has relied upon the military–security complex to frustrate the will of the population during elections. As it was argued:

> After the referendum defeat in February 2000, Mugabe turned to the military to shield himself from attacks and to mobilise support around him …. He also relied heavily on the military in organising the 2002 election. (Ibid.:8)

For that purpose, Mugabe appointed key military personnel to run the Electoral Supervisory Commission (ESC) which organised the 2002 election. The military-security complex set up a National Command Centre (NCC) which collated the election results provoking charges of rigging by the opposition and some observer teams. In 2008, the complex was credited for running a violent run-off election campaign after Mugabe had lost the first round in March 2008.

In addition, the military–security complex has been increasingly involved in running government ministries and departments, parastatals, commissions and various ad hoc military-style operations. There were a number of military officers appointed as ministers (for example, Mike Nyambuya, Ambrose Mutinhiri, Hubert Nyanhongo) and as permanent secretaries, ambassadors and directors and board members of parastatals (Ibid.). These appointments reflected the extensive patronage at the president's disposal to reward and retain loyalty.

The military–security complex was involved in business activities as individuals but also government business operations. Senior military figures got involved in business ventures in the Democratic Republic of the Congo (DRC) at the height of the war there in 1998–2001. They were involved in mining and timber operations which provided a lucrative source of accumulation (UN 2003). Although the results were disappointing, if not disastrous, nearer home, the military was involved in Operation *Taguta/Sisuthi*, a version of 'command agriculture' in rural areas in 2005. Their conception and execution of Operation *Murambatsvina*/Restore Order in 2005 was widely condemned for its ruthless excesses (UN 2005).

Overall, the military-security complex has not been successful in its various projects and operations with the exception of securing political tenure for Mugabe, and self-enrichment. Their entry into politics has far-reaching significance and repercussions for the structure and administration of the state especially during the period between 2000 and 2008. The institutions in which the military–security complex members were represented soon eclipsed the role of Cabinet until the advent of the Inclusive Government in 2008. The Joint Operations Command (JOC) and the National Security Council (NSC) were the two powerful institutions that rivalled the authority of Cabinet. As it was observed:

> With the JOC taking centre stage in all decision-making processes, Cabinet (which is vested with executive power) has increasingly become a rubber-stamping organ that endorses policies generated elsewhere .... For example, when Operation Murambatsvina was launched in 2005, Cabinet ministers were not aware of the programme. (UNDP 2008:214)

Some analysts went as far as characterising JOC as a 'kitchen cabinet' due to its central role in policy setting (Ibid.). Complementing the role of JOC is that of the NSC which was set up by Mugabe and the military-security complex in 2005 to oversee the economy. Dominated by members of the complex, security ministers, and the RBZ governor, the NSC also became a *de facto* cabinet in the realm of economic matters. With nine departments and task forces reporting to it, its remit covered all economic sectors and policy areas such as foreign exchange and monetary matters. As a consequence, by 2008 the military–security complex virtually controlled the major institutions of the state and formal policy-making structures and processes in the country (Zimbabwe Institute 2008). As we explore in a later chapter, it has become a significant part of the domestic bourgeoisie with many commanders teaming up with politicians and businessmen to form political and economic interest groups venturing into lucrative commercial ventures.

The military–security complex remains a shadowy but powerful group which is not subject to elections. Nor does it submit itself to requirements and standards of accountability and transparency that are expected of those in positions of governance authority and power. It is insufficient for them to justify their intervention in governance on historical grounds of their role in the liberation struggle. It is unfortunate that decline in Zimbabwe's governance and democracy standards during the lost decades has been associated with the devaluation of the role of key state institutions such as Cabinet due to competition from and elevation of the military-security complex.

The Phenomenon of the Party-State

One insightful study on Zimbabwean politics published in 1990 argued that even a party such as ZANU-PF, which had played a much more powerful role over a longer period of time in contesting for Independence than was the case for most parties in Africa, later became irrelevant in so many of Zimbabwe's decision-making processes (Herbst 1990). With the benefit of hindsight, this observation was premature. In fact, the ideology and practice of ZANU-PF was to insist on what was termed the 'supremacy' of the party in the setting of policy. The ruling party viewed itself as a superior institution in governance vis-à-vis the cabinet, parliament and the public service (Cliffe and Stoneman 1989). Articulating this position, Mugabe claimed that ZANU-PF:

> is more important than the government, and ... the Central Committee is above the Cabinet because Ministers derive their power from ZANU-PF.... In

the future, there will be no separation of the party from state organs, because after the August 1984 national congress, government programmes will be based on the resolutions of the Central Committee. (Quoted on ZBC News, 18 February 1984)

There was thus a strong aspiration within ZANU-PF to ensure party supremacy in the governance sphere. It was an aspiration shared by other parties and liberation movements elsewhere in Africa in the 1980s, at least before the transition to the multi-party state system. For instance, during that decade, the Tanzanian constitution devolved specific state powers to the party, while in Algeria it was not possible to disentangle the party from the state.

Indeed, certain ministries specifically catered for ZANU-PF party interests during the 1980s and 1990s. This was the case with the Ministry of Political Affairs, later renamed Ministry of National Affairs. Although they were partisan outfits, they drew on the national budget and it was only due to criticism from opposition parties and civil society that the ministry was subsequently dismantled. Even so, two other ministries, of youth and gender, continued to cater mainly for ZANU-PF constituencies right up to 2008. At the height of land reform, it became difficult to disentangle party structures from state structures regarding the allocation of resources; there was inter-penetration of the two sets of structures, especially at local levels.

The Zimbabwe experience of fused party–state structures is reminiscent of structures in communist/socialist states in Eastern Europe and China. Prior to their dismantlement in Eastern Europe, the doctrine of supremacy of the party in a context of one-party state reigned supreme. ZANU-PF sought to replicate the ideology and structure of the party–state, hence the creation of a 'Central Committee' and a matching 'Politburo'. It is significant that none of these party organs are reflected in the national constitution which makes their intended 'supremacy' contradictory in relation to the latter. An explanation that has been advanced is that the Western concept of party puts it outside the state: the parties are, at most, groups which occupy the state for certain periods of time (Herbst 1990). However, in developing countries such as Zimbabwe some parties have evolved to such an extent that they become part of the state resource-allocation process.

There have been structural and governance drawbacks as a consequence of the party–state. Partisan considerations in recruitment of staff into the public service and award of tenders and other resources have violated criteria of merit, fairness and efficiency. An audit in 2010 revealed that the Mugabe government recruited 13,000 additional personnel in 2008 without following laid down procedures in the public service. Most of the recruits were youth who were deployed in the 2008 ZANU-PF election run-off campaign. What mattered more was whether they belonged to the ruling party rather than their competence, skills and efficiency. Consider this order made to civil servants in 1995 by Kumbirai Kangai, a ZANU-PF provincial chair:

> No one should say I work for the government and not for the party. If anyone should say this, he will be removed from Manicaland. (Quoted in the Herald, 14 January 1995)

This threat was repeated on numerous occasions in the post-2000 period as various government ministries were purged of public servants who were suspected of supporting opposition parties (Hammar 2003). The decline in performance in the public sector during the lost decades can be traced partly to these adverse effects of the operations of the party-state.

Corruption

No assessment of the Zimbabwe state would be complete without reference to the phenomenon of corruption. It reached endemic levels during the lost decades. Perhaps the most notorious early episode of corruption was by ministers in what became known as the 'Willowgate' car scandal, when some ministers and senior government officials misused their office to profiteer from the purchase and re-selling of luxury vehicles from the state-owned Willowvale car assembly in 1987 and 1988. Although a government-appointed commission found the concerned ministers guilty of corruption, most got off lightly, with little more than censure from President Mugabe.

Significantly, the Willowgate scandal showed the growing web of interests between some politicians and the business class. The latter included white- and Asian-owned businesses as well as local black and multinational businesses. More generally, this episode of widely publicised corruption was not only indicative of the emergent post-independence political economy of cronyism but was also a harbinger of the more widespread corruption to come. The widespread abuse of the War Victims Compensation Fund by politicians, mostly from ZANU-PF, and by war veterans in the mid-1990s epitomised the spreading cancer. Later instances of corruption related to award of tenders for projects such as the construction of a new international airport in Harare. Parastatals became notorious not only for their incompetence and mismanagement but also for corrupt dealings, which led to the decline of large ones like the Zimbabwe Iron and Steel Corporation (ZISCO) in the 1990s. The land redistribution in the post-2000 was also marked by considerable corruption, with most politicians, senior bureaucrats and military officers grabbing the best farms. Ominously, the discovery of diamonds at Marange was accompanied by allegations of corrupt dealings by companies and state officials, resulting in the reduction of revenue flows into the national fiscus. Regrettably, the failure to nip corruption in the bud in the 1980s sent out the hugely negative signal that there was impunity for those engaged in corruption. This was accompanied by a dangerous sense of entitlement by politicians, war veterans, party officials and militia, who believed they could seize other people's property without paying for it. One of the chief legacies of the lost decades, corruption and entitlement became part and parcel of the Zimbabwe body politic.

Conclusion

This chapter has explored the structure of the post-colonial state in Zimbabwe through a close analysis of its institutional components. For a state inherited by a liberation movement, it has been remarkable how much of the old state apparatus was inherited almost lock, stock and barrel. More disquieting has been the inheritance of the more unsavoury aspects of authoritarian structures and tendencies in the security ministries. Similarly far-reaching has been the centralisation of powers in the executive. This excessive centralisation of powers in the presidency was unprecedented in the post-colonial period even within the Southern Africa region. But this proved a major structural weakness as the country slid into a dictatorship between 2000 and 2008.

Concomitant with this authoritarian centralisation of authority and power was the weakening of checks and balances between key institutions of parliament, the judiciary and the executive. Although the process started earlier, the authority of parliament and judiciary was steadily eroded during the post-colonial era. Clashes between the executive and the judiciary became frequent and pronounced, especially between 2000 and 2008, to the detriment of the rule of law.

The chapter also explored the significance of the military-security complex in politics and economics noting its increasing self-interest as a bloc and influence over the executive. While its professionalism diminished, its partisan tendencies grew stronger as its intervention during the 2008 presidential run-off election dramatised. Against the tenets of the constitution, there had arisen a party-state in which institutions of ZANU-PF wielded more power and influence in decision-making and implementation than constitutionally mandated institutions. This was to the detriment of accountable and transparent governance.

Postscript: The Inclusive Government Experiment

Although, strictly speaking, the Inclusive Government (IG) formed in 2009 on the basis of the Global Political Agreement (GPA) does not fall under the purview of the period covered in this book, it nevertheless merits some attention. This is largely because its composition and performance between 2009 and 2011 reflected the impact (or lack thereof) of changes on the state and wider society. Of course, the immediate background and impetus to the formation of the IG made up of ZANU-PF, MDC-T and MDC-M was the inconclusive poll of 2008 in which Robert Mugabe lost in the first round of the presidential election, as observed in Chapter 4. A great deal of violence was unleashed during the second round campaign, forcing Morgan Tsvangirai to withdraw his candidature.

The structure and performance of the IG left a great deal to be desired. First, it did not reflect the parliamentary weight of the two MDC parties. ZANU-PF clung to the more powerful ministries; it retained control over all the 'power' ministries including Defence, State Security and Justice. Furthermore, although the GPA sought to enforce civilian oversight over the military through the National Security Council (NSC), which includes MDC representatives, the power of the Zimbabwean military and intelligence services was not curtailed (Mavhinga 2011:8). Indeed, apart from a few meetings that it has held, the NSC has remained marginalised and dysfunctional while the partisan JOC has continued to pull strings behind the scenes, as we observed above. Furthermore, ZANU-PF has maintained its stranglehold on the public media, radio and television as well as a number of newspapers through which it de-campaigned other parties and poured attacks on cabinet ministers from those parties. The two MDC factions were given the social and economic ministries with limited power and scope.

There has been little change at the top echelons of government bureaucracy, which is critically neither apolitical nor suffficiently professional. This has sometimes resulted in obstruction of policy initiatives from the MDC parties. Without key strategic changes in leadership and personnel running state institutions, there will be resistance to changes, especially those relating to a transition to a more democratic environment.

The stalemate over the reappointment of Gideon Gono to the RBZ and of Johannes Tomana to the Attorney-General's Office, and the denial of Roy Bennet of the MDC-T to be sworn in as Deputy Minister of Agriculture were emblematic of the gridlock in the IG. Unilateral appointments by Mugabe included those of provincial governors without the concurrence of MDC-T and MDC-M.

Finally, political polarisation continued in the formulation of policies and programmes. This surfaced more clearly over the constitution-making process, as we explain in Chapter 4, and over the scheduling of the next election as well as the handling of public finances. The IG may continue to muddle through to the next election, which may take place in 2012. However, rather than provide an opportunity for better working relations between parties and their leaders, the record of the IG underscores the unilateral and authoritarian instincts of Mugabe and his party. As a result, it is unlikely to survive beyond the next election.

3
Political Parties

Introduction

The last two chapters have demonstrated how party politics have been central in Zimbabwe's political development in the past 50 years. Political parties were leading actors in the nationalist/liberation struggles as well as in the post-colonial era. Surprisingly, however, there have been very few studies on parties as pivotal institutions in the political process during that period (Sachikonye 2005). It is somewhat strange that, despite their centrality in the electoral and governance processes, there have been no detailed monographs on parties such as ZANU-PF, PF ZAPU, UANC, ZANU-Ndonga, ZUM or the MDC. Not only have academics and journalists demonstrated little inclination to undertake such an enterprise, but surprisingly, so have the parties themselves. In our survey of the lost decades, we recognise the pivotal role which parties have played in the processes which culminated in authoritarianism, and in the resistance that has grown against it.

This chapter begins by exploring the concept of political party and the contemporary context of parties in Zimbabwe, their ideologies and role in the political process. What are the principal elements of the party system, and what are the ideologies and platforms of the major parties? How do their internal functioning and tendency towards factionalism and violence affect political development and democratisation? These are the key questions we address.

Background

Political parties are distinctive organisations whose principal aim is to acquire and exercise political power through gaining control of the government apparatus. Parties aggregate diverse demands into coherent programmes. In modern political systems, parties therefore focus on acting as agencies for articulating different views and interests; serving as vehicles for selection of leaders and cadres for positions in state institutions; organising personnel around the formulation and implementation of government policy; and mediating between individuals and their government (Ndulo 2000).

In Southern Africa, parties are important instruments in encouraging, indeed mobilising, participation in the political process. However, most citizens in the region tend to associate parties largely with 'elections'. It is mainly around election time that more parties are formed explicitly to contest elections. The formation of such 'election time' parties is a general trend in the region, not least in Zimbabwe. An 'opportunistic' and 'entrepreneurial' approach appears to underlie the formation of such parties. However, even well-established parties have a tendency to be 'dormant' between elections, only springing to life in intense activity towards the next electoral contest. Thus a certain amount of 'electoralism' appears to pervade the strategic thinking and outlook of both ruling and opposition parties, old and new.

The Contemporary Context of Parties in Zimbabwe

The development of parties in Zimbabwe needs to be set in a broad context. As previous chapters have shown, Zimbabwe's political system was shaped by black nationalism in the 1950s, and by the liberation struggle between 1966 and 1979. The colonial legacy of white settler rule also left an imprint on the system. During the first decade of independence, the Lancaster House Constitution set out the framework of the political system of the new state.

First, the party system was a multi-party one as spelt out in the constitution. The definitive 1980 elections had resulted in majority rule under a ZANU-PF dominated government. With 57 seats in a 100-member parliament, ZANU-PF was the majority party, but between 1980 and 1982 it ran a government of national unity with PF-ZAPU. As we observed in Chapter One, with the eruption of the conflict in Matabeleland in 1982, the pact collapsed. It was not until 1987 that the two parties bargained a rapprochement resulting in a Unity Accord. Second, the abolition of 20 reserved seats in the House of Assembly in 1987 had a direct impact on the political system. It marked the demise of predominantly white-based parties. In the same year, a constitutional amendment created an executive presidency which awarded wide-ranging powers to the president. These developments laid the seeds of future authoritarianism (Makumbe and Compagnon 2000).

Third, although the system remained nominally a multi-party one, there was pressure to introduce a one-party state system in the late 1980s. Only sustained campaigns from opposition parties, especially ZUM, and from civil society organisations (CSOs) prevented the adoption of the system. Even so, multi-partyism was grudgingly accepted and retained while a strong one-party state ideological tendency continued to persist in ZANU-PF. During the 1990 and 1995 elections, ZANU-PF easily proved to be the dominant party by securing more than 95 per cent of seats in Parliament. During the period, 1990-1999, Zimbabwe was therefore a dominant-party system.

In 2000, there were an estimated 25 political parties in Zimbabwe; this was scarcely surprising as this was an election year. For instance, in 1999, there were 33 parties in South Africa, 34 in Zambia and 18 in Mozambique. However, the number of seriously organised parties was often a handful. Zimbabwe was no exception. It had its own fair share of 'briefcase' political parties that surfaced during election campaigns but disappeared soon afterwards.

The main parties at Independence were ZANU-PF, PF ZAPU, ZANU-Ndonga, UANC and the Rhodesian Front (later called the Conservative Alliance of Zimbabwe (CAZ)). By 1990, although the merger of ZANU-PF and PF ZAPU resulted in an enlarged ZANU-PF, the number of parties did not diminish. In addition to ZANU-Ndonga and UANC, parties continued being active such as the case of ZUM that was founded in 1989 by Edgar Tekere who had formerly been the Secretary-General of ZANU-PF. However, in 1991 some ZUM members broke away to form the Democratic Party (DP) under Emmanuel Magoche. Another party of note in the early 1990s was the Forum Party of Zimbabwe (FPZ) founded by a former Chief Justice, Enoch Dumbutshena. Towards the end of the 1990s, the Zimbabwe Union of Democrats (ZUD) was formed by Margaret Dongo who represented it in Parliament herself. Nevertheless, until the formation of the MDC in 1999, none of these parties posed a serious challenge to the dominant party system presided over by ZANU-PF. Later parties included *Mavambo/Kusile* formed in 2008 by Simba Makoni, a former Minister of Finance and the new ZAPU under Dumiso Dabengwa, also a former Minister of Home Affairs in a ZANU-PF government.

Box 3.1 – The aims and objectives of ZANU-PF

- *To preserve and defend the national sovereignty and independence of Zimbabwe*
- *To create conditions for the establishment of a democratic political and social order which shall guarantee in perpetuity that the government of the state shall be answerable to the people through periodic and fair elections based on universal suffrage*
- *To uphold and apply fully the rule of law, equality before the law, and equality of opportunities for all the people in Zimbabwe regardless of race, tribe, sex, religion or origin*
- *To establish and sustain a socialist society firmly based on our historical, cultural and social experience and to create conditions for economic independence, prosperity and equitable distribution of wealth of the nation*
- *To continue to participate in the worldwide struggle for the complete eradication of imperialism, colonialism and other forms of racism*
- *To oppose resolutely tribalism, regionalism, nepotism, racism, religious fanaticism, xenophobia and related intolerance.*

Source: ZANU-PF 1999

The History, Ideology and Platforms of Parties

Let us put each of the major parties under the spotlight, tracing their history, ideology and platforms. We assess ZANU-PF, MDC, and then its offshoots namely MDC-T and MDC-M. In addition, we trace the fortunes of three small parties which were vocal in 2005 but fell almost silent in 2010.

ZANU-PF

Founded in 1963, the party was a splinter group from ZAPU which was headed by Joshua Nkomo who, in later years, came to known as 'Father Zimbabwe'. Although banned in 1964, ZANU continued to operate in exile while prosecuting the liberation struggle. The party re-surfaced in the country in 1980 in an election which it won handsomely, as we saw above. ZANU-PF espoused a radical version of nationalism and pronounced adherence to pan-Africanism and socialism.

It is useful to underline that liberation movements such as ZANU-PF experience challenges in transforming themselves into parties. As one analyst pointed out:

> *the task of transforming liberation movements and guerrilla fighters into*

mass movements or democratic parties proved difficult in most of Africa. Movement political parties are, by and large, populist, nationalist and based on the ethos of liberation ideology. (Salih 2003:18)

It was further observed that liberation movements which transformed themselves into political parties tend to behave like one-party systems, often blurring the distinction between party and state. Chapter 2 explored the phenomenon of the party-state. Movements that became parties:

continue to be an embodiment of nationalist-populist politics in which the person of the president and the liberation struggle are constant reminders for voters to stay the course. (Ibid.)

There is also a strong streak of authoritarianism borne of the commandist methods used during the liberation struggle. Furthermore, there is often recourse to coercive strategies used by these parties in mobilising voters during elections. ZANU-PF has displayed these features and tendencies during the nearly 50 years of its existence (Kriger 2005).

The advantage that ZANU-PF has had over other parties is that it had an opportunity of 28 years to implement its aims, objectives and agenda. In reality, it experienced huge difficulties in attaining them.

The Movement for Democratic Change (MDC)

The MDC was founded in 1999 but the process of foundation began a few years earlier. The party had firm roots in the labour and civic movements. The rationale for the formation of a party has been spelt out in these terms:

When workers cannot earn a living wage and decent working conditions through industrial action at the workplace, they will go beyond the shop-floor and bring their issues to the national stage, thus politicising the issues. (ZCTU Resolution as quoted in Raftopoulos, 2000)

The leadership of the ZCTU, principally Morgan Tsvangirai, Gibson Sibanda and Gift Chimanikire, and of the NCA, chiefly Welshman Ncube and Tendai Biti, organised a National Working People's Convention in January 1999 in Chitungwiza, near Harare. The Convention resolved to build consensus on the formation of a vigorous and democratic movement for change. This was followed in May 1999 by another Convention at which the ZCTU was mandated to facilitate the establishment of a party. One analyst observed that the newly-born movement made judicious use of the structures of 'its parents, the ZCTU and NCA, as it penetrated the hith-

Box 3.2 – The aims and objectives of the MDC

- *To be an all-inclusive, dynamic political party with a truly national base and which shall seek to win political power and form a government of the people through free, fair and direct elections*
- *To seek the mandate of the people to govern the country and work for a dynamic economy built on principles of mixed economy with a strong social conscience*
- *To build an open democracy in which national government is accountable to the people through the devolution of power and decision-making to the provinces, local institutions and structures*
- *To seek equal representation of women as far as possible in public office and within the party*
- *To pursue the principle of active civic participation in public affairs and in the pursuit of this principle working with unions, business and employers' organisations, human rights organisations and other civic groups in the formulation of national policies.*

Source: MDC Constitution 1999

erto rural strongholds of ZANU-PF with the active support of some white commercial farmers and rural-based public service workers like teachers' (Masunungure 2004:178). It was noted that:

> *a distinctive quality of the MDC was that it was a new party in almost every sense. It was not a breakaway party nor was it founded from existing parties. It was born out of civil society's struggle against the party-state. Its leadership was therefore not tainted through associations with other parties. The MDC was a new party, with a new leadership and with a new agenda. (Ibid.: 178)*

In 2000, the MDC emerged as the strongest opposition party to ZANU-PF since Independence, giving the ruling party a stunning challenge when it won 57 of the directly contested seats in parliament. Its election perform-ance improved significantly in the 2008 election; the combined vote of MDC-T and MDC-M was greater than that of ZANU-PF which lost its parlia-mentary majority for the first time since 1980.

ZANU-Ndonga

There were a plethora of small parties that were active during election years but dormant during other times. The oldest amongst them is ZANU-Ndonga, an offshoot of ZANU-PF founded by Ndabaningi Sithole, the first

Box 3.3 – The aims and objectives of ZANU-Ndonga

- *To establish and maintain a democratic and non-racial state in Zimbabwe*
- *To ensure that the people's right of one-man-one-vote is freely and regularly exercised at periodic national elections*
- *To promote the social, economic, political, educational, cultural and religious welfare of the people of Zimbabwe*
- *To promote national consciousness and national unity in diversity*
- *To ensure the possession and use of equal opportunity by all for all*
- *To pursue in our foreign relations a policy of positive non-alignment.*

Source: ZANU-Ndonga Constitution 1999

president of ZANU in 1963. Largely confined to Manicaland province in eastern Zimbabwe, the party has never won more than two seats in Parliament since its formation. Since 2005, it has had no representation in Parliament.

ZANU-Ndonga has not had an opportunity to translate its objectives and agenda into policies and programmes because it has not had any power since 1980. However, it is of interest that it shares the values of nationalism and democracy. Its patriarchal founding leader, Ndabaningi Sithole, died in 2000 and was succeeded by Wilson Kumbula, a long-time member and office holder in the party, who represented it in Parliament in 1985–2005.

The Democratic Party (DP)

For its part, the small Democratic Party, under the mercurial leadership of Wurayayi Zembe, has aims and objectives that strike a tone attuned to the discourse on liberal democracy. However, the DP has not won any parliamentary seats since its formation as a splinter party from ZUM in 1991. A distinguishing feature of DP is that it boycotts elections on the grounds that there should first be constitutional reform to ensure that an electoral contest is truly free and fair.

The National Alliance for Good Governance (NAGG)

The National Alliance for Good Governance was created in 2000 out of a loose grouping of former ZANU-PF politicians who had lost nomination as ZANU-PF parliamentary candidates for the 2000 election.

Box 3.4 – The aims and objectives of the DP

- *To strive for the maintenance of a multiparty democratic order in Zimbabwe and to constantly oppose the tendency toward dictatorship in any form*
- *To cultivate a democratic political order in Zimbabwe by constantly encouraging self-criticism and guarding against commandist tendencies at all levels in our party as well as within society in general*
- *To promote the observance of the constitutional separation of powers between the Executive, Legislative and Judicial branches of state by maintaining constant vigilance and oppose the tendency in the Executive branch to overstep its jurisdiction*
- *To strive for the preservation and promotion of the freedom of association, expression, press, conscience, worship and right to privacy*
- *To ensure that our nation pursues pragmatic economic policies*
- *To strive for the eradication of unemployment, hunger, poverty, ignorance and disease.*

Source: DP Constitution 1991

Box 3.5 – The aims and objectives of NAGG

- *To preserve and defend the national flag and sovereignty of Zimbabwe*
- *To offer itself for election to political power in Zimbabwe through free, fair and direct elections*
- *To achieve and maintain good governance by adhering to principles of social democracy, transparency and accountability*
- *To promote and maintain the economic empowerment of all Zimbabweans*
- *Promote equal access and maintain organized and equitable distribution and enjoyment of the country's resources, especially land.*

Source: NAGG Constitution 2000

They rallied under the leadership of Shakespeare Maya, who was its founding president.

Although the party contested the 2000 elections, it failed to win any seats; nor did it fair better in the 2002 elections. In 2004, its founding president resigned to join the MDC.

The Internal Functioning and Structure of Parties

Although the five parties covered in this chapter vary enormously in size and age, some of their internal structures are remarkably similar. For the DP, NAGG, MDC, ZANU-Ndonga and ZANU-PF, the supreme organ in their structures is the congress. Sometimes termed a 'national people's congress' (by ZANU-PF) or simply 'congress' (by most parties), it is held once every five years and handles major issues such as the election of the top leadership, amending the party constitution, as well as formulating party policies. The congress also supervises the implementation of party policies, principles and programmes, considers the audited financial statements of the party, and appoints or re-appoints auditors.

It is significant that some parties hold their congresses towards the next round of elections (which are held at five-yearly intervals). The last ZANU-PF congress was organised in December 2004. The timing in such instances would be strategic in terms of party strategising for the upcoming elections. However, some parties hardly organise a congress; for example, the last one organised by ZANU-Ndonga was in 1979, while the DP and NAGG appear not to have held any. Most parties specify an annual party conference as one of the institutions of the party, but only a few parties are able to organise one. Smaller parties such as the DP, NAGG and ZANU-Ndonga cited resource constraints as the major reason for not holding congresses.

The second highest structure is a central committee, which handles administrative and policy issues through regular meetings. Its size ranges from 100 in the case of the DP to 232 in ZANU-PF. The term 'central committee' is reminiscent of socialist or communist party structures. Some parties such as the MDC and NAGG give a different name to this structure although its functions are similar. The MDC calls it a 'national council' while NAGG terms it a 'national high council'. The functions of the council are chiefly administering and implementing party decisions and policies. In most parties, an executive committee plays a more active role in this administrative and implementing role. It is called a 'national executive committee' in the MDC, ZANU-Ndonga and DP, while ZANU-PF takes on a Soviet-era term of 'politburo'. Acting as an administrative organ of the central committee, the 49-member politburo is tasked with implementing all decisions, directives, rules and regulations of the central committee. It meets monthly or 'in special session' as determined by the party president. Its equivalent in ZANU-Ndonga is the 'president in council' chaired by the party president, with authority to appoint members to the central committee and national executive council.

Below these executive or administrative bodies and committees is the national consultative assembly that draws on the wider party membership between annual party conferences and five-year congresses. The assembly's role varies between parties. Whereas it has little power in ZANU-PF, it has substantial power in the DP where the assembly can fill vacancies in the central committee and prepare for elections.

All the above parties have provision for women's and youth wings, sometimes called leagues (by ZANU-PF) or national assemblies (by the MDC). The MDC National Assembly of Women and that of Youth have the tasks of mobilising their respective constituencies to join the party, as well as ensuring that women and youth are fully involved in all party activities, including policy making. The women's and youth leagues of ZANU-PF have elaborate organs, namely a national conference, national assembly, national executive committee as well as a provincial conference. For its part, ZANU-Ndonga not only has women and youth leagues but also a men's league. The leagues are expected to hold annual meetings, receive and distribute party literature and information, as well as to uphold, defend and propagate the principles and policies of the party. NAGG has a national women's council and a national youth council, which seek to perform a role similar to those of leagues in other parties.

Other parts of the structure are the provincial and district committees that carry out the directives of the party in mobilising membership and propagating and implementing party policies and programmes. The provincial, district, ward and branch structures tend to replicate (at lower levels) the posts and functions of the top structures. For instance, a branch in the MDC consists of a minimum of 100 members. The lowest layer of most parties is the unit or cell (or a village committee in rural areas) with ten members. It would not be easy to ascertain how active they are.

However, in the past few years there have been efforts at conducting surveys of Zimbabwean public opinion on political and socio-economic issues. The more notable efforts have been those of the Helen Suzman Foundation based in Johannesburg, and the Mass Public Opinion Institute (MPOI) in Harare. Both organisations conducted surveys on political attitudes in 1999 and 2000. MPOI is a Zimbabwean polling organisation founded in 1999 by the late Masipula Sithole, who was a well-known and respected political scientist. It has released surveys on public attitudes towards issues such as land policy, corruption, political parties and the support for major political figures, namely, Robert Mugabe and Morgan Tsvangirai.

Most parties do not conduct public opinion surveys independently and instead tend to rely on the survey reports of such organisations as the MPOI, the Helen Suzman Foundation and Afrobarometer surveys (conducted by Idasa, a South African NGO). However, ZANU-PF and the MDC have the capacity to conduct opinion surveys for in-house purposes. Such surveys do not enter the public domain.

Party Funding

The viability of parties largely depends on whether they generate or receive satisfactory funding for their activities. Little funding cripples a party's operations and reach. Clearly there are major differences in scale in the amount of funding that different parties are able to generate and mobilise. We observed in a previous section that a major source of party funding in Zimbabwe is the public purse. The Political Parties (Finance Act) originally stipulated that only parties with a minimum of 15 seats in parliament were entitled to funding. This was later modified in 2001 to extend funding to a party which received at least five per cent of the vote in the previous election. However, only three parties – ZANU-PF, MDC-T and the MDC-M – have been beneficiaries under this formula. The smaller parties complain about their exclusion from funding; they argue that unless they get funding, they will not perform well in elections to the extent of garnering at least five per cent of the total vote. In 2000, some Z$100 million was disbursed and shared between ZANU-PF and the MDC.

It is significant that since 2001, parties have been prohibited from receiving foreign funding. The Political Parties (Finance) Act spells out that: 'No party, member of political party or candidate shall accept any foreign donation, whether directly from the donor or indirectly through a third person.' This prohibition appears to have hurt small parties because they have no source of steady income. At the same time, the bigger parties themselves have lost a considerable source of revenue – both ZANU-PF and the MDC had received significant donor support in the past.

What then are the other major sources of funds for the parties? ZANU-PF has raised considerable sums of money from its business interests that include shareholdings in companies, and from wealthy supporters who have included bankers and industrialists. For its 2004 congress, it was set to raise about Z$5 billion from both business interests and supporters. Its original target, however, had been Z$20 billion. Membership dues are another major source of revenue. The sale of membership cards, especially in the run-up to elections, also generates considerable amounts of funds.

For its part, the MDC relies on business donors, membership dues as well as rental revenue from leasing properties in Harare and several provincial centres. The party views those Zimbabweans in the diaspora as potentially a major source of funding and has therefore been making appeals to them.[60] In terms of breakdown, the party stated that about 60 per cent of its funding is from the state, 20 per cent from membership dues, 10 per cent from business donations, and the balance from party business interests. These revenues were utilised in publicity work (20 per cent), salaries for secretariat and other staff (30 per cent), transport (25 per cent), research and policy work (25 per cent) and legal fees (10 per cent). Financial constraints were a perennial problem for smaller parties.

Gender Equality

Only the MDC and ZANU-PF have set quotas for nominations or posts for women, but the quotas are voluntary. It is required that a third of the members in ZANU-PF's politburo should be women, but significantly no similar quota applies to central committee membership. Nor is there a set quota for women election candidates. An innovation was an amendment to ZANU-PF's constitution to have a woman as one of the two party vice-presidents. This was ratified at the 2004 December Congress of ZANU-PF, paving the way for the election of the first woman vice-president, Joyce Mujuru.

In the MDC, there is no formal quota for women election candidates or for the various party posts. The exception is the membership of the national council. The party's constitution states that in the event of there being less than eight women among the 24 members of the council, the national executive council has powers to co-opt women so that they form a third of the membership. In general, parties have not formulated clear positions on quotas for various special groups including women, the youth and people with disabilities. The First Past The Post (FPTP) electoral system appears to have discouraged a trend towards a party list, such as obtains under the Proportional Representation (PR) system. There is, however, recognition that a quota for women would be one of the first steps necessary on the path towards gender equality. One woman party member observed that in view of the fact that women constitute 65 per cent of the membership in her party they deserved a quota of at least 35 per cent in posts and election nominations.

Some of the parties were taking proactive measures, such as organising training programmes to hone women's political and campaign skills. These were to increase confidence among potential women candidates. In another party, the issues of gender mainstreaming in party programmes were being taken seriously. But concerns of personal security of women party members and candidates loomed large, particularly among opposition parties. There is still a long way to go before political parties in Zimbabwe establish conditions that are conducive for gender equality in political representation.

Factionalism in Parties

Zimbabwe's political parties have been particularly prone to factionalism. As we saw in Chapter 1, the nationalist movement itself was bedevilled with factionalism in 1963 leading to a split which resulted in the formation of ZANU. In 1975, factionalism in the African National Council (ANC) produced a number of different parties such as the United African National Council (UANC) and ZANU-Ndonga. The formation of factions led to splits in both the MDC (in 2005) and ZANU-PF (in 2008) with disastrous consequences for both parties.

Clearly, factionalism has a long pedigree in Zimbabwean politics. It should not be viewed as an aberration. The presence of factions in a party reflects differences in style, ideological outlook and tactical positions and leadership attributes amongst different groups that constitute a party. Parties are 'broad churches' with different tendencies amongst the membership. Leaders emerge to lead those different tendencies, which might have a class, regional, ethnic, generational and ideological dimension. However, some of the motivations centre around ambition and competition for power. Hence there is a tendency for a faction to cluster around a strong man or woman to compete with the party leader or another faction. In most parties, the party leader often creates his or her faction, or allies himself with one of the factions. An early analysis of factionalism in the post-colonial era argued:

> there is nothing unusual about the existence of conflicts between factions within the governing class, differences being a reflection of the uneven development of the economy, different relations of the factions to the domestic and external economy and differences in the economic bases or positions of these factions. (Mandaza 1986:55)

There were factions in ZANU-PF as well as within opposition parties. Factions are sometimes an avenue to power and resources but also to marginalisation. An early diagnosis identified regionalism as a major basis of factionalism in ZANU-PF. Amongst the factional leaders using their region or province as a base were figures like Edison Zvogbo in Masvingo and Simon Muzenda who later displaced Zvogbo and installed his own henchmen like Josiah Hungwe. As time went on, power struggles were expressed through provincial factions not only in Masvingo but also in Manicaland, Midlands and Mashonaland West. Commenting on factionalism, it was observed that:

> The nature and content of the leadership contest that has characterised post-independence Zimbabwe has in general not been overtly ideological .... However, the tendency for party barons with their local bases to compete with each other at the national level posed several kinds of difficulties within the party. First, the sustaining of their local base and the furthering of their national standing determined their tactical calculations rather than the furtherance of any coherent strategy. They had to be opportunist and acquisitive to gain the spoils to be able to pass them on, and there were thus in-built tendencies apart from their own personal interests, to corruption and nepotism. (Cliffe and Stoneman 1989:85)

This competition between the barons stirred up a factionalism among leaders and top officials that was supposedly based on ethnic grounds, as we saw above.

Factionalism in ZANU-PF and the MDC

During the period from 2000 to 2008, both ZANU-PF and MDC experienced serious factionalism. In ZANU-PF, the main factions were grouped around two figures with a strong background in the military and security sectors. The late Solomon Mujuru who headed one of these factions was a former Chief of the Defence Staff, while Emmerson Mnangagwa was Minister of State for Security, and later Minister of Defence. Both had unassailable liberation credentials. It is significant that the Mujuru faction drew most of its support from the three Mashonaland provinces (East, West and Central). Mnangagwa's support was strong in the party's branches in Midlands, Masvingo and Matabeleland. The basis of the competition between the two factions is a struggle for power with its focus on succession after Mugabe relinquishes power. Both Mujuru and Mnangagwa had reportedly extensive networks within the party. They have become extremely wealthy through investments and rents in the mining sector but have interests in other sectors as well. Their sparring for power has not broken out into open conflict but it remains fierce behind the scenes.

Perhaps, the fiercest clash between the two factions was in the run-up to the 2004 ZANU-PF congress. Seeking to place its leader in the most favourable position for succession, the Mnangagwa faction sought to garner support from at least six provinces in its bid for post of Vice-President at that congress. It had succeeded, but Mugabe was rattled by that manoeuvre and proceeded to annul it. He then rewrote the rule on succession to the vice-presidency insisting that one of them be a female. This provided the rationale for the ascendancy of Joyce Mujuru, thereby eliminating the candidature of Mnangagwa.

The contestation between the two factions sharpened again in the build-up to the 2008 election. The Mujuru faction was suspected of being lukewarm in its support for Mugabe's re-election bid, and to have surreptitiously backed Simba Makoni. Mugabe countered this by placing Mnangagwa as chair of the Joint Operations Command (JOC) which spearheaded the run-off election in which a great deal of violence was meted out against the opposition. Subsequently, Mnangagwa was appointed Defence Minister while the Mujuru faction seemed to have been marginalised. Party leaders like Mugabe have cynically played each faction against the other when it has been convenient to do so. Factionalism remains alive and well but the great conundrum is what will happen when Mugabe is no longer in power. The breaking out of open conflict between the factions cannot be ruled out.

The MDC also experienced turbulent factionalism during the period under review, especially between 2004 and 2005. Although a relatively young party, factions congealed early in the party: one was the cluster of trade unionists who had done the spadework for the formation of the party, the other of professionals and middle-class intellectuals and careerists who came into at the opportune time to occupy key positions. Loosely grouped, the first cluster was closely associated with Tsvangirai himself, and the second with Welshman Ncube, the party's Secretary General.

However, the first major clash between the factions occurred in 2005 over whether or not to participate in the Senate election of that year. The tactical differences over this issue generated a split in the party leading to the formation of MDC-M (named after Arthur Mutambara, who was elected President of the splinter group). The larger faction was called MDC-T after Morgan Tsvangirai. Perhaps the most penetrating account of the factions and their split is that by Brian Raftopoulos written a few months after it had happened:

> the debate over the Senate became an ugly public spectacle carried out in the state-controlled and private press, and characterised by disturbing levels of character assassination on both sides. Accusations and counter-accusations of corruption, violence, tribalism and complicity with the ruling party were thrown about liberally. Moreover, in a further ironic twist the internal battles in the MDC have ended up in the courts of the Mugabe regime. (Raftopoulos 2006:17)

Several other observations are made about the basis of the factional split. First, although the Senate issue provided the immediate pretext for the split, it had not been the fundamental cause of factionalism in the MDC. It was a site at which the two factions fought out long-standing problems and differences of organisation, structure, accountability and strategy within the party. The simmering issues that contributed to factionalism and the eventual split centred around the problem of a parallel structure in the president's office – the 'kitchen cabinet' appointed by the president – the growth of youth violence, conflict and competition between the offices of the Presidency and the Secretary General and infiltration by the state security agency. In sum, however, the factionalism in the MDC exhibited challenges of immaturity in institutionalising the party, a pervasive sense of insecurity in a context of authoritarianism as well as naked ambition for power.

For its part, ZANU-PF expelled two of its leaders, Simba Makoni and Dumiso Dabengwa, who were widely respected within it. The subsequent disorganisation and confusion caused by this development partly cost the party the 2008 election. This was not the last that was heard of factionalism in these two large parties. The Mujuru and Mnangagwa factions still have a lease of life, and so do the MDC 'kitchen cabinet' and factions around Tendai Biti and Morgan Tsvangirai. We return to their sparring in the following section, which deals with inter-party violence.

Inter-party Conflicts in 2000–2008

We have explored elsewhere the historical roots of inter-party violence in the contest for the political high ground between ZAPU and ZANU in the townships and rural areas in 1963 and 1964 (Sachikonye 2011). The legacy of those attacks on each other for support among the masses were conflicts in 1982 and 1987 between the same parties. In the more quiescent period between 1990 and 1999, the stakes were much lower because the potential and actual opposition was much weaker. This changed with the birth of the MDC in 1999 and with its first foray in a closely fought election contest in June 2000.

This chapter will not attempt to highlight the major features of inter-party violence between 2000 and 2008 because there are comprehensive dossiers that exist already (see various reports of ZHR NGO Forum 2001-2008, Amani Trust, Amnesty International, HRW, ZPP, and SPT. Here we will only pick on changing and constant patterns during the period. The main contestation was between MDC and ZANU-PF, although from 2005 there was also contestation between MDC-T and MDC-M. In 2000, violence by ZANU-PF was mainly directed at MDC election contestants and organisers but also against farmers and farm workers. In 2001, the key features of violence included retribution against MDC supporters who testified in the many MDC election petitions that were brought before the High Court. There was also systematic use of state violence drawing upon war veterans and CIO with beatings of MDC supporters in the presence of senior party figures such as Elliot Manyika. A reign of terror by 'Border Gezi' national service graduates was reported in Harare's high-density suburbs. In addition, there was increased use of abduction and extra-judicial execution as the murder of Trymore Midzi of MDC and of Cain Nkala in 2000 exemplified, as well as perfection of torture methods with the spread of the *falanga*, hooding and suffocation, and sexual torture. ZANU-PF perpetrators of violence continued to enjoy impunity.

In 2002, inter-party violence, mainly orchestrated by ZANU-PF, prolif-erated due to the presidential election of that year. There was a marked upsurge in the number of bases set up for use by militia and war veterans for mobilisation and torture as well as the use of gang rape as a political weapon against opposition supporters. Amongst other specific actions against the opposition were reported evictions of MDC supporters from their urban houses to make way for ZANU-PF supporters or their bases, violence against MDC polling agents and their displacement from areas of residence, and systematic terror against MDC local council candidates leading to their withdrawal from elections. Other aspects of violence were disenfranchisement of opposition supporters through destruction of their identity documents. In addition, food came to be increasingly used as political weapon while 'protection money' was demanded from MDC vendors in the Mbare suburb of Harare (ZHR NGO Forum, various issues, 2003).

In 2003, there was an upsurge in inter-party violence during by-elections with abductions, detentions and torture being more widespread than before. The use of the Public Order and Security Act (POSA) as a repressive legal instrument to harass and arrest opposition and CSO activists grew in frequency. Using maximum force, there was systematic crushing of marches by NCA and WOZA while close co-ordination of repression by the police and army, CIO and militia was evident in the blocking of the 'Final Push' campaign in June 2003. Shadowy militia groups like 'Chipangano' surfaced in Mbare. An upsurge in cases of rape against MDC women activ-ists and supporters continued. There were also reported instances of the barring of MDC candidates from entering Nomination Courts to file for election contests. In 2004, there was a marked trend towards police raids on MDC offices and homes ostensibly to paralyse the party. As we see below, violence was also directed at CSOs with beatings having become more brutal; the militia targeted student leaders in particular.

Inter-party violence continued unabated between 2005 and 2007. For instance, there was eviction and displacement of MDC support-ers in some areas in the build-up to the 2005 election. Harassment of opposition supporters included demand to produce ZANU-PF cards and bellicose threats from leaders such as Saviour Kasukuwere to get rid of MDC 'filth' (ZHR NGO Forum, May 2005). In 2007, state paranoia reaches new heights with arrest of alleged coup plotters as well as brutal beat-ings and torture of MDC leaders. Repeated raids were carried out on MDC offices, including its Harvest House headquarters, ostensibly in search of literature and weapons. Finally, there was a new trend towards abductions by state agents in unmarked vehicles with activists being dumped outside the main cities after beatings.

However, a new element in inter-party violence during this phase was the conflict between the two wings of MDC, namely MDC-T and MDC-M. This conflict began with the party split in 2005 but it continued to rear an ugly head during the next two years. Clashes between the two parties occurred in Harare, Bulawayo, Gweru and Mutare. While the clashes were not as ferocious and deadly as those between ZANU-PF and other parties, they nevertheless remained disturbing.

Another significant feature of inter-party violence during 2000 to 2008 was a trend towards counter-violence to ZANU-PF and state violence. This was basically retaliatory, and on a relatively small and unsystematic scale. In 2002, there was retaliatory violence aimed at Joseph Mwale who had been implicated in the murder of Chiminya and Mabika of MDC in the 2000 election campaign. Mwale's house in Ngangu village in Chimanimani was the target of a petrol bomb attack (ZHR NGO Forum, April 2002). Mwale was unhurt. In the same year, there was a report of a gang rape by MDC youths in the Graniteside area of Harare; the woman was subsequently hospitalised. In 2003, there were reports of MDC youths chanting their party's slogans as well as indiscriminatingly intimidating and assaulting civilians in high-density suburbs of Kuwadzana, Budiriro and Glen View in Harare (ZHR NGO Forum, May 2003). Later in that year, MDC youths arrived at a shopping centre singing and chanting slogans and forced patrons in a bar to chant the slogans (Ibid., November 2003). In another incident, MDC youths assaulted four police officers at a bar in Msasa, Harare, and fled after stealing money from the bar (Ibid., June 2004). Also later in the year, 15 MDC youths reportedly assaulted a ZANU-PF official who was wearing a Women's League T-shirt, while another group attacked a group of ZANU-PF supporters led by Pamela Tungamirai in Mabvuku (Ibid., October 2004).

Following the general election in 2005, the MDC held a demonstration that became violent resulting in shops and other property being destroyed (Ibid., April 2005). In 2006, 300 MDC supporters reportedly went on a rampage destroying a house in Glen View belonging to a ZANU-PF woman supporter who had been visited by a man wearing a ZANU-PF T-shirt (Ibid., April 2006). Cases of counter-violence by MDC supporters continued in 2007 and 2008 although they remained limited in scale. In February, some MDC supporters assaulted police officers in Ximex mall in Harare. There were reports of formation of Democratic Resistance Committees (DRCs) in 2007 by the MDC. These were essentially self-defence bodies ostensibly formed to protect MDC members from attacks from ZANU-PF and state-linked agencies.

In sum, inter-party violence was overwhelmingly one-sided. The phalanx of forces ranged against the MDC was formidable in that ZANU-PF coordinated its violence with various state agencies. The violence resulted in loss of life and injury of persons on a far greater scale than the violence perpetrated by the MDC. The latter was largely amateurish and limited in scale and mainly carried out by its youth members. However, the disturbing features of the counter-violence were their imitations of ZANU-PF methods of forcing people to chant party slogans, attacking members of the public wearing party T-shirts and gang-raping political opponents.

Intra-Party Conflicts in 2000–2008

As we observed elsewhere, internal struggles in parties have spiralled into violence in Zimbabwe (Sachikonye 2010). Intra-party violence in the period 2000–2008 is therefore not something new. We saw how the violence within the MDC contributed to a split into two parties in October 2005. The origins of that intra-party violence have not been fully publicly accounted for by the party leadership but there have been several accounts to explain how it evolved (Raftopoulos 2006; Le Bas 2005). The organisational response to the deepening repression had been the creation of a parallel structure within the MDC. However, the activities of this structure not only resulted in major problems of violence and accountability in party structures, but became the central site of struggle for the control of the party between its President and Secretary General.

The first major sign of the problems that were ignited by this parallel structure was the violence that occurred at the MDC headquarters in 2004. This structure had been formed as part of the mass action campaign 2003, but over time it became what was allegedly termed 'a source of force or militia for use in party struggles by unscrupulous politicians'. There were further outbreaks of intra-party violence in 2005 in spite of several party Commissions set up to resolve the issues that caused it in the first place. The youth were the major actors mobilised by a section of the party leadership to unleash violence against opponents. As in ZANU-PF, it is significant that much of the violence was caused by the youth under direction of certain figures in the party leadership.

Although it was a disturbing development, this intra-party violence never reached the same scale as that unleashed by ZANU-PF against MDC. Furthermore, although inexcusable, this emergent 'culture of violence' in MDC could not be dissociated from the wider context of political violence as orchestrated by ZANU-PF.

Although in the period after the split in 2005 there was a noticeable decrease in intra-party political violence, skirmishes continued within the two faction-driven parties. In-fighting sometimes flared up during party primary elections. One contemporary report explained that:

> intra-party violence broke out at Harvest House. It follows clashes between MDC supporters loyal to ousted Women Assembly's Chair, Lucia Matibenga and those in support of her replacement, Theresa Makone. A group of women besieged Harvest House demanding an audience with Tsvangirai whom they challenged to explain why Matibenga was ousted. (ZHR NGO Forum, November 2007)

This was an example of a serious clash in which seven people were assaulted. On previous occasions, party factional clashes had occurred in Masvingo, Mutare and Chitungwiza. In general, however, this intra-party violence was of a mild, unsystematic and sporadic character. While it could be contained, the danger nonetheless remained that it could spiral out of control and the impunity of perpetrators was a dangerous development. Similarly, intra-party party violence in ZANU-PF was not as ferocious as that directed at opposition parties. However, some of it was serious enough to warrant appointment of a Zimbabwe Republic Police Board of Enquiry. This was the case in the aftermath of violence in Makoni in eastern Zimbabwe in 2004. The task of the Board was to investigate violence between supporters of Didymus Mutasa and those of James Kaunye, his opponent in a ZANU-PF primary election contest in Makoni North. Kaunye himself was stripped and assaulted and 42 people were arrested for violence (ZHR NGO Forum, August 2004). In this instance, it was observed that the instigators of violence often used youths as 'foot soldiers' who are later prosecuted for perpetrating violence while instigators themselves are not held accountable (Ibid.). In another instance of violence in 2007, a former Governor of Masvingo, Josiah Hungwe, and other ZANU-

PF members were injured in a skirmish between two factions during Masvingo provincial party elections (ZHR NGO Forum, April 2007). Party leaders at that meeting were attacked with stones by delegates. Earlier, there had also been skirmishes between ZANU-PF supporters and war veterans in an incident in Gweru in 2004. Youth supporters of ZANU-PF destroyed offices belonging to war veterans in protest against the non-availability of food handouts that they had been promised in exchange for their demonstration against Roy Bennet, an MDC official (ZHR NGO Forum, May 2004).

In one case of violence, four youths mistaken for MDC supporters were abducted and severely assaulted by CIO agents in Bulawayo. The ZANU-PF youths suffered broken bones and serious injuries to their genitals (Ibid., September 2004).

Political Leadership

No chapter on political parties would be complete without some reference to the character and role of political leadership. The fortunes of parties depend considerably on the quality and tendencies of leadership. Although there have curiously been few studies on political leadership, certain tendencies have been common in most parties. First, there is often a strong will on the part of the founding leader to perpetuate his or her position. As a result, congresses and annual conferences are not genuine vehicles for discussion or negotiation of political succession. Political parties in Zimbabwe are indeed strongly identified with their founding leaders: Mugabe with ZANU-PF, Tsvangirai with MDC-T, the late Nkomo with ZAPU, the late Tekere with ZUM, Dongo with ZUD and Makoni with Mavambo.

Second, there is a strong element of personalisation of leadership, and this is in line with the trend in most African political parties. In Zimbabwe it reached its apogee in ZANU-PF where there is strong constituency that campaigns for Robert Mugabe to be the party's president for life. Other symbols of personality worship include the activities of the 21st February Movement that celebrates his birthday every year, and the emblazoning of his face on caps, T-shirts and dresses. A personality cult on a similar scale is not noticeable in MDC-T, but the situation could change if the party came into power. A relic of the one-party state era, personality cults are an outdated aspect of authoritarian leadership and politics. T

Conclusion

This chapter has shown that except for two or three parties, most parties were small, stunted and somewhat unstable with their proliferation largely confined to election periods. To that extent, parties have not been very active agents in the incubation of a democratic civic and political culture.

The different ideological tendencies of the parties were spelt out with reference to their constitutions and manifestos. However, despite their ideological rhetoric, most parties tend to share similar values and a single-minded focus on pursuit of power, hence the pivotal importance of elections in their various strategies. Most parties share a tendency and weakness for personality cults around their leaders as well as for factionalism. The chapter provided illustrations of some the dangers of factionalism in the larger parties, ZANU-PF and MDC-T.

4

Democracy, Constitutionalism & Participation

Curiously, the predominant political discourse in Zimbabwe soon after Independence was not about democracy but 'socialism', and the possibility of 'transition' to that state of affairs. The discourse was strongly 'ideological'. The rationale for that leap in discourse was that the sequel of the 'liberation struggle' and 'Independence' would be a transition to socialism (Mandaza 1986; Davies 1988). There was no priority and focus on how to build democracy in the newly independent state. For almost a decade, political parties and scholars ruminated on Marxism–Leninism and debated whether it could provide the basis for a socialist society. Discussion of a national democratic revolution was remarkably absent. It was towards the end of the first decade that rumblings against the one-party state concept included demands for a multi-party democracy. This was the immediate context in which civil society organisations and opposition parties such as ZUM pitched their campaigns. However, towards the end of the 1990s the discourse on democracy became fully fledged. The constitutional reform process which was initiated in 1998 raised the debate to a new level as issues of democracy, constitutionalism and participation became central to the outreach campaigns of that year.

In this chapter we explore the scope and limitations of this discourse and explain why the attempt at constitutional reform flopped in 2000. The slight opening of the constitutional debate and outreach processes were soon eclipsed by a reversion to authoritarianism and violence which transformed the country into a pariah as far as the West was concerned. It would only be during the third decade that the country would seriously address issues of democracy, constitutionalism and participation. However, the process of constitutional reform was still fluid and fragile at the time of writing.

Defining Democracy

Democracy should be contextualised. The concept and practice of democracy is customarily traced back to ancient Greece. The phenomenon of representative government – based on the participation of common citizens in political debate and consultation – characterised democracy in the city-state of Athens. However, this was selective democracy. Slaves and some citizens were barred from the process. This early flowering of selective democracy was short-lived. It was submerged in the long history of feudalism, territorial wars in Europe, and the imperialist annexation of Asia, Africa, the Middle East and the Americas by the emergent European industrial and maritime powers, principally Britain, France, Spain and Germany. However, liberal versions of historiography assert that the American Constitution of 1789, the French Revolution of 1789 and the English Reform Act of 1832 were significant landmarks in the development of democracy in the West.

Even so, in the cradle of the first bourgeois revolution in England, the right to vote was not extended to all until the twentieth century. In the United States, the 'democratic model' co-existed for many years with the institution of black slavery. It was not until the twentieth century that the US extended the right to vote to its black population. Even then it required a massive civil rights struggle to protect and consolidate that right.

The colonial system that was imposed over much of Africa, the Caribbean and Asia exposed the limitations of the democratic model touted by the Western powers. Colonialism entailed the expropriation of natural resources, the extraction of taxes and wage-labour together with the exclusion of the colonised peoples from political and decision-making processes. Memories of the historical experiences of African countries partly explain the retort by some of its leaders that Western countries cannot teach Africa about democracy. It should be stressed that even in the West, the existing democratic rights – to vote, to join trade unions or other associations, and the freedoms of association and speech – were the culmination of formidable struggles by workers and other classes over centuries. Similarly, the struggles for Independence in the colonies represented democratic aspirations which colonialism had denied to the majority of the citizens of these countries.

But how has contemporary democracy been defined? In a minimalist sense, democracy relates to a political system that allows citizens to freely choose their representatives and therefore government through fair elections; accords them adequate participation in national affairs; and ensures transparency and accountability in national governance. Some analysts have distinguished between a 'procedural' and 'substantive' meaning of democracy (Bratton, Gyimah-Boadi and Mattes 2005). A procedural perspective stresses the political dimensions such as the election process and the guarantees for political as well civil rights. A substantive view emphasises specific content such as economic and social rights. As one analyst argued:

> Democracy is not simply about satisfying theoretical expectations. For example, it is not about the electoral defeat of unpopular or discredited incumbents (the euphoria of 'regime change' does not last long) or, for that matter, about holding periodic elections. Rather, the democratic project is about and for citizens who have stakes in the project and expect dividends from it. Ordinary citizens who queue for long hours to cast their votes, or take part in riots and demonstrations to oust authoritarian governments ... expect immediate and long-term dividends. (Osaghae 2004:2)

According to this line of thought, one conceptually profound effort to bridge the gap between formal and substantive democracy is the 'developmental democracy' perspective. This rejects the notion that democracy should be desired for its own sake, and ties the necessity and utility of democracy to its promotion of just and equitable development (Ibid.). Even so, although the fallacy of electoralism, that is, the equating of democracy and elections, is acknowledged, this does not diminish the importance of elections. This is especially so in a context of democratic transition where they potentially serve as a foundation and vehicle of transformation. Arguing that elections remain fundamental to the democratic process, it was remarked that 'while you can have elections without democracy, you cannot have democracy without elections' (Bratton and Posner 1999). This is reflected in the Zimbabwe debate on democracy and the one-party state at the opening of the 1990s (Mandaza and Sachikonye 1991).

We have stressed elsewhere the need to view democracy as a process rather than as a static condition or end-point (Sachikonye *et al.* 2007). It is a protracted process by nature and can span generations. The process involves progress towards a rules-based, more consensual and more participatory type of politics.

The Zimbabwe Debate on Democracy

The Zimbabwe debate on democracy was a narrowly based one. The issue was not whether democracy was desirable and appropriate, but rather whether it was compatible with the one-party state system. The immediate context and imperative was a debate in ZANU-PF on the one-party state system in the wake of the Unity Accord in 1987.

There were two principal strands to the debate. The first endorsed democracy without any equivocation, while the second questioned the suitability of the model in the African context. However, neither strand could ignore an attempt to close the debate altogether. The attempt took the form of uncompromising rhetoric from Robert Mugabe, who argued that:

> *If you look at all of them, whether they are Germans or French or Belgians or Italians or Americans, what have their past performances been in Africa? Did the British leave us democracy? We had to take up arms to go to fight against an oppressive system and now they want to be accepted as teachers of democracy. (Mugabe, as quoted in the* Sunday Mail, *8 July 1990)*

This was an attempt to foreclose the debate. While colonialism was undemocratic, there was such a phenomenon as British democracy, however imperfect. The fact that colonialism was undemocratic did not mean that there was no imperative to build democracy in post-colonial societies. Rather the shrill rhetoric betrayed discomfort amongst some African authoritarians with the concept and practice of democracy.

Amongst the proponents of a multi-party state was Masipula Sithole. He strongly argued that it was superior to the one-party state:

> *which invariably leads to political complacency, unchecked corruption and government by the police. What makes things worse is that those torch-bearers occupying key positions at various levels of the vanguard party ... can manipulate democratic centralism to defend their interests. (Sithole 1991:77)*

Contrasting a *de jure* one-party state with a *de facto* one, he observed that the latter involved a popular party continuing to govern after every election with a renewed mandate from the people who had the freedom to choose other parties but preferred the ruling party instead. Concluding his argument, Sithole asked *'Ko yanga yakaipei?* (What is wrong with that?) (Ibid.). Arguing from a different perspective but reaching a similar conclusion, Fay Chung asserted that because of ZANU-PF's mass support from the peasantry, its ability to contain different ideological leanings and its 'pragmatism', the party was set to remain dominant for the next few decades (Chung 1991:137). The other parties were unlikely to achieve a plausible mass base for the foreseeable future:

> *In these circumstances, a one-party state is an unnecessary distraction from the more critical issues of the redistribution of land and wealth. (Ibid.)*

Other analysts questioned the focus of the democracy debate: it was argued that the conception of democracy was very restrictive and formalistic, concerned primarily with party political systems (Rukobo 1991). According to this perspective:

> *democracy is reduced to either the multi-party system or the one-party system. One system is equated with democracy and the other with dictatorship …. The debate is not only about political democracy, but about which development option Zimbabwe should follow. In this respect, the debate has assumed a clear ideological dimension. As a result, one cannot, in attempting to participate in that debate, avoid the ideological question. (Ibid. 121)*

It was argued that although individual rights and freedoms were central to any democratic order, they did not constitute the essence of democracy.

In later years, it was difficult to find a similarly passionate but decent level of debate on democracy in Zimbabwe. The debate was replaced with polemics in the post-2000 period. Those who espoused democracy and human rights were painted as parrots of Western governments and donors while those who argued against these concepts were viewed as authoritarians. The polemics became abusive as time went on, especially in state media such as the *Herald* and *The Sunday Mail* where lengthy columns poured scorn on democracy and human rights as foreign constructs. During the lost decades, Zimbabwe missed an opportunity to deepen a major debate that would have shaped views on the relevance of key concepts and values, and even laid a basis for a national consensus on them.

Democratisation

Constitutionalism

The change in focus from constitutionality to constitutionalism relates to constitutions being seen as tools for bridge-building between civil society and the state. In order to formulate African political cultures grounded in human rights and social justice, an organic link was needed between the constitution as a rule of law instrument primarily concerned with restraining government excesses and protecting ordinary citizens, and the constitution as a legitimation of power structures and relations based

Table 4.1 – Constitutional Amendments, 1981–2007

Year	Amendment
1981	Reduced qualification period of lawyers to the judiciary and Senate Legal Committee to make such offices accessible to black lawyers.
1981	Created a separate Supreme Court from the High Court. Also specified qualification period for judges, making this more attainable by blacks.
1983	Afforded Parliament the power to abolish dual citizenship.
1984	Introduced Office of Ombudsman and reconstituted the Judicial Services Commission to give the President more control over it.
1985	Allowed for appointment of Provincial Governors by the President.
1987	Ended the separate roll for whites.
1987	Created the Executive Presidency and abolished the office of Prime Minister.
1989	Provided for the AG becoming a member of Cabinet, thus bringing the judiciary under Executive influence.
1989	Abolished the Senate, making way for a one-chamber Parliament.
1990	Created a second Vice-Presidency.
1990	Terminated land provision for 'willing buyer, willing seller' in favour of 'fair compensation'.
1993	Reorganised the prison and public services and armed services, reducing their independence.
1993	Reversed a Supreme Court judgement on the death sentence, stating that delayed execution did not amount to a human rights abuse.
1996	Reversed a Supreme Court judgement on women marrying foreign men – such spouses no longer automatically became citizens.
1998	Changed the start date of the government financial year from 1 July to 1 January.
2000	Land provision transferred responsibility for compensation from Zimbabwe Government.

on a broad social consensus in a diverse society (CDD 2000). The task is to move away from old constitutionality which over-emphasised law and state power towards a new constitutionalism that has more relevance to the needs of African citizens and is ultimately owned by them (Ibid.).

Zimbabwe has a chequered history of Constitution-making. The Lancaster House Constitution which ushered in Independence was negotiated under duress, and perhaps reflected the balance of forces involved in the country and the region at that time. As a compromise, it pervaded the process and structures through which the new state sought to consolidate national independence and provide the basis for economic and social development. However, as it was observed:

> The conduct of the Lancaster Conference itself, the various concessions that the guerrilla representatives had to make which is the basis of the Agreement itself all tended to reflect a result less than that which might have been expected of a national liberation movement had it won outright victory on the battlefield. (Mandaza 1986:2)

The Lancaster House Constitution was not to have its significant provisions amended for ten years. It was therefore surprising that from 1990 to 1998 there was no attempt to review it, despite many burning issues relating to democracy, land reform and social rights. Instead, the executive branch introduced constitutional amendments mainly to centralise and consolidate its power and authority (Table 4.1). The period between 1990 and 1998 was one in which political positions had not yet become too adversarial. In that sense, it was a lost decade as far as constitutional reform was concerned.

This lack of urgency can be partly explained by the fact that the President himself was a major beneficiary of amendments made after 1987. The constitutional amendment of 1987 created the position of Executive President and vested near-absolute powers in him in critical areas of the constitutional and political process, thereby creating a 'presidential monarch' (*Sunday Gazette*, 19 March 1995). Others contended that the constitution gave the President wide discretionary powers to dismiss Parliament without having to justify his decision; and that in conducting state affairs, the President did not have to seek advice even from his Cabinet (Makumbe and Compagnon 2000).

There emerged a penetrating critique of the manipulation of the method of constitutional amendment to centralise power in the executive. It was argued that the political leadership had problems living with notions of limited government:

> This has resulted in a rejection of some of the principles underpinning consti-tutionalism. The 'power map' of the independence Constitution which created a 'controlled' executive has been revised in such a way that power has been shifted in favour of the executive arm of the state …. Elsewhere in Africa, the process of achieving executive hegemony involved the constitutional 'over-throw' of the legislature by the party which then asserts its superiority over all organs of state power. (Ncube 1991:171)

Debate on Constitutional Reform

It was scarcely surprising that the initial clamour for constitutional reform emerged from outside ZANU-PF. In the view of civil society organisations and opposition parties, no significant political and social change could occur without rewriting the constitution. More generally, the regional conjuncture of the mid-1990s was one in which progressive constitutions were being crafted in such countries as Botswana and South Africa. The first salvo was fired by a broad alliance of CSOs which founded the Nation-al Constitutional Assembly (NCA) in 1998. The NCA spelt out its objectives as follows:

- *To identify shortcomings of the current Constitution and to organise debate on possible constitutional reform*
- *To organise the constitutional debate in a way that allows broad-based participation*
- *To subject the Constitution-making process in Zimbabwe to popular scrutiny in accordance with the principle that Constitutions are made by and for the people. (NCA 1999:8)*

More specifically, the NCA singled out several clauses in the constitu-tion which it argued were not justifiable in a democratic society. It was observed, for example, that the protections in the Bill of Rights were not as wide as they should be (NCA, 1998). It was further contended that the electoral system and process as defined and prescribed in the constitu-tion was not conducive to the holding of 'free and fair elections'. Some 14 amendments had been made in 17 years and such a piecemeal approach undermined the constitution, it was asserted.

How did the ZANU-PF government respond to this growing pressure? Although it was reluctantly persuaded that such reform was overdue, its authoritarian tendencies made it difficult to craft a consensual approach; the government sought to monopolise the process at every stage.

There were at least three positions, at the beginning of 1999, on how constitutional reform should be conducted. Two of these emanated from within ZANU-PF itself. Drawing from Robert Mugabe's approach, the first was termed the 'Mugabe Way':

> the procedure which all along I thought we would adopt is one which would first enable our party at the provincial and then at Central Committee levels to address the matter and come to some initial conclusions on the various parts of the Constitution needing amendment. The views of other organisations will be collected in the process but only for consideration by us and in comparison with our own. (Mugabe, 21 March 1998)

Broadly speaking, this was the position and intention of the Zimbabwean leader and some of his party's top leadership. It was an autocratic position which could be described as 'constitutional reform from above', a process that would largely be driven by the ruling party. A party congress resolution of the previous year reflected that paternalistic sentiment.

A variant of that approach was termed the 'Zvobgo Way' after the then leading constitutional expert in ZANU-PF, Eddison Zvobgo (Hlatshwayo 1998), which sought to integrate the above-mentioned party congress resolution with one that called on the executive to introduce a mechanism to review the constitution. The position conceded that ZANU-PF should not monopolise the constitutional reform process entirely but should instead allow others to contribute to the process. However, it envisaged that ZANU-PF would still be the dominant player.

The NCA approach was the main challenge to the envisaged 'constitutional reform from above'. Arguing for broader participation, this would be inclusive and open. While there was basic agreement on the case for a new constitution, there was polarisation on the process to follow in crafting one. The resultant stalemate on this issue led to an unprecedented, parallel constitution-making exercise. The ZANU-PF-dominated exercise was represented by a government-appointed Constitutional Commission (CC) that consisted of 400 members of whom 150 were parliamentarians. This Commission gathered views from the public for about four months and then submitted its findings to President Mugabe. However, the provisions under which the Commission was set up still gave considerable powers to the president to amend the draft constitution. This is what subsequently transpired.

The NCA outreach exercise involved an extensive civic education campaign to explain why an inclusive approach was necessary. Identifying the limitations of the Lancaster House Constitution, it solicited suggestions and proposals on what a new constitution should contain. There was a strong element of competition in the gathering of views in the two parallel outreach exercises, and their findings were subsequently woven into two different constitutional drafts.

Eventually, however, the credibility of the CC exercise was thrown into serious doubt when its draft omitted and misrepresented some of the citizens' views. For instance, consistent sentiments had been expressed in public hearings as well as in other submissions that the powers of the President should be reduced considerably, as should the size of the Cabinet, and that an independent electoral commission should be appointed. When most of these and other recommendations were ignored or fudged, the public and voters were not amused. To complicate matters, the President unilaterally inserted certain provisions, including those on land reform. The draft of the CC was decisively rejected in a vote in February 2000. The NCA had contributed to that rejection through its 'no' campaign which found resonance amongst the electorate. What followed for the next eight years was a stalemate on the future direction of constitutional reform.

Can any wider lessons be drawn from this abortive reform process? The first lesson is that if the process is seriously contested and flawed, it will be difficult to obtain a constitution that stands the test of time and creates an acceptable contract between a government and its people (Austin 2009). It is of crucial importance that all major stakeholders (or at least a substantial majority) endorse the process prior to its implementation. As one observation team remarked, the debate about the constitution:

> could have provided an opportunity for Zimbabweans to have taken a deeper look more calmly and soberly into key questions that define their body politic and shape their political configuration: issues that have to do with national unity, power sharing etc. This was a missed opportunity to reach a historic settlement that would constitute the basis upon which the way forward would be charted. (CDD 2000:11)

This was a sentiment later shared by a leading politician who had headed the 'no' campaign against the constitution draft (Tsvangirai in Chan 2005:93). The constitutional reform debate should have been handled differently, Tsvangirai admitted, and added that 'it was a lost opportunity' (Ibid.).

The second lesson is that the engagement of international actors in Zimbabwe's constitution-making process has been contentious, if not intrusive. This might explain Zimbabwe's almost schizophrenic political environment, 'where the language and attitudes of liberal democracy vie with the dogmatic slogans of anti-imperialism, sovereignty and militaristic discipline' (Austin 2009:85). Constitutional reform should be primarily a national responsibility, even in a globalised world.

The third lesson is that until the advent of the GPA in September 2008, there had not been a broadly shared and solid agreement on guiding principles for reforming the constitution. The idea of agreeing on a particular mechanism, 'much less an inclusive mechanism, for settling the agenda, procedures or committees by which a consensus on problems and their solutions might be reached had not been attempted' (Ibid.).

These lessons were borne in mind in the constitutional reform exercise of the Inclusive Government. Although it was a protracted exercise to launch the process in mid-2009 and implement the outreach programme in mid-2010, there existed consensus amongst the key stakeholders on the framework and modalities, and the reform exercise was spelt out in the GPA itself. Instead of the President, it was Parliament, through the Constitutional Parliamentary Committee (COPAC), which spearheaded the process. However, it was still under way in the second half of 2010; despite the inter-party consensus, problems had been faced related to funding, party-inspired disruptions, disputes over the status of the Kariba Draft of 2007, and sporadic instances of intimidation and violence.

Although the 2009–2011 constitutional reform process replicates some elements of the 1999–2000 exercise, there were distinctive differences. In addition to the centrality of Parliament in the exercise, substantial investment was directed towards involving key stakeholders at all stages. Hence the convening of Stakeholders' Conferences at the inception and conclusion of the outreach process. But in contrast with the previous exercise, which was largely state-funded, the second depended mainly on donor funding. Early estimates put this at US$18m, but it was expected to go up in the last quarter of 2010. Although this might have looked embarrassing for a government which asserted claims of sovereignty at every opportunity, there appeared to be no alternative.

Another difference was the backing given by a large part of civil society, including some of the CSOs that had boycotted the 1999 exercise. The few exceptions that boycotted for the second time in 2009 included the NCA, ZCTU and a faction of ZINASU, but their activities were severely diminished, due to reduced funding, and they were ineffective in their campaign. By mid-2010 the NCA was a shadow of its former self.

A further difference with the 1999 exercise was the prevalence of intimidation and low-intensity violence, particularly in rural areas. Most reports agreed that ZANU-PF and sections of state security were behind the campaign to coerce voters to support the party's position on the Kariba Draft (which left the powers of the President more or less intact). It remains to be seen what the final draft will contain, and whether the referendum in 2011 will endorse it.

The Electoral System

Prior to 2008, the context of authoritarianism presented obstacles not only to democratisation and constitutionalism but also to substantive electoral reform. Particularly after 1987, there had been a ring-fencing of the system to maintain the advantages of the President and the incumbent government. It was scarcely surprising that one of the principal arguments of those who advocated constitutional reform was that Zimbabwe's electoral system was defective and prone to patronage. For many years the election management bodies (first the Electoral Supervisory Commission (ESC) and then Zimbabwe Electoral Commission (ZEC)) were viewed as part of state bureaucracy. This was out of line with the trend toward autonomous election commissions elsewhere in southern Africa.

The institutional framework of election management was cumbersome, consisting of a Delimitation Commission, the Electoral Supervisory Commission, the Election Directorate and the Registrar-General's Office. Sitting at five-yearly intervals and prior to a general election, the Delimitation Commission determined constituency boundaries, but there was no involvement of stakeholders such as parties, civic groups, and women's and youth organisations. The Commission's report was submitted to the President, who might raise objections if he was in any way dissatisfied with it, but the public was denied the same privilege (ESC 1997).

Until 2004, the ESC had little power, although it was tasked with the responsibility of supervising the electoral process. Like the Delimitation

Commission, it was appointed by the President. Its functions were to supervise the registration of voters, to conduct elections and to consider any proposed legislation that may be referred to it relating to presidential, parliamentary or local authority elections. Funded through the then Ministry of Justice, Legal and Parliamentary Affairs, it had a miniscule budget despite the vast scope of the electoral process. After each election, the ESC submitted a report to the President on the conduct and outcome of the election. As some analysts argued, it was largely impotent because the constitution did not confer any executive power to it (Makumbe and Compagnon 2000). In view of its limited and ambiguous powers, and meagre budget, the ESC was severely constrained in exercising its supposedly 'supervisory role'. The powers, authority and resources that should have accrued to the ESC were instead dispersed to the Election Directorate and the Registrar-General of Elections. Indeed, one election watchdog body argued that the 'election process is not managed, administered and controlled by the ESC but by the Registrar-General' (ZESN 2002).

The Election Directorate, created in 1990, was staffed by civil servants who operated under the Public Service Commission (PSC). It co-ordinated the activities of ministries and departments in electoral matters, and gave instructions and made recommendations to the Registrar-General regarding the exercise of his functions under the Electoral Act. The independence of the Election Directorate, by virtue of its being part of state structures, was suspect.

Finally, the Registrar-General of Elections was actually the key player in the electoral process. A public servant, he was responsible for almost the entire electoral process from the registration of voters and provision of electoral staff to the declaration of results and the custody of election materials. The impartiality and efficiency of the Registrar-General's office were questioned by opposition parties, NGOs and media, especially with regard to its conduct of the 2002 election.

Against the background of a sustained critique of the electoral system, the government introduced the Zimbabwe Electoral Commission (ZEC) in 2004. The 2005 elections were the first to be administered by the ZEC. During the 2008 elections, its capacity and credibility were severely tested and the institution was found wanting. How did the electoral process fare in 2008? On the whole, the election, and especially the run-off election, was poorly organised. It was not sufficient to have a restructured administration body; the electoral framework remained in need of urgent attention (ZESN 2008), and for four principle reasons.

First, the voter registration process only started late in 2008, the voters' roll was not up to date, and the prevalence of 'ghost voters' remained a major challenge. In some instances, insufficient and incorrect information was provided to citizens about the registration process. Second, while the ZEC had direct responsibility for the delimitation exercise, its management of the process was far from satisfactory. The Delimitation report itself was tabled in Parliament too late in the process for the public to be educated about boundary changes. Third, postal voting was shrouded in secrecy, and inaccessible to observers, and the ZEC did not enable Zimbabweans in the diaspora to exercise their right to vote. Fourth, the Electoral Court was not capacitated to hear and make timely judgements on all election-related appeals within six months of their submission.

In sum, it was concluded that:

> ZEC's management of the delimitation, nomination, voter education, voter registration and inspection processes and release of the 29 March presidential results was a cause for concern. ZEC's neutrality and ability to work without being influenced by parties is highly suspect (Ibid.: 12).

These shortcomings were fully displayed in the chaotic 2008 presidential election, as various studies and observer reports have shown (EISA 2008; Masunungure 2009).

The overall verdict on the 2008 presidential election was that it had been 'militarised' and badly managed. It is appropriate to draw from the observations of a regional election observation body in this regard. First, the election was marred by the interventionist role of security forces. It was therefore recommended that in future, 'political powers of the day should ensure the effective management of all security to prevent the de-legitimisation of elections and ensure a climate of freedom to contest' (EISA 2008). Second, the election was severely flawed in terms of access to information. It was recommended that both short- and longer-term corrective action was needed: 'as a starting point, the state media needs to be overhauled in order to eradicate partisan orientations' (Ibid.). Third, it was observed that excessive numbers of ballot papers were printed. The urgent implementation of sufficient preparatory measures to ensure the integrity of ballot production and safeguarding was recommended.

Despite having paid lip service to the SADC Principles and Guidelines on Democratic Elections, the Zimbabwe state authorities reneged on their implementation. The militarisation of the election process which began in 2002 became more pronounced during 2008. In the last analysis, the existence of a nominally autonomous election management body is not a sufficient condition for a credible and fair election. The incumbent government should be fully committed to the implementation of the relevant electoral legislation in a transparent and accountable fashion. The government of Zimbabwe failed this test in the presidential run-off election of 2008 (AU 2008; PAP 2008).

It was in response to this critique that a new ZEC was appointed in 2009. Parliament was for the first time directly involved in the selection process. Candidates for the Commission were invited to apply and undergo a public interview and were assessed by an all-party parliamentary committee. The names of successful candidates were then forwarded to the President for the final selection.

Participation

To what extent have Zimbabwean citizens participated in the processes of democratisation, and constitutional and electoral reform? What other forms of participation exist? These are complex issues but nevertheless pivotal in assessing to what degree authoritarianism has stifled participation during the lost decades. In our view, the major aspects of participation relate to governance affairs, civic life and socio-economic activities.

Citizens participate in governance and law-making through the election of members of parliament (MPs) who represent their interests and views in the legislative chamber. Citizens also lobby for laws through various channels and networks that include CSOs, business associations and political parties. It is, however, debatable whether the election of MPs by citizens necessarily translates into representation of their interests in the law-making processes. MPs tend to neglect their constituencies much of the time, only surfacing during an electioneering period to donate goods and equipment and to 'buy' votes. In an MPOI survey of Parliament in 2006, close to 40 per cent of respondents stated that they did not know their local MP (MPOI 2006). Sixty-five per cent stated that their MPs did not organise regular meetings with their constituencies. A similar pattern of distance between local authority councillors and citizen ratepayers was discernible.

MPs tend to concentrate on projects that deliver short-term political capital to them, such as the distribution of food handouts and commis-

Box 4.1 – Common problems with participation

- *The term 'participation' is used to give respectability to inadequate development programmes*
- *Many Zimbabweans lack material conditions for participation*
- *Many institutions are too weak to support participation*
- *Bureaucratic, professional and political blocking can hinder participation*
- *Practice of participation is rare due to continuation of a 'top down' approach*
- *Participation raises expectations which can be frustrated (those with power and resources often block participation by citizens as they find it too threatening)*
- *Participation is hard to measure*
- *Participation is usually accepted in trivial issues but rarely invited on vital issues such as choosing priorities and making major political and economic decisions*
- *Attitudes such as superiority, inferiority and dependency hinder participation*
- *There is a great deal of apathy*
- *Participation is a necessary but insufficient condition for democracy.*

Source: ZHDR 2000:89

sioning of donor-funded projects; although these may generate some immediate popularity, they rarely deliver sustainable development to communities. Generally speaking, community participation in local affairs is not high. Some analysts have argued that a combination of economic decline between 2000 and 2008 and the severe curtailment of civil liberties has contributed to a general disengagement of the citizenry from civic participation, a situation that is not healthy in building democracy (Sachikonye *et al.* 2007).

On the whole, participation in governance affairs has been constrained by the paraphernalia of authoritarian legislation, such as POSA, as well as a flawed electoral system. But the right to participation depends on other rights, such as the right to freedom of speech and expression, freedom of assembly and association, the right to public information, and access to public institutions and education (Saki 2010). Thus it is the totality of the environment which has restricted popular participation in Zimbabwe. In any case, participation and authoritarianism tend to be incompatible: the one threatens and undermines the other.

Participation in civic affairs, however, has been more widespread, from village and local community affairs to residents' associations and CSOs. It is difficult to measure the depth of this type of participation. As we explain in greater detail in a later chapter, there are CSOs involved in various sectors, including housing, co-operative enterprises, education, and human rights. They also engage in lobbying, advocacy and policy discussion. It is debatable how effective they can be, however, particularly those which concentrate their activities in major towns, thereby isolating people in the smaller towns and rural areas.

Levels of participation in socio-economic activities are shaped by the wider macro-economic environment, and in the decade from 1998 were affected by a sharp increase in unemployment, to an estimated 80 per cent. Similarly, participation in policy-making and budgeting at local and national levels has been restricted.

Government ministries do not release their annual financial reports to the public, yet at the opening of each financial year they are given allocations of state funds and are also issued with supplementary budgets. Local authorities impose budgets on their residents without prior consultation or their involvement. The central government does not involve the public in its planning process. The release of budgets and expenditure is a mere formality, and there is no questioning or enquiry by the public. (Chiware 2010:21.)

When budgets are made and announced, they remain opaque to the average person; this lack of knowledge and transparency constrains participation. However, some social groups are more marginalised than others, especially women and youth (Munando 2010; Chitanana 2010). There is a considerable distance to go before participation as a key element in building democracy becomes entrenched in governance and civic affairs as well as in socio-economic life. In the last analysis, however, participation is not given by the state to citizens but has to be demanded by those who have previously been excluded as they begin to organise themselves and muster negotiating skills.

Conclusion

In exploring the linkages between democracy, constitutionalism and participation, the objective of the chapter was to highlight a uniquely Zimbabwean discourse that emerged in the 1990s. Processes of democratisation are often accompanied by increasing debate within the academic and political classes. It was argued, however, that there were missed opportunities in setting national priorities in the building of democracy and constitutional reform in the first two decades of independence. The focus on socialism evaporated with the collapse of the Soviet and Eastern European model of development in the late 1980s. The governing party was lukewarm towards constitutional reform, creating a vacuum that CSOs were able to fill in the late 1990s but in a more polarised context. That polarisation handicapped an opportunity for a consensual approach to constitutional reform resulting in a stalemate created by the referendum result in February 2000.

The analysis of the flaws in the electoral system and the 'militarisation' of the 2008 presidential election confirmed the enormous constraints on the democratisation process in Zimbabwe. Resistance to democratisation by ZANU-PF and key institutions in the state was massive and co-ordinated. Nevertheless, the impetus for popular participation continued. In 2009–2010, there was renewed momentum for constitutional and electoral reforms despite attempted blockage by the authoritarian state.

Part II

5
Development Deferred

Introduction

Nowhere has Zimbabwe performed as poorly as it has done as in economic development since it gained independence in 1980. The country's economy shrank from an estimated USD9 billion in 1997 to USD4 billion in 2008. This is as surprising as it is disappointing. The surprise stems from the country's inheritance of the second most industrialised and diversified economy, and with an enviable infrastructure, on the African continent. Its economy was also the most balanced, with the manufacturing sector contributing about 25 per cent of GDP. Compared to its immediate neighbours Botswana, Mozambique and Zambia, Zimbabwe was well-endowed with natural and human resources, resources which would have provided it with a head start in growth and development.

Yet whatever growth occurred in the first decade of independence was, at best, mediocre; stagnation set in the 1990s while contraction marked a substantial decline between 2000 and 2008. If Zimbabwe's growth had been steady, its GDP would now be about USD15 billion, or three times the current GDP (*Zimbabwe Independent*, 4 June 2010). What went wrong? Why is Zimbabwe now the 'sick economy' of Southern Africa? These are complex questions that this chapter seeks to address. Answers to the questions provide a clue to understanding the processes that unfolded during Zimbabwe's lost decades.

The Economy at Independence

The inherited economy had particular strengths and weaknesses. One of the strengths was the forcefulness and coherence of state economic strategy, especially during UDI (1965–1979). This consisted of carefully chosen and systematically targeted instruments 'in support of an essentially privately controlled economy, in which the major economic interests exhibited little dissonance with the nature, objectives and methods of the state' (Khadhani 1986:104). The intervention was primarily prompted by the systematic need to keep a tight rein on fiscal and external account balances and maintain stability in the labour markets. Market forces were carefully attenuated in order to protect the high income levels and living standards of the white minority on which the Smith regime depended for legitimacy and technical and administrative skills. Despite sanctions, there was an economic boom from 1965 to 1972 which enabled a rapid restructuring of the economy at sectorial level, producing an annual GDP growth of six per cent.

Second, UDI had the effect of widening the economy's access to investible financial surpluses, primarily in the shape of the large blocked balances that would otherwise have been remitted abroad. In such circumstances, foreign firms were compelled to redirect surpluses towards reinvestment and thus retain them in the overall domestic system. This facilitated investment in product diversification.

Third, the sanctions and other siege conditions facilitated the emergence of the Treasury and the Reserve Bank as the central loci of influence and authority in the running of the economy. This became evident in the tight control that was exercised over the use of foreign exchange and the level of the budget deficit as well as in the deliberate direction of resources towards productive sectors. Such sectors were designated to spearhead diversification and greater import substitution capability, particularly in metal and engineering products, mineral beneficiation and agro-industrial linkages.

There were, however, several weaknesses in the UDI economy. These became quite evident in the mid-1970s when a prolonged recession set in. Capacity utilisation dropped to 75 per cent in 1978 and employment growth stalled. Import substitution and product diversification ran into problems, the first of which was the structure and limited size of the domestic market and the second the constrained scope for growth given the economy's limited capacity to finance imported inputs. There were large expectations, therefore, that the lifting of the economic embargo at independence would provide a major stimulus to the economy.

Defining 'Development' and an 'Economic Strategy'

Zimbabwe's lacklustre economic performance was not due to a lack of economic plans and clearly articulated policy objectives. Amongst early statements and plans of intent were the Transitional National

Box 5.1 – Growth with equity objectives

- *To achieve a high rate of growth to raise incomes and expand employment*
- *To restructure the economy in ways which will promote rural development*
- *To achieve greater and more equitable degree of ownership of natural resources*
- *To promote participation and ownership of a significant portion of the economy by the state*
- *To improve basic economic infrastructure*
- *To improve and extend social services to lower income groups*
- *To reform the fiscal and monetary systems in order to achieve greater equity and efficiency*
- *To fully exploit opportunities for oil substitution*
- *To promote regional co-operation in various spheres with our neighbours.*

Source: Government of Zimbabwe (1981)

Development Plan (TNDP) (1982–1985) and the First Five-Year National Development Plan (FFYNDP) (1986–1990). Prior to these two documents, the Mugabe government had published the Growth with Equity statement, which spelt out broad economic policy objectives as being:

> to establish progressively a society founded on socialist, democratic and egalitarian principles ... to end imperialist exploitation, and achieve greater and more equitable degree of ownership of natural resources including land; promote participation in, and ownership of, a significant proportion of the economy by nationals and the State .... However, Government recognised the vital role which foreign investment can play in the development of industry. (Government of Zimbabwe 1981)

For its part, the TNDP spelt out similarly ambitious economic targets. The Plan set out to expand the linkages within and between the manufacturing sector and other sectors in the economy; the promotion of import substitution policies wherever possible; the decentralisation of industries; the promotion of labour-intensive industries; the increase in local participation; and the promotion of energy efficiency. Expansive objectives were also spelt out by the FFYNDP. One of its major objectives was achieving an annual growth rate of 5.1 per cent, creating 28,000 jobs per year and a USD7.13 billion cumulative investment plan to be funded 60:40 from domestic and foreign sources.

What were the outcomes of the two national plans? Consensus among economists was that the plans flopped. Presenting some of the first post-mortem analysis on Growth with Equity and the TNDP, it was observed that:

> they were more matters of elucidating the pleasant ends than setting out the means of getting them. Growth rates were set, investment targets in the state and private sectors, and the needed sums of foreign finance were all set out. But in the absence of instruments to implement these, the plans amounted to not much more than elaborations of how the paths to the desired ends would look if they occurred, but offered little help with making them occur. (Stoneman 1988:53)

An earlier analysis had pointed out that the TNDP had ceased, as early as 1982, to serve as a significant reference point for planners in public and private sectors except in the case of social programmes (Khadhani 1986:110).

The logic of the TNDP was to maintain high levels of output to maximise revenues that could be tapped from the capitalist sector and then used to fund social service expansion. However, the degree to which the private sector could be taxed without losing the confidence of skilled white labour and capital was limited:

> by 1982, the continued viability of the transitional strategy was becoming problematic, caught in the squeeze of budgetary expansion, ebbing commercial confidence and low growth. (Gordon 2004:128)

Thus economic planning had quickly proved to be a major weakness of the Mugabe government. There was not only a shortage of planners but also a poor understanding of what planning entailed (Stoneman 1988). As one example of lack of real planning content in the government's economic plans, projected growth depended on achieving an export growth rate of seven per cent per annum without addressing constraints in the domestic economy preventing the implied shift in gear (Cliffe and Stoneman 1989). In addition to lack of realism in target setting, the process was in no sense 'central planning', as there were no attempts to use indicative planning techniques to ensure compatibility. Finally, there were no mechanisms for ensuring compliance with plan targets beyond an implicit assumption that by maintaining tight control over foreign exchange and imports, the state could indirectly thereby control investment decisions.

Nevertheless, the tradition of loose and unrealistic planning continued.

It featured in the Economic Structural Adjustment Programme (ESAP) of 1990–1995 which set a target of five per cent annual growth. Subsequent programmes and plans did not deviate from this magic figure despite its lack of realism. This made planning lose credibility as an economic instrument. One analyst argued that the real issue was the design of the plans and programmes themselves: 'the targets set are quantitative, not qualitative; it is important to focus on qualitative, human-centred indicators which reflect the ultimate goal of development' (Kanyenze 2004:138).

As a consequence as well as an indicator of failure in planning, the Mugabe government relied on the annual budget as its principal instrument of economic policy. The annual budget became not only the central and independent instrument for resource mobilisation and distribution but also the major mechanism for the structuring of economic and financial policy (Khadhani 1986). During the lost decades, economic management took an essentially short-run, fiscal and external balance stabilisation orientation. Crisis management of the economy reflected an ad hoc approach, especially during the period 1997 to 2008. This was an eloquent reminder that the state had failed to design a coherent development strategy since independence. Together with poor planning, the absence of such a strategy resulted in a policy drift which undermined the economy during the lost decades.

Explaining Contradictions and Shortfalls in the 1980s

In this section, we assess how the development plans and targets failed in the first two decades of independence and also explore the main factors behind the shortfalls experienced. At best, growth was erratic during the 1980s. Although the first two years of independence saw a boom of 11 per cent GDP growth in 1980 and ten per cent in 1981, never again would the economy reach such growth levels in the following 29 years. In fact, this two-year boom increasingly came to look like a one-off spurt. The explanation for it was it was the consequence of the opening of the economy after 14 years of sanctions and the liberation war. Additional factors behind the boom were renewed access to international loans and aid as well as increased aggregate demand arising from agricultural and wage incomes (Kanyenze 2004).

However, the remainder of the 1980s experienced slow growth, increased budget deficits and rising debt. There was a two per cent GDP decline in 1982, followed by another of 3.5 per cent in 1983, before a slight recovery in 1984. It was observed that:

> *purely on the basis of the disequilibria that emerged in external account and fiscal balances, clearly the 1980–81 booms could not be sustained. The constraints of capacity ceilings and weather shocks added impetus to the downswings that followed from 1982 to 1984 .... The economic crisis of 1982–84 was expressed through production bottlenecks, sharp reductions in government revenue resources and pressure on balance of payments – reflect-ed in inability to sustain imports of essential inputs. (Khadhani 1986:108)*

As a consequence of this crisis, the objectives and targets of the Growth with Equity policy and the TNDP were abandoned by the government. To resolve the crisis, an approach was made to the International Monetary Fund (IMF) for a loan, resulting in an 18-month IMF standby agreement to support a stabilisation programme in March 1983. However, it was subsequently suspended following disagreement over the issue of gov-ernment's suspension of remittances of dividends and profits as well as cutbacks on foreign exchange allocations.

Other indicators of an economy in the doldrums were a rise in total debt from USD786 million in 1980 to USD2.3 billion in 1983. In addition, the budget deficit had risen from 6.6 per cent in 1981–82 to 8,7 per cent in 1984–85. Defence commitments in Mozambique and expenditure on drought relief and social services ensured that the budget deficit would remain relatively high during the 1980s.

Between 1986 and 1990, growth averaged four per cent per annum against the background of population growth of 2.9 per cent. It was a growth that fell short of the projected 5.1 per cent. Some analysts estimat-ed that real growth rate during this period was about 1.5 per cent, which implied that income per capita was stagnant or falling (Stoneman 1988). Average real income was barely above 1975 levels while the proportion of people employed was much lower. Disappointingly, employment grew at an annual average of 2.7 per cent during the same period, thus failing to absorb new entrants into the labour market in a context in which the labour force was growing at about three per cent per annum (Kanyenze 2004).

The remainder of the macro-economic picture in the 1980s was scarce-ly brighter. Projected foreign investment inflows had failed to materialise. Servicing debt required about USD800 million (about 30 per cent of total exports). In real terms, exports in the 1980s had risen one per cent per annum, requiring a continuing fall in the real value of imports as the debt service increased seven-fold (Stoneman 1988). In sum, Zimbabwe was caught in the same structural trap as most developing countries:

> it was not earning enough foreign exchange both to service its debts and to invest for expanded exports, but it can only escape through a massive expansion of exports. (Ibid.:59)

This was the broad context in which the Mugabe government sought a comprehensive response to this situation of anaemic growth, lacklustre export performance and slow trickle of investment inflows. In response, it designed the ESAP as a blueprint for accelerated growth.

However, before we assess the ESAP and its outcomes, let us conclude this section by positing the factors that derailed the plans and strategies that had been crafted at the beginning of the 1980s. A number of policy blunders contributed to the economic crisis of the early 1980s. First, immense pressures were generated as a result of the reversal of UDI to liberalise exchange controls. This resulted in outflows of payments and remittances from USD72 million in 1980 to USD206 million in 1982. This policy stance on liberalisation reflected what was termed 'a significantly reduced cohesion relative to the pre-1980 era in the macro-economic strategies of this period' (Khadhani 1986). As a consequence, net foreign assets declined from USD178 million at the end of 1980 to negative levels in 1982, with the debt service ratio increasing thrice, to about 30 per cent by 1983 (Ibid.). Some analysts were more forthright in their critique of the government's policy stance:

> the partial opening of the economy after 1980 was harmful, exposing it to a hostile world market, raising dependence on the export of primary commodities which were unstable in price, opening up a capital outflow through repayments of loans and factor income from foreign investment, allowing in unnecessary imported especially luxury cars, and focusing on the external market at the cost of failing to develop the impoverished internal one in rural areas. (Cliffe and Stoneman 1989:163-4)

Some caution was therefore necessary before the rapid opening of liberalisation soon after independence. It is possible that the new but inexperienced government did not fully understand the consequences of their liberalisation policy. If that was the case, there is no evidence that some useful lessons were drawn from the policy failure. There would be a repetition of a similar policy mistake under the ESAP in 1990–1995.

Second, lack of clarity on industrial strategy was another weakness identified by some analysts. For instance, it was observed that 'a clear industrialisation strategy has not yet emerged' in the 1980s. The co-ordinating capacity of the state still left much to be desired, especially in 'defining and disseminating an ideology of industrialising and industrial programmes, and successfully implementing and co-ordinating them' (Della 1986). Third, the overall development strategy of the 1980s was one based on what was termed the least common denominator of radical and reformist proposals. As it was observed:

> it attempted to postpone, avoid or finesse the hard strategic choices that were being urged upon it from various sides. It was a strategy that depended upon the creative use of political ambiguity and one that threatened policy indecisiveness. It was a strategy that failed to satisfy any group completely. (Gordon 1984:128)

Consider the tension between investments in social services and in the productive sectors. By committing the government to heavy expenditure in social services, recurrent expenditures skyrocketed. The policy of avoiding hard choices exacerbated the problem, meaning that the 'cost of avoiding political conflict was the loss of control over expenditures' (Ibid.).

Finally, by the end of the 1980s, the ideology of socialism co-existed uneasily with capitalist reality. The former appeared more and more anachronistic in view of domestic developments of emerging *embourgeoisement* and corruption, and the collapse of the socialist model worldwide. In that lost decade of the 1980s, Zimbabwe failed to consolidate its growth constituency as well its equity constituency.

Economic Adjustment and its Limits

The recourse to adjustment in 1990 was an admission by the Mugabe government that its development strategy and economic policy had not been successful. For instance, the budget deficit was in excess of ten per cent of GDP during much of the 1980s; government debt had reached 71 per cent of GDP by 1989, of which 36 per cent was external (Government of Zimbabwe 1991). Private sector investment remained at ten per cent of GDP during the decade. The cumbersome foreign exchange allocation system, the tightly regulated business environment in relation to pricing, labour and investment controls together with uncontrollable fiscal deficits deterred investors (Ibid.).

Export growth at 3.4 per cent per annum between 1980 and 1989 coupled with debt service repayments, which reached a peak of 34 per cent of export earnings in 1987, severely constrained the growth of imports. This in turn undermined utilisation of existing capacity and possibilities of re-equipment, and also discouraged fresh investment. In short, whatever growth had occurred in the 1980s had been fragile given the structural weaknesses built into the economy. A continuation of the economic policies of the 1980s was unlikely to lead to a dramatic and sustainable transition such as had occurred in the newly industrialised countries in Asia (Stoneman 1989).

The Mugabe government therefore decided to seek financial flows from international financial institutions (IFIs) and bilateral funding agencies. It was required to meet certain conditionalities that are standard in adjustment programmes. These primarily related to:

- *Budget deficit reduction*
- *Fiscal and monetary policy reforms*
- *Trade liberalisation*
- *Public enterprise reforms (including privatisation)*
- *Deregulation of investment, labour and price controls* (Government of Zimbabwe 1991:4)

The ESAP optimistically projected that implementation of these measures over a five-year period would lead to:

- *Five per cent annual growth*
- *A reduction of the budget deficit to five per cent of GDP by 1995*
- *A reduction of the external current account deficit to four per cent of GDP*
- *Reduction of the debt service ratio to 20 per cent by 1995. (Ibid.)*

Furthermore, direct subsidies and transfers to public enterprises would be reduced from ZWD629 million to ZWD40 million by 1995. A comprehensive programme for improving efficiency and management, and of commercialisation and privatisation of public enterprises, would be implemented as a matter of urgency.

A phased process of trade liberalisation would be instituted to move from a state-administered, forex-based allocation system to a market-based one so that with a few exceptions all importable items would be importable on the Open General Import License (OGIL). This measure and others were expected to contribute to greater investment inflows that were projected to rise to 25 per cent of GDP by 1995. It was also projected that GDP per capita and consumption per capita would rise by two per cent during the ESAP period. Finally, the adjustment period would contribute to reduction of high unemployment, by 100,000 new jobs being created in the formal sector in the period 1992–1995.

Was the ESAP 'wish list' successfully implemented? Unfortunately, the ESAP met the same fate as previous government economic programmes. It encountered huge problems at the implementation stage. The difference, however, with the ESAP was that it was jointly owned by the IFIs, chiefly the World Bank, and the Mugabe government. And although not always timely, some significant resources were poured into the programme. So what went wrong? Most of the projections were not met.

One study concluded that the ESAP 'failed miserably':

> *GDP averaged just 1.2 per cent from 1991 to 1995. Inflation averaged more than 30 per cent during the period and never dropped anywhere near the ten per cent target. The budget deficit was more than ten per cent of GDP during the period. (Bond and Manyanya 2003:32)*

Most indicators pointed to lack of success of the ESAP measures. A process of de-industrialisation occurred (Sachikonye 1999). In an extended survey of factors that conspired to derail ESAP, one analyst identifies them as:

- *technically deficient implementation owing to poor design*
- *speculative surge in imports*
- *late disbursements of funds by donors including the World Bank*
- *punitive interest rates and contraction in foreign investment*
- *a major drought in 1990–91 necessitating food imports. (Gibbon 1995:13)*

On the whole, the ESAP was distinguished for missing its targets and exposing the weakness of the model as an economic strategy.

In a previous longitudinal study on the effects of the ESAP on the economy, I arrived at several conclusions which confirmed that the programme had been a failure (Sachikonye and Zishiri 1999). For a programme that was launched with such a huge political fanfare, the outcome was not impressive. First, growth was almost stagnant at less than one per cent on average per year between 1990 and 1995. The volume of manufacturing output, for example, sank below the pre-adjustment period (ZCTU 1996). In our longitudinal case studies, we observed that the combination of high interest rates, devaluation and low domestic demand hurt certain sub-sectors, especially textiles, clothing and metal. Exports plummeted. The value of exports, which had grown at an annual average of nine per cent between 1985 and 1990, declined to an estimated three per cent between 1990 and 1993. Statistics on the production volume in 1995 showed that half of the manufacturing sub-sectors had witnessed their volume fall to, or below, the levels recorded in 1980.

However, a measure of progress had been accomplished in areas of investment and trade liberalisation, and in the de-regulation of financial, labour and market controls. Nonetheless, as we observed in our case studies, there was no attempt to synchronise trade liberalisation and sustainable modernisation of the manufacturing sector. The implementation of trade liberalisation may have been ahead of schedule but it was a hollow achievement given the setbacks that some manufacturing sub-sectors experienced owing to unregulated flows of competing imports.

The World Bank was candid enough to concede the unsatisfactory outcome of the ESAP. It agreed that Zimbabwe's adjustment experience pointed to the importance of the proper sequencing of such a programme. In its own words:

> trade liberalisation and the rationalisation of tariff, tax and export incentive regimes need to be sequenced carefully. The failure in Zimbabwe to properly synchronise these measures and to establish the conditions for rapid expansion of exports early on, placed many domestic firms at a disadvantage and delayed the supply response. (World Bank 1995:11)

Of course, this newly found wisdom was an attribute of hindsight, for the World Bank itself had originally been dogmatic about a 'big bang' approach to stabilisation and adjustment. As in similar cases of adjustment programmes that had gone awry, it was the implementing government, not the IFIs, who picked up the tab for the expensive blunders. A performance audit report by the World Bank further acknowledged the constraints that had arisen halfway through the ESAP:

> many firms feel that they have been given a less than level playing field as a result of having to contend with increased competition while confronting tax and tariff regional trade anomalies. (Ibid.)

Yet, there was no attempt to readjust these policy measures which were contributing to the woes of the manufacturing sector. In spite of its role in the designing of the ESAP, the World Bank would later seek to distance itself from the flawed outcome.

Finally, in the public enterprise sector, reform seriously lagged behind, with largely negative macro-economic consequences. For instance, in 1993–1994 the total operating deficit of the nine major enterprises amounted to 3.3 per cent of GDP. In 1995, the government inherited parastatal debts amounting to ZWD four billion. Persistent lacklustre performance and losses by parastatals weighed heavily on public finances, necessitating increased government debt through domestic borrowing and reduced availability of finance for private sector investment. The ESAP objectives relating to public enterprises did not, therefore, materialise. In sum, government expectations that the ESAP would result in increased investment, accelerated growth and rising incomes were not met.

Stalled Agrarian and Industrial Transition

There was a link between the failure of the ESAP to transform the economy through growth and the stalled agrarian and industrial transition. In the absence of land reform that supported the growth of agro-industry and creation of many jobs, and of increased linkages between agriculture and industry, there was little likelihood of a successful transition. In those two crucial decades of the 1980s and 1990s, despite the availability of the key ingredients of relatively advanced industry and commercial agriculture, Zimbabwe failed to rise to the occasion to implement a land reform process that dovetailed with a growing manufacturing industry. During these lost decades, policy-makers missed an opportunity to set commercial agriculture on a sustainable path by deliberately drawing more small farmers into agriculture production and small industries. The opportunity to enlarge the domestic market for various inputs such as seed, fertiliser, equipment, irrigation materials and consumer goods amongst smallholders was missed. So was an opportunity to extend and consolidate backward and forward linkages between industry and smallholder agriculture. This would have been one path to break the dualism embedded in the Zimbabwean economy and society since colonialism.

A strategy for making the transition was argued along these lines:

firstly, the increased demand for industrial goods would result in an expansion of output in the industrial sector thereby increasing profits and savings or re-investible earnings to spur further expansion. Secondly, the supply of cheap wage goods in the form of food and cheap raw materials from the rural sector would lower costs of production in the industrial sector, thus reinforcing increased productivity and output expansion in the industrial sector as well as increased profits. (ZCTU 1996:17)

In addition, the increased demand for goods in rural areas could be used as an opportunity to promote the decentralisation of industry to smaller towns and growth points. The resulting general expansion in the industrial sector coupled with the release of labour from the rural sector as a consequence of the increased productivity would result in the increased absorption of cheap labour in the industrial sector, thereby further widening the market for both food produced in rural areas and wage goods from the industrial sector. Thus the combination of the chain reactions in the rural and industrial sectors, if consciously nurtured and guided by proactive government policies, would lead to the resolution of allocative and technical inefficiencies and to the blurring of the enclavity and dualism that was the legacy of past development processes (ZCTU 1996:18). This conceptualisation of development strategy was unfortunately missing from government plans and programmes and from the ESAP. This meant that the question of agrarian and industrial transition was avoided, despite it being central to any strategy of transformation. This also explains the limited priority attached to the land reform issue during these two lost decades.

The Collapse of the Social Contract in the late 1990s

The cumulative failure of economic plans and programmes created a crisis for the social contract in the second half of the 1990s. The crisis related to stagnation and decline in living standards, unemployment and dim prospects for growth and transformation. Various social groups ranging from labour to commercial farmers and informal economy operators and industrialists to war veterans were pessimistic about the capacity of the Mugabe government to manage the stalled transition. One symptom of the gathering storm was the eruption of strikes by labour unions and demonstrations by war veterans in 1996 and 1997. As it was pointed out:

> 1997 was the turning point because it was the year civil society groups agitated visibly for their rights, which had been eroded under ESAP. In 1996, the longest and most acrimonious public sector strikes since independence occurred, especially involving health workers and teachers. And in 1997, some 232 strikes were recorded, the largest in any year since 1980. Because of the widespread nature of these strikes and high levels of mobilisation, EMCOZ and ZCTU agreed to hold a summit before negotiations with workers commenced. (Kanyenze 2004:130)

In a rare consensus, EMCOZ and ZCTU agreed that the erosion of workers' purchasing power was largely due to the imprudent fiscal policies of the Mugabe government.

For their part, war veterans demanded a pay-off from their service during the liberation struggle. This was perhaps the most expensive and disastrous of any pay-off sought by any social group. The gratuities of ZWD50,000 and pensions wrestled from the government under duress forced the largest devaluation of the Zimbabwe dollar, triggering a crisis that would become full-blown in 2000. Little did the Mugabe government and the war veterans know that the consequences of their decisions and actions would be a decade-long economic crisis resulting in a severe contraction that would wipe off between 40 and 50 per cent of GDP. This was exacerbated by an expensive military intervention in the DRC in 1998 which gobbled about USD30 million a month. Food riots broke out in 1998 as prices went up. The social contract had never before been under such serious strain.

For what it was worth, there was an attempt by the labour movement to persuade the Mugabe government to resuscitate the social contract in 1996–1997. A union proposal to set up a tripartite Zimbabwe Economic Development and Labour Advisory Council was, unfortunately, rebuffed by the government. Polarisation set in. From within civil society, there grew pressure for constitutional reform with the founding of the National Constitutional Assembly in 1998. From within the labour movement, the momentum developed for the formation of a party, culminating in the founding of the MDC in 1999. The stage was thus set for a bruising struggle, one that few foresaw lasting a whole decade! Last but not least, sections of the peasantry became more militant and began to organise land occupations from 1998 in districts such as Svosve. This would be co-opted and broadened into a land reform process carried out in an unsystematic fashion as *jambanja* between 2000 and 2003. The next section explores how the economy was affected by the decade-long crisis.

The Depth of the Economic Crisis, 1998–2008

There has been an explosion of writing and analyses of the crisis that Zimbabwe underwent during the lost decade of 1998 to 2008 (ICG various; Meredith 2002; Bond and Manyanya 2003; UNDP 2008; World Bank, various; IMF 2007). It is an era that attracted a great deal of commentary given the depth of the crisis. We will confine our attention to the economic dimension of the crisis, notwithstanding the clear inter-connections that it had with political developments. What made this particular decade unique was that the Mugabe government was literally fighting for its survival after the constitutional referendum defeat in 2000 and the substantial erosion of its majority in the 2000 election. Unfortunately, economic decisions and programmes formulated from 2000 onward had the primary rationale of prolonging its stay in office. The Mugabe government's overall objective was to delay, if not avoid, what was colloquially termed 'regime change'. Sensing its vulnerability at the polls, it deployed two key instruments. The first was patronage which consisted of material rewards to retain supporters and to buy votes. The second was intimidation and violence against recalcitrant opposition supporters. In such a context there was little likelihood of economic policies and programmes remaining rational and retaining a medium- and long-term perspective.

The political factor thus loomed larger than ever before in economic policy design and implementation during this decade. As a major survey confirmed:

> *political imperatives took precedence over economic goals, most marked in the land reform programme but also in exchange rate policy, the pricing policies of parastatals ... and the Indigenisation and Economic Empowerment Act .... Economic policies seem to have been driven by the need to secure immediate and medium-term political goals, while paying scant attention to collateral social and economic consequences of such actions. (UNDP 2008:211)*

These developments not only illustrated the extent to which the state had been captured by vested interests but also the apparent transition from *state capture* to *predatory state*. In a predatory state, conventional macroeconomic and regulatory policy levers are deemed inadequate and authorities seek to secure direct control over markets and economic actors (UNDP: 2008).

We explored in Chapter 2 the implications of state capture by key interests within the then ruling ZANU-PF party, the military–security complex and the state bureaucracy ensconced in the public service and parastatals. In different ways, each took advantage of accumulation opportunities and engaged in asset-stripping in both the private and public sectors.

There was a deliberate decision to make political appointments to strategic institutions such as the Reserve Bank of Zimbabwe which provided finance for further accumulation on partisan grounds.

Table 5.1 – Zimbabwe's economic performance, 1980–2006

Indicators	1980–1990 (per cent)	1991–2000 (per cent)	2001–2006 (per cent)
Average annual growth	4.3	0.9	-5.7
Employment growth	1.9	0.4	-7.5
Formal employment	12.2	10.9	7
Manufacturing (percentage of GDP)	20.3	17.7	15
Agriculture (percentage of GDP)	16.2	14.9	17
Mining (percentage of GDP)	4.3	4.2	4

Source: UNDP (2008:13)

A principal feature of this decade was the abandonment of any pretence to medium- and long-term economic planning and programming. The ESAP was the last major sustained effort at economic reform. Designed as a successor programme to the ESAP, the Zimbabwe Programme for Economic and Social Transformation (ZIMPREST) was stillborn. It was not implemented. Successive ones with such high-sounding terms as the Millennium Economic Recovery Programme (MERP) of 2000, the National Economic Revival Programme (NERP) of 2003, and the National Economic Development Priority Programme (NEDPP) in 2006 were implemented haphazardly. From 1998, donors had demonstrated little interest in providing substantial loans and grants. In the wake of land reform in 2000–2003, there was reluctance by IFIs to commit large lending and aid in the absence of what was termed 'rule of law' and respect for 'property rights'. This stimulated the development of a 'siege mentality' bordering on paranoia on the part of the Mugabe government. Henceforth, all subsequent economic failures and hardships (Table 5.1) were blamed as stemming from 'illegal sanctions' by the West.

In the absence of medium and long-term planning, the government resorted to ad hoc crisis management, especially from 2000. As we observed above, short-term programmes with catchy acronyms such as MERP and NERP were cobbled together and implemented in a rather haphazard fashion. In reality, the annual budget remained the principal instrument of economic policy during this decade. Ministers of Finance had short tenure as the President sought greater influence on economic policy and national budget setting. Some of the symptoms of the depth of the crisis were endemic shortages of inputs such as fuel, resulting in legendary winding queues, and also of basic consumer goods:

> real costs to society were high ... there is a thriving parallel market for basic commodities, where the price is much higher than the controlled price. This is the market where a significant part of our population is sourcing basic commodities. The beneficiaries of the price controls are the speculators and dealers and not the targeted vulnerable groups. (Minister of Finance's budget statement, 2003:14-15)

The ripple effects of the crisis included production of lower quality goods as producers were forced to 'shave' inputs in order to maintain profit margins and loss of employment opportunities as companies downsized production (Ibid.).

Conventional responses such as devaluation were ruled out by the Mugabe government, to the chagrin of some of his finance ministers. Inflation went out of control. Budget deficits shot up unrelentingly. Balance of payments problems mounted. There was an increasing resort to informal methods of economic transactions such as barter trade as well as the mortgaging of resources such as land and minerals to certain countries like China and Libya in opaque deals.

This was the context in which Gideon Gono was appointed as Governor of the Reserve Bank of Zimbabwe (RBZ) in 2003. He soon usurped the authority of and powers normally wielded by the Minister of Finance.

Quasi-fiscal Activities

The immediate context in which the RBZ became a major player in the economy between 2003 and 2008 was one in which there was a great deal of disdain of conventional methods of economic management, which were often dismissed as 'textbook or bookish economics'. The rationale for interventionism of the RBZ was that:

> where a national economy experiences real, persistent and unprecedented structural shocks and where those shocks transform the market economy into a bubble-driven casino economy as happened in Zimbabwe from 2000 onwards, monetary policy must then necessarily do more by getting out of the traditional mandate toolbox in order to take into account the contextual factors on the ground from a pragmatic point of view. (Gono 2008:139-40)

Table 5.2 – Quasi-Fiscal Activities of the RBZ, 2003–2008

Date	Purpose
2003	Productive sector finance facility
2004	Troubled Bank fund
2005a	Parastatals and local authorities reorientation programme (PLARP)
2005b	Agriculture sector productivity enhancement facility (ASPEF)
2006	Agricultural mechanisation programme
2007a	Basic commodities supply-side intervention facility (BACOSSI)
2007b	Commissioning of a bio-diesel plant
2007c	Assistance to ZINWA to improve water supplies
2008	Provision of finance for the public transport sector (e.g., ZUPCO and NRZ)

Source: Gono (2008:148-52)

Gono defined the mission of the RBZ as adopting a deliberate policy to stimulate productive economic activities by providing concessional funding to key sectors of the economy, most notably the agricultural sector. This meant devising 'extraordinary and innovative measures and interventions to stimulate economic activity, ensure food self-sufficiency, stabilise energy supplies, arrest further decline and rein inflation' (Ibid.:145). It was an agenda that conceded that conventional economic policy had failed. To rescue the situation, the RBZ pumped resources to ailing sectors such as agriculture, parastatals, finance, local authorities and water (Table 5.2).

As it was acknowledged, the RBZ thus found itself at the centre of virtually all activities in the economy. This included the financing of agriculture; stabilising supplies to the health sector; supervising national examinations in 2008; logistical support in the fight against the 2008 cholera outbreak; providing basic commodities for rural communities and urban households in the high-density areas under BACOSSI; importing electricity, fuel, agrochemicals, fertiliser and grain, among many other necessary operations that would otherwise fall on the national budget (Gono 2008).

Several pertinent observations can be made regarding the RBZ financing these activities and projects which should have been the prerogative of government ministries and the private sector. First, the resources that were required were significant. Second, it was mostly those who were politically connected that had access to those financial resources. Third, the accounting and transparency mechanisms for these resources remained opaque. Finally, it is difficult to establish the total amount that was spent on each of the various quasi-fiscal programmes. Part of the amount was drawn from printing of notes which then found their way onto the parallel currency market where they were exchanged for US dollars and South African rands, amongst others.

It was observed that while Central Bank losses in most countries have not exceeded ten per cent of GDP, Zimbabwe's flow of realised central bank quasi-fiscal losses was estimated at 75 per cent of GDP in 2006 (IMF 2007). Corroborating the evidence above, it was noted that losses rose from a range of activities, including monetary operations to mop up liquidity, subsidised credit, foreign exchange losses through subsidised exchange rates for selected government purchases and multiple currency practices and financial sector restructuring (Ibid.). The power to create money to finance losses quickly ran into conflict with any recognised monetary policy objective, with official inflation reaching 1,600 per cent in January and 232 million per cent in mid-2008.

Evidence that RBZ expenditures were well beyond its resources consisted of the USD1.2 billion debts that it was saddled with by 2010. Before a new law was introduced in that year to pre-empt further auctions, the RBZ had witnessed some of its assets being auctioned off in order to pay the debt. The debt and these episodes graphically illustrated that the quasi-fiscal activities were both unsustainable and ill-advised.

The Rise of a Parallel Economy and Informalisation

The decade-long crisis caused significant de-industrialisation as well as capacity underutilisation, which had sunk to about 15 per cent in some sectors in 2008. Retrenchments were widespread. These developments, combined with around 80 per cent unemployment, contributed to the growth of the informal economy. This segment of the economy was the fastest growing during the period 1998 to 2008. Although up-to-date and reliable statistics were difficult to obtain, this parallel economy absorbed workers and small entrepreneurs in vending, cross-border trade, gold panning, sewing, carpentry, currency trading, maintenance and construction, amongst others. Most of the activities were part of survival and coping strategies at the low-scale end of the market. Conditions and incomes in these sectors were often precarious. A survey conducted on employment trends in 2008 indicated that 87 per cent of the sample was mainly involved in the informal economy, with only 12 per cent engaged in the formal sector (Luebker, 2008).

As a consequence of the broader economic crisis, most of those engaged in the informal economy led a hand-to-mouth existence. As it was observed:

> the most common activity was retail trade, and in particular street vending. Respondents were also engaged in small-scale manufacturing that includes female-dominated activities such as crocheting and tailoring, and male-dominated activities like the production of furniture and household hardware. Many of those interviewed work excessive hours and yet generate incomes that are insufficient to meet even their most basic needs. The survey found no indications that workers enter the informal sector to secure a competitive advantage versus formal sector enterprises. (Ibid.: 53)

We return to the pivotal issue of livelihoods in the informal economy in Chapter 8. For now, we may conclude by observing that the shrinkage in formal sector employment has partly resulted in reduced tax revenues for the state.

The Debt Burden

A chapter on Zimbabwe's economy during the lost decades would be incomplete without some some consideration, no matter how brief, of the mounting debt millstone (Table 5.3). In August 2010, the total external debt amounted to USD6.5 billion which constituted nearly 120 per cent of GDP (Kanyenze, Chitambara, Kondo and Martens, 2011). Some 37 per cent of the debt is owed to multilateral creditors such as the IMF, 34 per cent to bilateral creditors with 29 per cent owed to commercial creditors. Arrears have become a major element of the debt, which was expected to climb above USD7 billion by 2011.

The implications of this millstone are far-reaching. First, they include a major constraint on government finances; payment of arrears is a great burden. Some USD3.2 billion (or almost half) of the debt is in arrears. This

Table 5.3 – Zimbabwe: selected economic indicators and estimates, 2008–2011

	2008	2009	2010	2011
Real GDP growth	-14.5	42.	2.0	2.0
Nominal GDP (USDm)	3.92	4.39	5.14	5.48
Consumer price inflation	-1	6.5	5	5
Central Government (percentage of GDP in USD)	3.4	22.2	26.1	26.8
Total external debt (percentage of GDP)	147.5	162.5	149	148.3

Source: IMF (2010:31)

has curtailed further borrowings and inflows thus placing a major constraint on growth and recovery. One analyst has argued that the debt burden is the 'biggest albatross' around Zimbabwe's neck, and that its resolution requires domestic leadership and political will (Muchena 2011:22). Furthermore, the international community needs to be supportive and creative towards debt alleviation in the realisation that economic stabilisation is still in its nascent stages, and key social sectors still recovering from a decade-long malaise (Ibid.). There have been calls from within civil society for an audit of the debt to determine which of it could be 'odious' and thus illegitimate (Sachikonye and Bricking, 2009). There should be some consideration of mechanism to forgive or cancel some of the debt, and provide the country with a breathing space to make a fresh start.

Conclusion

Marking the end of the decade-long crisis in 2008 was the formation of an Inclusive Government and the beginning of a recovery underlined by growth of about five per cent in 2009. This was the first reverse of contraction in ten years. Even so, the recovery was still fragile, as this assessment made clear:

Zimbabwe's external position is precarious. The current account has been in deficit for the past decade. Exports have stagnated over the past ten years on account of the disruptive economic environment. Investment in key export sectors is handicapped by inadequate infrastructure, high operational costs are exacerbated by wage pressures and poor business climate makes Zimbabwe less attractive to investors. Agriculture's share in exports has fallen substantially. (IMF 2010:31)

In 2009, the current account deficit was estimated to have reached 30 per cent of GDP and external debt rose to USD7.1 billion (162 per cent of GDP), with external arrears accounting for about 64 per cent of the external debt. The consequences of a large external debt are far-reaching in terms of economic and social effects (Sachikonye and Bracking 2009). Thus Zimbabwe is not out of the woods yet. It would be naïve to expect this in the aftermath of the economic haemorrhage of the past decade and the cocktail of unsuccessful policies and programmes of the past three decades.

In concluding, we observe the centrality of three factors, amongst several, in accelerating Zimbabwe's economic decline. The first related to an increased sense of entitlement to opportunities and resources by the ruling elite from the mid-1990s onwards. This entitlement largely focused on material accumulation and aggrandisement which ranged from drawing from the national treasury for liberation war compensation to confiscating white farmers' property (land, equipment and housing) and jostling for finance and other assets from the RBZ. The total amount of resources accumulated in these ways by the ruling elite may not be accurately established but they were very substantial. Whatever term may be applied to the process ranging from so-called 'primitive accumulation' to 'asset-stripping' and plain 'theft', a certain recklessness characterised the elite's scramble for resources and the Mugabe government's handling of the economy. A similar approach was discernible in the extortion scheme against manufacturing companies in 2001 and later in the formulation of the Indigenisation and Economic Empowerment Act. The principles of rule of law and sanctity of private property were thrown overboard. In such a context, it would have been naïve to expect foreign investment inflows to be significant. This created large disadvantages for the country in terms of competitiveness within southern Africa. One net result was that while other countries in the region registered growth, Zimbabwe experienced contraction. While 26 African countries achieved growth rates above three per cent in 2000, the number increased to 40 in 2002. Zimbabwe was not among them. It missed out on this growth wave due to poor policies as well as the self-aggrandisement mentioned above.

However, an external factor also played a role during the decade-long crisis, although this was a primary or sole one, as the Mugabe government often claims. Although estranged relations with the West and the IFIs did not lead to a break in trading relations, it did adversely affect Zimbabwe's access to loans from such institutions as the IMF and World Bank. For instance, in 2002 the country was suspended from the IMF for its substantial arrears. This also reduced its access to concessional finance and grants. In addition, companies owned by members of Zimbabwe's ruling elite had restrictions clamped on them by some Western countries through what were termed 'targeted sanctions'. The removal of those sanctions was conditional, being dependent upon the Mugabe government dismantling authoritarian legislation and measures. The message was that there was a price to pay for riding roughshod over the rule of law, violating property rights and disregarding bilateral and international agreements.

6

Land Reform & its Aftermath

Introduction

A large part of the explanation of the stagnation and decline of Zimbabwe's economic development, as assessed in Chapter 5, relates to the changing fortunes of its agriculture. No account of Zimbabwean politics, economics and social development would therefore be complete without assessing the significance of the land question. The issue of land – its ownership, control and utilisation – has been central to Zimbabwean politics for over a century, indeed since the country was colonised in 1890, and granted independence in 1980. Thus the history of the land question unfolded over many decades, depositing a residue of memories of dispossession, trauma and hardship amongst deprived blacks, and of conquest, superior production techniques and subsequent dispossession amongst white landowners (Palmer 1977; Moyo 1995; Sachikonye, 2004).

State-sanctioned evictions of blacks from better-endowed land began in the 1890s and continued well into the 1950s and 1960s. Memories of dispossession were stoked by the liberation struggle which was mainly waged in the rural areas, including areas where there was commercial farming land, in the 1960s and 1970s. During the lost decades, there was no serious effort to resolve the land question. It was only in 2000, the year of the parliamentary elections, that it became a major political resource for ZANU-PF. For the first time since independence, its hold on power was seriously threatened by a fledgling opposition party, the MDC. The survival of the Mugabe government in the 2000 election ultimately hinged on the use of both the 'carrot' of land reform and the 'stick' of violence.

In this chapter, we will not attempt to provide a full review of how the land question was addressed after 1980. There is plentiful literature on this (Raftopoulos, Hammar and Jensen 2003; Alexander 2006). We will confine much of our assessment to the land reform of 2000 to 2003 and the wider ramifications that constituted its aftermath.·

Without ignoring the key contours of the land question at independence and the significance of the largely peaceful and orderly first phase of reform in the first two decades, the chapter explores the consequences of *jambanja* (land occupation by force) and patterns of agrarian decline after 2000. We draw on some field research we carried out on the fate of farm workers and white farmers in 2003 as well as reflect on the subsequent rise of a black landed elite.

The Land Question and the First Phase of Reform

The structure of land ownership and use was clearly inequitable at independence. About 6,000 white commercial farmers owned 15.5 million hectares of land while 8,500 small-scale African farmers had 1.4 million. The rest, an estimated 700,000 communal farming households, subsisted on 16.4 million hectares. In other words, these households occupied less than 50 per cent of all agricultural land, of which 75 per cent was in the drier and less fertile agro-ecological regions 4 and 5. There was therefore a keenly felt sense of historical injustice and deprivation over the question of land, making it one of the most contentious issues negotiated at the Lancaster House conference. There were unconfirmed reports that the US and UK governments promised a package of USD1.5 billion to break the log jam in the negotiations about how land reform should be addressed.

Whatever the actual promise might have been, the pledge was not enshrined in the Lancaster House Constitution, which instead contained onerous clauses on the protection of private property, including land. Indeed, the Constitution proved to be the major brake on the speed and scope of land reform during the first ten years of independence. It restricted the purchase of land for redistribution by means of the stringent 'willing seller, willing buyer' provisions. In general, the cost of land was high, to the degree that the purchase involved immediate payment of full value in foreign exchange, which significantly restricted the government's room for manoeuvre on the land question during the first decade of independence.

This was the wider structural context in which the government's land reform programme operated, with its centrepiece being the resettlement of the poor and landless. It was a programme whose overall objective in 1982 was to resettle 162,000 households on nine million hectares of land over three years. This would have represented a transfer of 23 per cent of households from congested communal lands onto new land. This did not happen. Owing to resource constraints and limited political will, by 1989 only about 48,000 households had been resettled.

In the 1990s, on the whole, there was curiously less urgency attached to resolving the land question. This was perplexing in view of the earlier impetus and the expiry of the restrictive clauses of the Lancaster House Constitution in 1990. Fewer than 25,000 new households received land between 1990 and 1997. Although the total number of resettled households amounted to 71,000 by 1997, this was a far cry from the original target of 162,000. However, a significant parallel development was that by the mid-1990s about 500 black farmers had become fully fledged commercial farmers. Of these, about 80 per cent had bought farms with their own resources while the remainder rented leasehold farms from the state.

Assessing the First Phase of Land Reform

The official explanation for the slowdown in land reform in the 1990s was that land acquisition through the 'willing seller, willing buyer' approach significantly limited the scope of spatially matching land supply with the demand for resettlement. Land sold in small parcels was expensive to develop for resettlement. Scarcity of land, exorbitant prices of available land in the market and the inability of the government to pay the prices asked limited its capacity to achieve its reform targets (Government of Zimbabwe, 1998). It was estimated that by the mid-1990s land prices had increased three-fold since the late 1980s and that unless the amount of land for sale increased it was doubtful whether the government was capable for purchasing land in sufficient quantities to implement a new programme (ODA 1996). Although two key legal developments in the form of a Land Acquisition Act and the 14th constitutional amendment were passed during this period, there remained limited political will and little momentum for land reform.

At the same time, there was evidence that land redistribution through resettlement had achieved a modicum of success through substantially improved yields. For instance, a British evaluation mission that assessed the resettlement programme observed that:

> *it had made impressive strides towards achieving its principal objectives, in particular the short run political objective of contributing to post-war reconstruction and stability. The majority of families settled had benefited considerably through the provision of increased opportunities for income*

generation and the availability of services such as health and education.
(ODA 1996)

This assessment corroborated an earlier study conducted by the Zimbabwe Comptroller and Auditor-General, who concluded that the resettlement programme had been well planned, that it had benefited mostly the landless rural poor and that the standard of living of most settlers had improved as a consequence of increased incomes and access to clean drinking water, sanitation, housing and schools. By the 1990s, even the initially sceptical analysts who had made pessimistic forecasts appear to have changed their position in the face of evidence that land reform had 'helped beneficiaries to increase their level of household income significantly' (Kinsey, Deininger and Hoogeveen 2000).

It was against this broad background of this orderly and incrementally successful programme that political pressure for land reform in the mid-1990s was less intense than before. The Mugabe government had comfortably won the 1990 and 1995 elections, sweeping about 95 per cent of parliamentary seats. Opposition parties were fragmented and weak, and thus unable to mount a credible challenge to the incumbent party. Until 1998, there was little organised pressure for more land from peasants and the landless.

However, a significant development in the 1990s was the emergence of a growing group within the ruling elite which sought access to land ownership. The political and economic environment of economic adjustment was favourable to this aspiration, which found expression in the leasing of state land to cabinet ministers, parliamentarians, judges, army officers and civil servants. Although the majority of this elite lacked farming experience and did not derive their livelihoods mainly from land, state land was made available to them at concessionary rates while the more pressing needs of the poor and landless were given less attention. The subsequent publicity given to the long list of elite beneficiaries by a member of parliament, Margaret Dongo, provoked a heated discussion about the government's commitment to a land reform programme that benefited the poor. At this point in the mid-1990s, 90,000 households still needed land in order for the programme to reach its original target of 162,000 households. Unsurprisingly, there emerged a strong critique of the process of *'embourgeoisement'* through state-facilitated access to land. There was a strong likelihood of corruption or cronyism in this process, as well as a deepening of social inequalities.

This was the immediate background against which donors began to insist concertedly on transparency in any future land reform programme. An international conference with donors organised in 1998 by the government of Zimbabwe stressed that such a programme should be implemented 'in a transparent, fair and sustainable manner, with regard to respect for the law, and broadened stakeholder as well as beneficiary participation; and that it should be affordable, cost-effective and consistent with economic and financial reforms' (communiqué 1998). A mission which prepared a report in 1999 for the UK's Department for International Development (DFID) and the European Union (EU) was even more emphatic when it advised that conditions should be attached to any future support to 'eliminate gross abuses such as the use of funds for the purchase from landowners who may have been allocated state land under an earlier process' (DFID and EU 1999). Together with a widely publicised letter by Clare Short, then Secretary of State for International Development, on conditionalities on aid, this new insistence on transparency and accountability irked the Zimbabwe government. To it, this appeared as part of the broader discourse on 'good governance' which the Blair government propagated with more zeal than previous Conservative governments.

In this new donor approach, there was also greater emphasis on poverty reduction, which in turn required a more systematic selection of beneficiaries from among the poor, such as those living in congested communal areas, those with farming aptitude and vulnerable groups such as farm workers (communiqué 1998). The case for alleviating the marginalisation of farm workers in future land reform was also highlighted in several detailed case studies on the poor conditions under which they worked and lived (Amanor-Wilks 1995; Sachikonye and Zishiri 1999). In addition, it was argued that future land reform should address more adequately gender aspects, especially issues of equal access and ownership of land and the involvement of women in planning and implementation processes.

Jambanja and the Limits of Redistribution

As we have observed, *jambanja* was a term coined to designate the process of unplanned, coercive and chaotic occupation of commercial farms that began in February 2000. *Jambanja* thus refers to this process which the Mugabe government termed the 'fast track land reform' (FTLR) programme. To some analysts, however, christening the process as a programme lent it a systematic and cohesive character which it did not have in reality (GAPWUZ/RAU 2008). Nevertheless, in our assessment we will use 'jambanja' and 'programme' interchangeably to denote and evaluate this process.

The FTLR programme was undertaken in several phases. The first phase ran between the onset of the 'land invasions' – also termed 'land occupations' – soon after the constitutional referendum in February 2000 and continued in the build-up to the parliamentary elections in June 2000. This was a phase in which there was neither an officially defined programme nor clear direction to the 'invasions'. The elements of orchestration, coercion and violence were strong in this first phase.

The post-election period beginning in July 2000 marked the second phase in which the government defined the parameters of the FTLR more clearly. The programme was to be implemented at an accelerated 'fast-track' pace and the programme targets were specified. The amount of land to be redistributed increased from the five million hectares specified in a land policy of 1998 to nine million hectares. This was later increased to 11 million hectares. The number of beneficiaries was increased from the 162,000 specified in previous land resettlement programmes to 300,000 under an A1 model (small-scale farms), and 51,000 under the A2 model (predominantly black-run commercial farms). This more expansive second phase lasted between July 2000 and September 2001, when the Abuja Agreement was brokered between the British and Zimbabwe governments under Commonwealth mediation. Under the Agreement, the government of Zimbabwe pledged to end farm invasions and violence, to restore the rule of law and undertake land reform in a gradual, fair and transparent manner (The Independent, 7 September 2001). For its part, the British government agreed to make substantial funds available to compensate displaced farmers and finance infrastructure in resettled areas (The Guardian, 7 September 2001).

The third phase of jambanja ran from the last quarter of 2001 to 2003, even though the Mugabe government officially announced that the FTLR had come to a close in August 2002. Since 2003, 'land invasions' have continued intermittently and seem to peak at election time, as in 2005 and 2008. Although these invasions are of a low-intensity nature, they mostly involve politicians, army officers and state bureaucrats seeking to increase their land holdings or acquire fresh and better-endowed land. To that extent, land invasions have continued into 2010, and could continue well after, even though the number of white commercial farmers has dwindled to less than 400.

As observed above, there is general agreement that the 'land invasions' were organised soon after the referendum result became known in February 2000. The immediate catalyst was the political setback of the 'No' vote to the Mugabe government. An unprecedented momentum for these invasions was initially unleashed by war veterans and later undertaken together with party youth and militia, peasants and certain agencies such as the army and the state intelligence agency. The role of war veterans was pivotal and legendary, as a state-leaning paper shows:

> it was clear that about 4,000 white farmers who clung to Zimbabwe's prime land had bankrolled the no vote campaign .... For the first time, white commercial farmers supped, dined and drank with their labourers in open air parties held to celebrate the victory of the 'no' vote .... In the quiet of the night of 16 February 2000, seven war veterans moved to occupy Yothum farm in Masvingo East commercial farming area. This effectively gave birth to the FTLR programme –the Third Chimurenga – which ushered a vibrant agrarian revolution for Zimbabwe. (Herald, 8 August 2000)

While there was some element of spontaneity in the first few weeks of *jambanja*, this soon changed as its orchestration by ZANU-PF and its government became more pronounced as months went by. As one analyst observed:

> in a carefully co-ordinated campaign starting on 26 February 2000, gangs armed with axes and pangas invaded white-owned farms across the country. Government and army trucks were used to transport them to the farms and to keep them supplied with rations once there. They were war veterans, but some of the participants were too young to have participated in the war 20 years earlier. Their immediate task was to peg out plots of land. But the wider purpose of their deployment was to crush support for the opposition in rural areas in the run-up to the 2000 election. (Meredith 2002:167)

So, by and large, the land invasions served a double purpose. The first was to seize the land and thus indiscriminately punish white farmers for their political stance, and the second was to close off the commercial farming areas to campaigning by opposition parties. The overall objective of the invasions during this phase was to prevent a repetition of the referendum defeat. This explained the emphasis on wartime methods of political mobilisation such as all-night meetings known as *pungwes* and considerable use of coercion and violence against farm workers and farmers. The first killings of farm workers and farmers occurred in the first week of March 2000. During this period, 400 farms were invaded. By June 2000, about 1,500 farms had been invaded, with the three Mashonaland provinces witnessing a relatively higher level of coercion and violence in the process.

The second phase between July 2000 and August 2001 witnessed a concerted implementation of what was termed 'an agrarian revolution' or 'Third Chimurenga'. How was the implementation carried out during this phase? A principal vehicle of implementation was termed 'Operation *Tsuro*' (Hare). It had three facets. The first was the dimension of 'command and control' which was undertaken by a co-ordinated group from the Police, Central Intelligence Organisation (CIO) and war veterans, and for brief period, the Ministry of Information and Publicity (Chitiyo 2003; Rutherford 2001). This group met for regular briefings to discuss the implementation and direction of *jambanja*. The second dimension was the 'operational zones' established to identify 'loyal' and 'opposition' zones and communities with the ultimate aim of converting rural areas into 'liberated' pro-ZANU-PF zones. While the 'loyal' zones were rewarded, the 'opposition' ones were punished. The third dimension related to 'ground troops' constituted by land-hungry peasants (armed with farming implements such as picks and axes) led by war veterans with the state acting as armourer (Ibid.). Operation *Tsuro* also deployed both a stick and a carrot, with land reform the carrot for peasants and other assorted beneficiaries.

This was the broad context in which a rift between the executive and the judiciary widened over the absence of the rule of law in the land reform process. For instance, there were strong verbal attacks on the judiciary by the Attorney General and the President. The Chief Justice, Anthony Gubbay, was forced to take an early retirement in the first half of 2001. A number of judges retired or left the country as judicial independence came under sustained attack. But there were differences amongst the judiciary itself over the FTLR programme. One of the leading judges argued that:

> it is no longer possible to give judgements on certain issues that are acceptable to both sides of the divide. In some instances, judgements of the judiciary [on land issues] that are highly praised by one side are gravely criticised by the other side of the divide. (Judge Chidyausiku, as quoted in the Herald,

9 January 2001)

There was a clear polarisation of opinion over how to handle 'land invasions', and this reflected the division of opinion in the wider society. President Mugabe exploited this polarisation to effect new appointments to the judiciary in a bid to ensure judgements more sympathetic to the government position on land. In December 2001, the restructured Supreme Court ruled that government acquisition of land and the rule of law prevailed in commercial farming areas (*Herald* 4 December 2001). This judgement gave legitimacy of the law to *jambanja*, a legitimacy which had eluded the executive since the process started in early 2000. By then, about 6,400 farms covering 9.2 million hectares had been seized.

During the third phase, from the third quarter of 2001 to 2003, the major development related to the uptake of the farms designated for the A2 model. Although this was a slower process it was more contentious. The speed of uptake depended on several factors. The first related to the availability of farmland and directly added to the urgency attached to the remaining white commercial farmers still resident on their properties in mid-2002. The second factor was a slower uptake of land due to the large investment necessary to restart production. Access to credit finance remained a major constraint for most A2 farmers. Far fewer than the envisaged number of black farmers (51,000) had settled on the farms by the cut-off date of August 2002. The then Minister of Lands, Agriculture and Rural Resettlement, Joseph Made, was obliged to warn that prospective farmers should confirm their willingness to undertake agricultural activities by 23 August 2002 or risk having their offer letters withdrawn (*Herald,* 6 August 2002).

Even so, there was a competitive scramble for land in prime agro-ecological regions by members of the ruling elite throughout 2002 and 2003. Due to the fact that this land was more fertile and served with good infrastructure, the competition for it was more intense. Amongst the prime farming areas that witnessed disputes stemming from the scramble were Merowe, Goromonzi, Chinhoyi, Shamva, Marondera and Beatrice. The scramble for A2 farmland was less intense in Manicaland and Matabeleland provinces, and there were few reports of it taking place in the Midlands and Masvingo provinces. Indeed, there was growing apprehension that a new, black, land-owning elite was emerging, a sentiment that found expression at the ZANU-PF national congress in December 2002.

The scale of the FTLR was huge by any standards. Approximately 11 million hectares were confiscated from white commercial farmers for redistribution. This constituted the largest property transfer in Zimbabwe and indeed Southern Africa in such a short space of time in recent history. However, it is noteworthy that the Mugabe government initially exaggerated the figures for FTLR beneficiaries. In 2001 and 2002, it claimed that 300,000 small farmers on A1 land and 54,000 black commercial farmers on A2 land been allocated land. In fact, the numbers were about 45 per cent and 15 per cent of these figures for A1 and A2 models respectively. By the end of 2003, some 127,000 small farmer households and 7,200 emergent black commercial farmers had been allocated land (Utete 2003). These have since grown to about 140,000 and 12,000 for A1 and A2 respectively.

The total amount of land allocated to small farmer households amounted to about 4.23 million hectares, and that to black commercial farmers was approximately 2,19 million. By July 2003, the amount of land used for large-scale white commercial farming had shrunk from 11.8 million ha to 2.6 million ha. This massive redistribution process did not, however, satisfy the continuing large demand for land. The Mugabe government itself acknowledged that 249,000 people remained on the A1 model waiting list while there were 99,000 under the A2 model list (*Financial Gazette*, 15 July 2004). If these figures are correct, then the demand for land under both models remained insatiable.

This explains the subsequent persistent land invasions and disputes between 2004 and 2010. They embraced land under the Bilateral Investment Protection and Promotion Agreements (BIPPAs) framework ostensibly protected by bilateral agreements between Zimbabwe and another country. For instance, between 2008 and 2010, some of the land belonging South African, German, French and Malaysian nationals, amongst others, and protected under BIPPAs was invaded, sparking a diplomatic furore. Persistent invasions of the remaining white farms resulted in some of them lodging their cases with the SADC Tribunal, which ruled in their favour in 2008. With about 225 farms occupied during 2008, the formation of a Government of National Unity in 2009 did not reduce momentum in land invasions (ZHR NGO Forum 2010). It was estimated that 152 of the remaining 300 white commercial farmers were targeted for eviction in 2010. Factors such as a propensity for greed and accumulation as well as genuine need have compelled these latter-day invasions. As it was observed:

by the end of 2009, many actors were responsible for property violation, from ordinary peasants to high-ranking politicians, the 'junta', government ministers and even ministers of religion. Some did it covertly while others chose to carry out violence secretly. All in all, this violence, which disrupted the once vibrant agricultural economy, had long-term effects materially and psychologically. (Ibid.:11)

In sum, the FTLR did not, as the Mugabe government expected, bring finality to Zimbabwe's land question. Land is a finite resource. Whether the government fully appreciated this reality is unclear. However, the persistence of the land question is also a consequence of the mode, cronyism and unfairness which characterised the FTLR. Several government-sponsored audits to address this cronyism and other shortfalls embedded in the FTLR failed in their purpose. In late 2010, another long-awaited land audit, as stipulated in the Global Political Agreement, had still not yet been undertaken. The perennial and sporadic invasions, disruption of farming activities, inexperience of new 'small' and 'large' farmers as well as limited investment into the farms combined to accelerate a significant decline in agricultural production during this lost decade. This is what we explore in the next section.

Decline in the Agrarian Sector

To what extent has the redistributed land been productively utilised for food and industrial crops? A distinctive trend in most agricultural production between 2000 and 2009 was, with one or two exceptions, a decline in output. For example, maize production declined from an average annual output of about 1.7 million tonnes in the mid-1990s to about one million tonnes between 2000 and 2004. During most of this decade, the country therefore needed to import to import maize to meet its full needs. Thus, from having been a regional breadbasket, Zimbabwe became a food importer during this lost decade. Similarly, wheat production declined from about 270,000 tonnes in 1998 to 62,000 in 2007 – thus falling well short of the national requirement of 350,000 tonnes. By June 2010, only about 13 per cent of the government stipulated hectarage had been planted; this would produce less than three per cent of national requirements (*Herald*, 1 June 2010). Declines in the production of soya beans and groundnuts were also recorded during this decade.

In industrial crops, there was a more mixed picture in production

Table 6.1 – The decline in agricultural production, 1998–2007

Crop	Commercial Production Tonnes (000)		Percentage of 1998 levels
	1998	2007	
Wheat	521	160	31
Soya beans	113	64	57
Tobacco	210	65	31
Coffee	10	1	10
Tea	18	15	83
Sugar	553	384	69

Source: UNDP (2008:156)

trends. From an average annual output of about 200 million kilograms (kg), tobacco production plummeted to 65 million kg in 2004. It declined further to below 60 million kg in 2008. However, it recovered to 110 million kg in 2010 although this was still about 50 per cent of average annual output some 10 years earlier. The production of sugar and tea generally remained steady, with only limited declines during the decade. This was precisely because the FTLR was not extended to the plantations on which they were grown. Their utilised land and infrastructure remained largely intact throughout the decade. Even so, it was estimated that tea and sugar production was pegged at 83 per cent and 69 per cent of their 1998 levels respectively (UNDP 2008). Finally, cotton production was little affected by the FTLR because most of it was produced by smallholder farmers.

Table 6.1 provides figures depicting the relative decline in agrarian production in selected commodities between 1998 and 2007. More generally, when Zimbabwe's agricultural performance is measured by per capita value added, it can be shown that:

> It has declined from its peak in 2001 to about half that level in 2006. This drop is explained not only by the impact of the FTLR on commercial production, but also by critical input constraints. (UNDP, 2008:156)

Exacerbating the input supply constraints were government-directed price cuts affected through 'Operation *Dikes Muting*' (Reduce Prices) of

2007. For instance, the actual cost of producing fertiliser was up to ten times the government-controlled price. At the same time, the capacity to produce fertiliser was crippled by frequent power outages at phosphorous mines (Ibid.). Persistent shortages of other inputs such as fuel, seed and equipment also contributed to the decline in production.

Additional factors that contributed to production decline related to the displacement of skills of white farmers and black farm workers and the underutilisation of acquired farmland. We explore the impact of displacement below. A considerable proportion of the 2.19 million ha for black commercial farmers was underutilised. The level of land use and intensity of production remained low, with significant portions of once highly productive commercial farms continuing to lie idle (FAO and WFP 2008). On the whole, the division of white commercial farms resulted in sub-economic units. This negatively affected production to the extent that the process did not take sufficient cognisance of the farms' layout and structure. The infrastructure of commercial farms had been based:

> on a homestead and centralised farm operations that included machinery, workshops, sheds and barns, as well as an irrigation system that was dependent upon a single water source and a system that branched out across the farm. The new subdivisions, however, cut across this infrastructure. As a result, many of the new farms do not have access to the former farm's resources and facilities, making them less efficient and viable. (Ibid.:158)

A combination of these factors contributed to the steep decline in agricultural production which in turn exacerbated the economic crisis that we explored in Chapter 5.

In assessing patterns of production decline, it is necessary to make some observations about productivity trends. Clearly, there is a huge difference between productivity levels on white commercial farms, black commercial farms and small resettlement farms. The productivity levels of the new, black commercial farmers are a fraction of those that had been achieved by evicted white farmers. On the whole, the land that was seized now produces much lower yields per cultivated hectare. As we observed above, the lack of skills, experience and finance have hampered the productivity of the new producers. It will take many years before the productivity levels achieved by white commercial farmers can be attained.

Finally, the decline in the agrarian sector had broad repercussions on the wider economy. There were numerous and complex downstream economic losses caused by this decline in Zimbabwe's backbone industry:

> Agriculture was the largest client for many Zimbabwean businesses, from pesticides, fertiliser and seed companies to legal and accountancy firms, from light engineering businesses and freight concerns to packaging and marketing houses. Many former agricultural towns are in a state of complete ruin as the business that sustained them has vanished. (GAPWUZ and JAG 2009:44)

The symbiotic relationship between agriculture and manufacturing ensured that the decline in the former was a major contributory factor to the economic crisis of this lost decade, as we observed above.

The Situation of White Farmers

There are very few parallels in recent history in which the economic fortunes of an established class have experienced such a sudden and inexorable reversal as did those of white farmers between 2000 and 2003. The Mugabe government was determined to break the backs of white commercial farmers from 2000, first as a political vendetta against the referendum defeat and pre-emption against future electoral reverse, and second as a strategy to pave way for the emergence of a black landed class. This twin strategy made the possibility of a compromise between the government and white farmers increasingly remote. This explains why conciliatory initiatives by the farmers were viewed by the Mugabe government as 'too little and too late'. Yet the initiatives were substantive. Consider the Zimbabwe Joint Resettlement Initiative (ZJRI) in 2001 which consisted of an offer of 561 farms covering one million hectares. The key aspects of ZJRI included not only one million ha of uncontested land for resettlement of small-scale commercial farmers, but also one hectare of free tillage for each of the families, a Z$60 million (about USD1.1 million) grant for agricultural inputs, and the establishment of a ZWD1.37 billion (about USD25 million) revolving fund. This was rejected.

The number of white farmers on land had diminished to less than 900, and to 400 by 2008, and to about 300 by 2010. What was their fate after dispossession? Significantly, the majority remained in Zimbabwe although they were no longer active in production. According to a survey conducted in 2009, the locations of the farmers were established as Zimbabwe (74.2 per cent), Australia and New Zealand (9.3 per cent), South Africa (six per cent), SADC (3.3 per cent) and the UK (2.9 per cent) (GAPWUZ and JAG 2009:14). It was observed that the fact that 74 per cent of the sample

Table 6.2 – Losses experienced by a sample of white farmers

Loss	Total in USD (million)	Average per Respondent in USD (thousand)
Moveable property	190	445
Crops	74	177
Property burnt	43	102
Earnings	677	1,621
Livestock	68	164
Medical expenses	3.3	808
Legal expenses	2,6	6,408
Total	1,066	2,530

Source: GAPWUZ and JAG (2009)

still resided in Zimbabwe suggested that the respondents had stronger ties to Zimbabwe than they did with any other country (Ibid.). The picture of Zimbabwean white farmers moving in large numbers to SADC countries and to Nigeria to conduct farming operations had therefore been 'an exaggeration' (Ibid.).

Interestingly, about eight per cent of the sample of 418 respondent farmers still lived on their farms, with 15 per cent continuing to conduct farming operations albeit on a reduced scale. However, the material and psychological losses suffered by the white farmers have been staggering, as Table 6.2 illustrates.

The gross estimate for total losses for the sample was about USD1.06 billion while estimated lost earnings from FTLR were at least USD4.4 billion or an average of USD1 million per farmer. As it was observed:

> as the last unrestricted farming year for many farmers was in 1999, this represents up to nine years of greatly reduced or non-existent operations. The loss to the economy has been massive. (Ibid.:53)

If the actual losses are broken down, a minimum of USD1.2 billion of moveable property was lost, property worth at least USD130 million burnt and livestock worth USD347 million lost (Ibid.). Finally, sampled farmers spent an average of USD1,000 on medical expenses as a result of trauma or physical violence.

Ironically, some of the beneficiaries of the expropriation of white farmers were the neighbouring African states of Mozambique, Malawi and Zambia, as well the West African state of Nigeria. Evidence suggests that the contribution of the white farmers to food production in these countries has been notable. The rise in maize exports from Zambia and tobacco exports from Malawi during this decade coincided with the arrival of white farmers. Meanwhile, the coping strategies and livelihoods of white farmers who remained in Zimbabwe have not yet been systematically explored. It would be particularly useful to document and assess their role in emerging tenant relations with the new black commercial farmers. For example, to what extent have tenant arrangements with former white farmers spread? In what ways have these arrangements made a difference in productivity and output in commodities such as horticulture and tobacco? This remains to be established.

The Situation of Farm Workers

The most adverse effects of *jambanja* or FTLR were experienced by farm workers. Most studies based on extensive fieldwork in the early years of FTLR have largely confirmed the displacement, disenfranchisement and disruption of livelihoods of farm workers (FCTZ 2001; UNDP 2002; Sachikonye 2003, 2004). Prior to FTLR, there were about 320,000 farm workers on white commercial farms, supporting a population of about two million. At the end of the reform period, an estimated 220,000 farm workers had lost their jobs as the numbers of white farmers dwindled to about 400. By 2007, an estimated 85,000 full-time workers were still in employment, mainly on agro-industrial plantations such as those producing sugar, tea and timber (Magaramombe and Chambati 2008). In addition, there were about 40,000 to 50,000 casual and part-time workers on various farms, including those of the remaining white farmers. The new, leaner labour force suggested that women workers were likely to have been the greatest losers since they had dominated the part-time labour force.

As we illustrate below, the impact of the loss of regular wage incomes has been predictably severe on former farm workers. Those workers who continue to stay on the farms have mostly lost their permanent worker status to become seasonal or itinerant workers who largely survive from doing piecework (Sachikonye 2003, 2004). The black commercial farmers have not provided employment opportunities on a significant scale. Clearly, poverty amongst farm workers was exacerbated and cases of their destitution increased. The majority of farm workers were rendered more vulnerable under *jambanja* because most of them did not receive land. Only about five to ten per cent of farm workers were able to achieve access to land to eke out new livelihoods.

Drawing on a survey that we undertook in late 2002, we recall that the consistent pattern was one of significant job losses as white farmers scaled back or closed down operations (Sachikonye 2003). A related survey of 235 farms established that over 40 per cent of farm workers had lost employment in Mashonaland East, 46 per cent in Mashonaland Central and 33 per cent in Mashonaland East (FCTZ 2002). Job losses amongst seasonal workers had been far higher, with about 50 per cent of them in the three Mashonaland provinces having been fired by the end of 2002. During the same period, farm employment levels had dropped by 70 per cent in the Midlands province. A few months later, 90 per cent of farm workers in Mashonaland West had lost their permanent status and mostly become casual workers on short stints (Ibid.). In the two Matabeleland provinces, data suggested that the farm workforce had been reduced by up to 65 per cent. About 80 per cent of workers interviewed in Mashonaland East had left permanent employment and large lay-offs were reported in Masvingo province. Thus the overall picture from field research was one of massive job losses much higher than the original estimate of 50 per cent. The net effect of the exodus of 90 per cent of white commercial farmers in the last quarter of 2002 was triggering further lay-offs.

Several factors explained the vulnerability and misfortunes of farm workers. First, about a quarter of the total farm workforce consisted of descendants of migrant workers from Malawi, Mozambique and Zambia. They were the target of xenophobic attitudes amongst some of the ruling elite. As one study observed:

> *farm workers have largely been shut out of the land redistribution process primarily because the government viewed them as politically suspect .... The* Citizenship Act of 2001 *barred 'migrant' farm workers from voting in the presidential election. The government suggested that up to a third of farm workers should be considered foreign despite that they have lived and worked in Zimbabwe for a generation. (ICG 2004:93, my emphasis)*

Table 6.3 – Coping strategies of farm workers after land reform

Coping strategy	Number	Percentage
Retraining	1	1
Informal deals	2	4
Cross border trading	4	5
Working in other countries	4	5
Becoming a beggar	5	7
Migrating to rural areas	7	9
Working for a new farmer	13	17
Migrating to town	17	23
Continue staying on the farm	21	28
Continue working for the old employer	22	29
Buying and selling	31	41

Source: GAPWUZ (2010:45)

A later survey conducted in 2010 concurred with these observations when it observed that their historical links to neighbouring countries had been one of the causes of farm workers being treated as second-class citizens and used as justification for their systematic disenfranchisement, exclusion and physical and psychological assault (GAPWUZ 2010). This explained the political retribution against them in the form of intimidation and violence during the 2000 and 2002 elections.

Let us explore some of the specific social effects of the FTLR on farm workers. The first relates to demographic changes. In a survey in 2010, farm workers reported living with an average of 2.8 family members compared to 4.3 members prior to FTLR (Ibid.). Of the 2.8, an average of 0.1 per cent were currently working on the farm compared to average of 1.4 family members prior to FTLR. The proportion of children attending school on farms had dropped from 40 per cent to 19 per cent, according to the survey. This new demographic picture demonstrated 'the dispersion and destruction of farm worker communities' (Ibid.:64).

As Table 6.3 shows, there was considerable displacement, migration and diversification of and by farm workers during this lost decade as a consequence of FTLR. As it was explained:

> with the greatest proportion of workers coping after eviction by 'buying and selling', we see how the informal economy began to thrive. It is very interesting too that few workers migrated to rural areas, with only nine per cent saying that they had chosen this strategy .... It is also interesting that 17 per cent stated that they worked for the new farmer. GAPWUZ statistics have demonstrated the enormous differences in wages earned by workers under the old employers and the wages paid by the new farmers. Finally, it is significant that 23 per cent of the workers stated that they had moved to town after their eviction. (Ibid.:46)

In addition, it should be emphasised that farm workers also suffered considerable losses during the FTLR, as Box 6 illustrates. Significantly, they are still seeking restitution of those losses.

Those farm workers who have continued to live on farms find themselves co-existing in an unequal relationship with resettled farmers. They provide labour to the new class of landowners, particularly black commercial farmers on A2 land. In the course of one survey, it was observed that the 'new farmer looks down on ex-farm workers. These workers are not, in any way, getting paid better than before' (Sachikonye 2003:75). On some of the farms, the compounds that originally housed farm workers were appropriated by the new landowners and the workers expelled. On others, the new farmers torched the houses of the workers to evict them en masse. This is corroborated in a later study that observed that 'eviction threats from these compounds by new farmers are persistent for those who are unemployed' (Magaramombe and Chambati 2008:224). Even where farm workers were not evicted, the number of jobs declined significantly because of a downscaling of operations. This resulted in them losing their compound houses if they went searching for employment from farm to farm. The picture of the farm worker class that has emerged is that of an 'itinerant', 'poor' and 'unstable' class.

Finally, further research on living conditions of the workers underlined several trends (Mbetu and Musekiwa, 2004). First, their insecurity was compounded by a lack of government policy on the situation of former workers who continued to live on farms where they had been employed. Apart from the threat of eviction, the farm workers were denied access to essential services such as water and electricity if they failed to comply

Box 6.1 – Damages suffered by farm workers due to *jambanja*

Living conditions today, quite apart from the fact that most farm workers are now unemployed, are much worse than before. Let us consider a few of the major changes. The loss of livestock is reported by 83 per cent of respondents, and crops by 78 per cent. Taking into account the high loss of other incomes (82 per cent) and the loss of subsidised rations (68 per cent), it is scarcely surprising that the farm workers, like the rest of the country, are now unable to feed themselves adequately. Medical care has dropped by 74 per cent, piped water by 61 per cent, access to clinic by 52 per cent and toilets by 42 per cent. Such conditions are very likely to have contributed to the severe cholera outbreak in 2008–2009.

Perhaps most significant, however, is the loss of a home (61 per cent) and wages (66 per cent). These losses are common to both farmers and farm workers, and are deeply felt by respondents. The destruction of one's livelihood and one's home is devastating, both physically and psychologically, and when done with intent, provide ample evidence of the state's callous disregard for the lot of many of its citizens.

Source: GAPWUZ (2010:47-8)

with the dictates of the new landowners. In some instances, verbal, physical and sexual abuse of workers was reported. Second, for those farm workers who were provided with employment, the jobs were offered mostly on a contract, casual or piecework (*maricho*) basis. Moreover, underpayment was widespread, with some workers going for several months without pay. In general, the new A2 farmers tended to pay lower wages and have poor employment contracts (Magaramombe and Chambati 2008). In such instances, it was scarcely surprising that the new landowners experienced a labour shortage. Third, as observed above, relations between farm workers and new farmers were characterised by mutual distrust. This contrasted with the situation on the remaining white farms where employment conditions such as wages and labour relations were better. Fourth, those who were employed by new farm-owners and those that had lost their jobs were all in a vulnerable situation that forced them to supplement their incomes through fishing, panning for gold, petty trading, theft and prostitution. Other types of relationship besides those between new farmers and farm workers may yet evolve. For example, besides providing labour, some farm workers may become new tenants or sharecroppers, especially on under-utilised land. Some resettled farmers might find it necessary to supplement their crop incomes by sub-contracting their labourers to more productive farms that are short of workers.

The Rise of the Black Landed Elite

The impetus behind the FTLR was not simply to satisfy land hunger amongst the poor and landless and those on congested communal land but also that of urban-based workers, the middle-class and the ruling elite. Those with aspirations for accumulation and diversification of wealth opportunities include about 500 black land-owners who had acquired land in the 1990s. The 'land rush' for wildlife conservancies between 2000 and 2003 also included the middle class and the ruling elite to whom land-ownership increased their portfolio of interests. These classes were able to muster their political power to have access to prime land with the best infrastructure, as we observed above. The FTLR offered a perfect opportunity for these classes to amass white farmers' thriving landholdings without prior investment in the form of purchase price or mortgage loans.

Most members of this class acquired land under the A2 model. Some 7,200 had done so by July 2003 when they had acquired a total of 2.19 million ha (Utete 2003). By 2007, the number of beneficiaries under this model had jumped to about 12,000, with an average holding of 200 ha each (Moyo 2007). It was acknowledged that the beneficiaries were 'relatively well-off and socially connected ... on the bulk of high-quality land (including irrigable land) and close to markets' (Ibid.:8). There was extensive evidence that the ruling elite used its political muscle to allocate to itself some of the best land (*Daily News* 6 September 2002). Newspapers were awash with stories of a frantic scramble for such land by cabinet ministers, governors, senior army, intelligence and police officers, top civil servants, war veterans and others connected to this elite. Thus, privileged members of the elite, through patronage and clientelism, have become beneficiaries of a process which should have been largely aimed at poverty reduction through the decongestion of communal areas. As white farmers relocated to towns or neighbouring countries, the elite and the urban-based middle class thus got their cut from the FTLR programme. This material imperative behind land reform might have been initially under-estimated because the political factor had loomed larger in the context of the 2000 and 2002 electoral contests. The imperative has since become quite significant in economic and political terms. As the sharing of spoils allows for 'instant accumulation' with state collusion, the beneficiaries were thenceforth more likely to be beholden to a ZANU-PF party and government than to parties that advocated transparency in the land reform process. However, it remained doubtful in 2011 whether this increased number of part-time and 'cellphone' elite and middle-class farmers would make their farms sufficiently productive to maintain the sector's contribution to GDP growth, foreign exchange earnings and food security.

It is precisely due to the under-performance by this landed elite that there has been recourse by some to tenancy arrangements, ironically with former white farmers. It is difficult to estimate with confidence the spread of such arrangements. The case for the arrangements was posited in these terms:

> farmers who wish to farm only a small section of their holdings (for example, those in flower production) should be allowed to let or cede the rest of their holdings to other farmers .... The adjustment of land allocations to new farmers and encouragement of the use of underutilised land through subletting may well be a critical mechanism for the production of a variety of crops among the few elite, given that agricultural financing is still low. (Moyo 2007:20)

Government policy on tenancy production arrangements remains unclear. In some instances, the arrangements have been sharply attacked, especially by President Mugabe himself, but in others the arrangements continue. In a fundamental sense, however, tenancy arrangements confirm the present incapacity of the landed elite to utilise their farms to maximum capacity.

Avarice and speculation have also been major characteristics of the black landed elite. Asset-stripping of farm equipment and crops standing in the fields, without compensation to white farm-owners, has been a distinctive feature of the elite. Unsurprisingly, this one-off accumulation has not provided a sustainable basis for viable farming. This was amply demonstrated in the asset-stripping at the Kondozi agro-industrial estate in eastern Zimbabwe in 2004. The plantation employed about 5,000 workers and had export markets for vegetables and flowers worth about USD15 million per annum. After its seizure by the state and stripping by politicians and bureaucrats, the export markets were lost and workers laid off as the plantation sank into dereliction (UNDP 2008).

Speculation in land has taken the form of ownership of multiple farms in prime agro-ecological regions. Politicians and other members of the elite have been blamed for this activity. As an exercise in damage limitation, several government-sponsored audits were commissioned beginning in 2002, but to no avail. Multiple farm ownership persisted as a problem, necessitating the Global Political Agreement (GPA) to prescribe a land audit as one of the urgent tasks of the Inclusive Government in 2008. By late 2011, the audit had still to be carried out. Clearly, some of the landed elite have an interest in an opaque land reform process, including multiple farm ownership.

7

State & Civil Society: A Changing Balance

Introduction

How have the political and economic developments assessed in the last six chapters shaped the growth of society and its relations with the state? Undoubtedly, the three decades of erratic growth, stagnation and crisis have left profound imprints on Zimbabwean society. These lost decades have affected the social contract between the post-colonial state and society and shaped the growth and orientation of civil society as well as the processes of democratisation and development. Chapters 7 and 8 explore the impact of these changes on society. While this chapter examines the impact on relations between state and civil society organisations (CSOs), the next chapter assesses wider and deeper changes that relate to new patterns of livelihoods and pressures for migration leading to the growth of a significant Zimbabwean diaspora over the last ten years. The migration of an estimated three million people (about a quarter of the country's population) is the most eloquent testimony of the deep and wide repercussions of the Mugabe government's economic and political measures during the lost decades.

Defining 'Civil Society' and the 'Social Contract'

A useful approach to the analysis of relations between the state and society is to focus on its interactions with organised sections of society in the form of CSOs, and the content of the social contract between them. However, let us begin by defining the concepts of 'civil society' and 'social contract'. Civil society relates to a non-state sphere comprising a plurality of public spheres that range from productive units and community-based organisations to professional and voluntary associations that are self-organising. It is an aggregate of non-state institutions that engage in economic and cultural production and voluntary activities, among others (Keane 1988). The relative autonomy of CSOs from the state is a feature of civil society, although this is a hotly debated issue. Despite its flaunted influence and potential role, civil society has limited capacity to protect rights, institute affirmative action or to control capital. Furthermore, it is unrealistic to view civil society as a collective opposition or alternative mechanism of government or a substitute for political parties or the state.

A more sophisticated rendering of the state–civil society relationship stresses its symbiotic aspects. It argues against a dichotomised view of state–society relations because such a view obstructs an understanding of how the two forces mutually constitute each other (Beckman 2001). It is necessary to look outside the state–civil society dichotomy to locate the constituting features of the way interests, movements and groups organise themselves:

> they cannot be seen as constituted primarily in relation to the state but within arenas of conflicting interests in society. Even if we, by virtue of our problematic, as when we concern ourselves with the social basis of democratisation, have good cause to focus on state–civil society relations, we must be able to address these relations in the context of such primary, constitutive conflicts. (Ibid.:56)

This argument will become clearer and relevant when we show how the balance in state–society relations swung from one position to another during the lost decades.

It is the contention of this chapter that relations between state and society in Zimbabwe were based on a social contract. This was an unwritten understanding and agreement on the respective roles, obligations and responsibilities of each of the two parties. The post-colonial state was expected to deliver basic social services, decent economic growth, allow for the exercise of democratic rights as well as provide security. The constituent elements of society were expected to provide political support to the party (or parties) in government, and contribute taxes and development levies. If both sides respected and met their obligations and responsibilities, the social contract thrived. As a more expansive definition of social contract puts it:

> social contracts in Africa have to be seen as the product of historical compromises forged out of relations of opposition .... A coercive social contract is one in which the right to govern is predicated on the capacity of the rulers to make intolerable the lives of their subjects. In extreme cases, the contract may look like a statist version of a protection racket in which people surrender their political voice in return for being spared from predatory acts .... A productive social contract is one in which the sovereign authority and the subjects/citi-

zens enter into some form of negotiation over how the rule by the former can contribute to the well-being of the latter. (Nugent 2010:43)

Finally, a permissive social contract represents a kind of halfway house. While the governing authority claims its sovereign rights, it chooses not to exercise them in return for a measure of de facto compliance (Ibid.:44.). During the first decade, Zimbabwe had a tenuous version of a productive social contract.

Civil Society, State and Social Contract

The composition of Zimbabwe's civil society has been extensively documented (Moyo, Makumbe and Raftopoulos 2000; Dorman 2001). The composition displays a great deal of diversity in terms of activities, sectoral spread and scale of operations, political and ideological outlook and the tone of relations with the state. It would be mistaken to view Zimbabwean civil society as homogeneous in composition and outlook. Its diversity is a source of both strength and weakness. In spite of operating within the same legislative framework, different CSOs have different missions and strategies as well as a variety of relations with the state. While some CSOs have reasonably good working relationships with state institutions, others have difficult, even mutually hostile relations.

CSOs can be broadly divided into several categories: *developmental, welfarist, humanitarian* and *governance-related*. Their core constituencies and goals have a direct bearing on design of strategies, tactics and programmes, in short, in how CSOs craft their relationship with the state. However, it would be naïve to expect a coherent approach to the policy and development processes (from design to implementation and evaluation) by CSOs because they are not a cohesive constituency. Nor are state institutions themselves coherent in their formulation of policies and programmes. In sum, the diversity among CSOs and incoherence between state institutions make the task of assessing their relations problematic.

One of the studies on CSOs in Zimbabwe argued that state–society relations should be understood and assessed not only in terms of the state's use of coercion and power but also its construction of consent (Dorman 2001). Furthermore, the study observed of CSOs that:

- *They operated within the framework of the hegemony of the state which depended on a context of 'legitimacy' created by a liberation war entrenched by post-war reconstruction;*

- *They operated under material and organisational constraints, as they are as much centres of employment as activism, which encourages them to develop working relations with the state but constrains them from contentious challenges to its authority; and*
- *Resulting from the foregoing, they exercise strategic pragmatism framing the challenges that they make to the political order in a depoliticising discourse in order to make themselves acceptable to their peers and the state. (Ibid.:137)*

This assessment of CSOs drew from research conducted in the mid-1990s, before the contest between them and the state became sharper, and before the counter-hegemonic thrust of some of the CSOs became clearer. In the post-2000 period, some of this analysis was superseded by events and processes.

7.3.1 The 1980s: an era of state–CSO partnership

Let us spell out the distinctive phases through which state–civil society relations have evolved since independence, bearing in mind the features of accommodation and conflict between the two sides. In the 1980s, the number of CSOs was smaller and more concentrated on development and welfare activities. They sought a low-profile, complementary approach 'to the interventions of the state …. They mobilised women in such areas as rehabilitation, relief and social services, developed close links with donors and sought a close working relationship with ZANU-PF. By the mid-1980s, as the government set out its first five-year plan, the focus of CSOs moved to income-generating projects' (Raftopoulos 2000:4).

A variety of CSOs provided agricultural and vocational training to address a deficit of skills particularly in rural areas. For these and other development-related projects, CSOs mainly drew upon donor assistance. Among the most active CSOs during this period were the Association of Women's Clubs (AWCs), the Organisation of Rural Associations of Progress (ORAP) and the Organisation of Collective Cooperatives in Zimbabwe (OCCZIM). Except for one or two organisations, no major CSOs existed in the governance and human rights sector in the 1980s. This partly explained why there was little domestic outcry and research despite massive human rights violations in Matabeleland between 1982 and 1987.

Even relations between the state and the labour movement were cordial during most of the 1980s. Pervasive state intervention in the regulation of labour relations during this decade was variously interpreted as 'progressive' and 'benignly paternalist'. Early government emphasis on the reconstitution of splinter unions into large industrial unions and on the restructuring of the national labour movement into the Zimbabwe Congress of Trade Unions (ZCTU) demonstrated the direct stake of the state in the domestication of the labour movement (Sachikonye 1995). The mediatory role of the state in capital–labour conflicts conveyed the impression that the state was an ally of the working-class. Further, its exhortations to labour unions to restructure and centralise their operations suggested that the state was 'pro-working class'. Throughout most of the 1980s, the working relationship between organised labour and the state was thus reasonably good, with the former as a junior partner. However, this partnership would not be permanent.

7.3.4 State and CSOs in the 1990s: from partnership to protest

The situation for CSOs changed significantly in the decade of the 1990s. This was an era of economic adjustment and a post-Cold War dispensation which created a momentum for advocacy on a variety of issues. As it was observed:

> the economic marginalisation of the majority of Zimbabweans under structural adjustment created an environment for advocacy on poverty issues. The labour movement, student groups, human rights and women's organisations began to organise effectively around issues of poverty, human rights and democratisation. This transition was characteristic of many [CSOs] which began as providers of welfare services for the poor and then evolved into organisations that questioned the basis of poverty in society. (ZHDR 2000:160)

In the area of public policy debate on poverty, the establishment of a Poverty Reduction Forum (PRF) in 1996 provided a valuable structure under which state officials, CSOs, donors and academics engaged in dialogue on poverty reduction strategies.

Quite active also in the 1990s were CSOs that organised around housing, health and employment conditions. For instance, there was a re-emergence of residence associations as a response to poor performance by local authorities regarding housing, infrastructure and services. There was also a proliferation of community-level organisations mobilising around specific local issues.

This steady growth of CSOs and extended range of their activities occurred in a context in which opposition parties were weak and disorganised. It was also a context in which economic liberalisation was the mantra, with international financial institutions playing a key role in the financing of adjustment programmes on certain conditions. That the state had ceded part of the control over national economic and social policies to such institutions later provoked a backlash from social groups affected by those policies.

Things came to a head from the mid 1990s to 2000, a phase during which there developed a confluence of grievances relating to economic and political issues. This was symbolised by the revolt of war veterans (under the Zimbabwe National Liberation War Veterans Association (ZNLWVA)) in 1997 which caused a government panic; by peasant restiveness over slow land reform; and by the founding of a constitutional reform movement (under the NCA). The growing maturity of CSOs was underscored by their capacity under ZCTU leadership to mobilise around economic issues through a series of general strikes in 1997, 1998 and 1999 respectively, and by the capacity of the NCA to prod the government into a Constitution-making exercise. The issues of living wages, democracy and good governance, human rights and gay and lesbian rights, amongst others, were on the table.

In particular, the years 1998–2000 were a definitive watershed in state–CSO relations. The CSOs briefly occupied space and roles that were normally dominated by political parties as there were no sufficiently strong and credible opposition parties. For a brief interlude, there was a momentous stalemate as each side manoeuvred for strategic advantage.

The constitutional reform issue was the catalyst and conjuncture for this contestation. The referendum result in February 2000 was interpreted as a victory for CSOs involved in governance and human rights campaigns in particular and for anti-government forces in general. It was the first major political setback for the long-ruling ZANU-PF since 1980. In the aftermath of these developments, not only did the constitutional reform process stall for nearly a decade, but there was also a clearly decisive shift towards authoritarianism.

The Decade of Repression, 2000–2008

This shift to a 'police state' included the use of political violence and electoral intimidation as tools for self-preservation by ZANU-PF, which resorted to 'land invasions' as a method of land reform and to 'factory invasions' as a strategy to bolster the status of a government-sponsored labour federation, the Zimbabwe Federation of Trade Unions (ZFTU).

Accompanying this was a pronounced shift in government attitude towards CSOs in general. CSOs were henceforth viewed as part of a wider anti-government bloc, and as actors in an alliance misleadingly claimed to be bent on 'regime change'. It was this hostile perception on the part of government that would influence its attitude towards CSOs for the remainder of the decade.

Civil Society: growth, orientation and challenges

At independence, civil society was relatively weak and inexperienced. There is a relationship between the level of economic and social development and the density of civil society. As the economy expanded and social services created growth in education and health infrastructure and number of professionals, there was an explosion in growth of CSOs in the 1990s. A critical mass of CSOs had emerged by 2000. Indeed, there were an estimated 850 CSOs in Zimbabwe in 2000 (ZHDR 2000). Of these, about two-thirds of consisted of community-based NGOs representing locally based self-help groups specialising in a particular activity. Some 18 per cent of them consisted of intermediary NGOs that assist in the operations of smaller groups and mediate between such groups, state and donor agencies. They worked in areas such as relief services, sanitation and water provision and providing back-up support for co-operatives in various sectors. The third category of CSOs is that of service NGOs, which represented nine per cent. They provided support for project formulation and implementation, consultancy and research in training and information. Constituting five per cent of the total, the fourth category was made up of trusts and unions. Belonging to this group were interest groups such as farmers, business, trade unions, women and youth organisations. Finally, making up about four per cent of the total, were regional and international NGOs spanning various sectors.

Growth and strength amongst CSOs in Zimbabwe has been uneven. Some have grown faster than others; for instance, professional associations such as those of teachers and health workers have shown steady growth. Student and faith-based organisations have demonstrated some resilience. Labour unions grew rapidly when economic conditions were propitious for employment growth. But others grew slowly or declined in those sectors that experienced crisis, especially after 2000. In one study on civic CSOs, it was observed that their major strengths were their resources of energy and the enthusiasm with which they undertook the struggle against the authoritarian state (Zimbabwe Institute 2008). For instance, against heavy odds, the CSOs were proactive in setting the agenda for constitutional reform in 1998. This galvanised government to launch a constitutional reform process, one that ultimately proved to be flawed. Energy, optimism and solidarity were the hallmarks of the leadership and secretariats of the early NCA, CZC, ZCTU and ZESN, for example. The credibility and strength of their cause put the state on the defensive, especially between 1998 and 2000. The elements of initiative and surprise were on the side of CSOs before the state went on the offensive and began to dictate the agenda from 2000.

Another strength of the CSOs related to their close working relationships and solidarity. This was mostly sustained through coalitions, particularly in operational areas such as electoral work, human rights and constitutional issues. The adage that there is strength in numbers was adopted in the strategies of civic coalitions. This was aimed at making them less vulnerable to state coercion than if they operated individually. Undertaking lobbying and advocacy on particular issues as coalitions strengthened their critiques and messages.

However, CSOs also experienced certain weaknesses and challenges. In situations in which struggles last for a limited period, the assets of energy and surprise can make a large impact. However, in situations of prolonged struggle, these can dissipate to be replaced by fatigue, burnout, reactiveness and diminution of resources. The decade-long contest from 2000 was one of attrition and sapped the energies of most CSOs. They were vulnerable to economic and social decline, and more acutely to harassment, detention and torture. In addition, a major weakness of CSOs has been the apparent absence of a medium- and long-term strategy against the authoritarian state. Such a strategy would require a great deal of planning, the weighing up of the pros and cons of tactics and methods to be employed. It would also presuppose that CSOs had assured access to resources to enable them to engage in medium- and long-term strategic planning. This has not been the case. Most have operated on a hand-to-mouth basis, which compelled them to pursue short-term projects and programmes. Hence their propensity towards 'spontaneous' militant activism in short, isolated outbursts. While this generates publicity for the concerned civic group and the specific issue (for example, women's rights), the momentum generated created quickly dissipates.

Finally, a prominent feature of CSOs is their dependence on donor assistance. This takes the form of funding of programmes and secretariats as well as staff salaries. Very few CSOs can claim to be locally or self-funded. Most are aware of and candid about the fact that that support from a donor promoted that country's values and foreign policy interests, and that the donor was often the stronger partner in setting the agenda of projects and programmes. The partnership was not one of equals, it was more 'a power relationship', with their control of resources enabling donors to play a more dominant role in 'agenda setting'. However, like fashion, the areas of donor interest vary and shift from time to time from gender to HIV/AIDS, human rights to climate change, good governance to children's rights. While CSOs discover that they have to tailor their programmes to areas defined as priorities by donors, in struggles for democracy and human rights, their objectives and values happen to coincide.

Civil Society, Democratisation and Development

Let us specifically focus on the experiences of CSOs in the processes of democratisation and development. CSOs have been pivotal in both, especially from the 1990s. It was primarily the civics, particularly human rights and governance CSOs, that were at the forefront of challenging the authoritarian, dominant, one-party system centred on ZANU-PF and pushing for a democratic transition. In the 1990s, the regional and global environment was propitious for political liberalisation and transition. South Africa was building a post-apartheid order and most states in the region were making the transition to a multi-party system. CSOs in Zimbabwe focused on constitutional reform, the protection of basic freedoms of expression and assembly and wider participation in policy-making and governance. The key CSOs involved in campaigns for democratisation include the National Constitutional Assembly (NCA), Zimbabwe Lawyers for Human Rights (ZLHR), Zimbabwe Human Rights Association, Transparency International Zimbabwe (TI-Zimbabwe), and the Media Institute of Southern Africa (MISA-Zimbabwe). In addition, a number of coalitions of CSOs focused on specific areas: for instance, the Zimbabwe Electoral Support Network (ZESN) on electoral matters, the Crisis Zimbabwe Coalition (CZC) on governance matters and the Zimbabwe Human Rights NGO Forum (ZHR NGO Forum) on human rights matters.

Formed in 1998, the NCA defined its mission as fighting for a people-driven Constitution. However, it also lobbies and advocates for broad democratic reform. Although repressed repeatedly by the state, the NCA organised demonstrations regularly to drum up support for a new Constitution. It campaigned against the 2000 draft Constitution and protested that the inter-party constitutional review exercise of 2009–2010 was not people-driven. For its part, the CZC was founded in 2001 as a coalition to address the country's 'multi-faceted crisis' while amplifying the collective voice of CSOs on governance issues. Formed in 2000 as a network of CSOs committed to transparent, free and fair electoral processes, ZESN's major programmatic activities have included election monitoring, voter education, and research and advocacy on electoral matters. Finally, the ZHR NGO Forum brings together human rights NGOs that pursue the objectives of deepening human rights provisions in the Zimbabwean Constitution, and pushing for the implementation and protection of international human rights norms as contained in the relevant international conventions.

However, the environment in which these CSOs have had to operate has been a difficult and hostile one. Two particular pieces of legislation, namely, the Public Order and Security Act (POSA) and the Access to Information and the Protection of Privacy Act (AIPPA), have provisions that have curtailed basic freedoms of assembly and expression. When POSA was promulgated in 2002, it was argued that it was a piece of draconian legislation intended to curtail the activities of CSOs and opposition parties. For its part, the Mugabe government publicly registered its discomfort with CSOs working in areas of democracy, governance and human rights, accusing them of being conduits of hostile international forces bent on 'regime change'.

CSOs lobby for democracy and human rights in various ways, despite the plethora of challenges that they face in an authoritarian environment. One of the strategies that they use in lobbying state institutions is through face-to-face meetings with officials where matters of concern are raised. Letters are also another medium of communication with relevant ministries. However, in general, the response of state institutions has been cool to frosty on governance and human rights issues, especially since 2000. Due to paranoia, most state institutions have been very suspicious towards CSOs involved in governance and human rights issues.

Another strategy used by CSOs has been to lobby regional and international human rights bodies such as Amnesty International, the

International Bar Association and the African Commission on Human and Peoples' Rights (ACHPR) on human rights violations within Zimbabwe. One such example relates to the work of the ZLHR, which has pushed for the implementation of international human rights norms as contained in international conventions; in pursuit of this, it has lobbied the African Union to censure the government of Zimbabwe for human rights violations through the ACHPR. The ACHPR undertook a fact-finding mission to Zimbabwe in June 2002 as a direct result of lobbying by CSOs. This resulted in the ACHPR releasing a report in 2005 which found government guilty of torture and other abuses. As it was observed:

> this was the first time that a reputable African body had officially reprimanded the Zimbabwe government. This has succeeded in keeping Zimbabwe in the spotlight, and the government under political pressure. (Alexander 2005:36)

Similarly, information and documentation about mass demolitions in Operation *Murambatsvina*/Restore Order provided by CSOs, both in interviews and written reports, contributed to a damning report by the United Nations in 2005.

CSOs have also been involved in development-related work. Many community-based organisations (CBOs) are involved in various types of local development projects in rural and urban areas. There is little published work on a systematic basis on these various local initiatives. This is a major lacuna in our knowledge of CBOs in local developmental work, which ranges from health and sanitation provision, school and dam construction to microfinance and women's income-generating projects. In general, however, the crisis in 2000 to 2008 undermined most of these developmental initiatives, particularly due to hyperinflation and endemic shortages of equipment, funding and labour. CSOs nevertheless continued to be prominent in the provision of humanitarian assistance. They provided food aid, crop inputs, medical assistance and home care schemes for those with HIV/AIDS. Foreign governments and international aid agencies preferred to use CSOs as conduits for developmental and humanitarian assistance because of their credibility, professionalism and non-partisan approach. This developmental and humanitarian role, especially in food assistance provision, was viewed with suspicion by the state. It is not difficult to understand this suspicion, given that the state itself was often accused of partisan tendencies in food distribution.

Links between CSOs and Parties

Conditions of authoritarianism make it difficult for CSOs to remain independent of political parties and political processes. Hence it makes a great deal of difference whether a particular CSO is engaged in development and gender-related work or in governance and human rights work. (The former are sometimes termed 'soft areas' and the latter 'hard areas'.) In the 1990s, it was not uncommon for some CSOs to co-operate with ZANU-PF in local development, social services and food aid matters. Furthermore, in 2006 and 2007, women's organisations worked closely with both the ZANU-PF Women's League and the MDC-T women's wing to draw support for the passage of the Domestic Violence Bill in Parliament. Women's rights organisations appear to have been innovative in lobbying both ZANU-PF and the two MDC parties on specific issues of concern to them. Similarly, the organisation called Women in Politics Unit provided a facilitation service to women parliamentarians and officials of all parties. In 2008, a CSO known as the Women's Trust took an initiative to provide campaigning skills to aspiring candidates from both ZANU-PF and the two MDC parties.

On the whole, however, there has been little engagement and co-operation between CSOs and ZANU-PF and state institutions. CSOs have historically been more closely aligned with opposition movements. Indeed, organisations such as the ZCTU, the NCA and the Combined Harare Residents Association (CHRA), among others, were active in the process that culminated in the founding of the MDC in 1999. There was a close organic link underlying the working relationship between CSOs and the MDC. Although there was no formal alliance between these CSOs and MDC, their co-operation contributed to the defeat of the referendum in 2000 and boosted the latter's electoral performance in 2000 and 2002. Indeed, the composition of the MDC parliamentary teams in 2000 and 2005 reflected the considerable presence of activists and leaders of CSOs such as the NCA and ZCTU.

It was thus possible to speak of *a special relationship* between CSOs and the MDC between 1999 and 2005. It was one ostensibly built on shared values and a common revulsion against authoritarianism. There was also a shared aspiration for a democratic transition from Mugabe's authoritarian rule. However, most CSOs involved in this relationship with MDC tended to be uncritical of its internal democracy and leadership. As one CSO observed, with the benefit of hindsight, following the MDC split in 2005:

> CSOs should not have gone to bed with parties. The relationship should have been at arms' length. We should be able to separate our role from that of parties. We romanticised the MDC. We were not critical towards it. CSOs subcontracted the struggle to MDC. Apathy and disillusionment have ensued. (Zimbabwe Institute, 2008:36)

There were two main catalysts for the change in this special relationship. First, the split in the MDC in 2005 caused a rift in some CSOs, while others took a distancing neutral position towards the two factions, namely, MDC-Tsvangirai (MDC-T) and MDC-Mutambara (MDC-M). The fact that the causes of the split related mainly to shortfalls in internal party democracy upset CSOs engaged in good governance, transparency and human rights issues. More broadly, the split was interpreted in some quarters as revealing power ambitions on the part of the MDC leadership and authoritarian tendencies reminiscent of those in ZANU-PF. There was little doubt that the 2005 debacle in MDC removed any lingering doubts that some CSOs might have had about the special relationship.

The second, larger catalyst in the CSOs' change of attitude towards relations with parties was the SADC-facilitated Inter-party dialogue begun in 2007. As early as September 2007, CSOs were agitating against the dialogue process and in 2008 against Constitutional Amendment No. 18. CSOs were particularly critical of the seeming bilateral deal between MDC-T, MDC-M and ZANU-PF to introduce constitutional amendments instead of pursuing a people-driven Constitution-making process.

State Strategies against CSOs

President Mugabe fired a salvo against CSOs in 2001. His warning reflected deteriorating relations; he charged that:

> the moment they seek governmental power and office ... we begin to view them differently as political opponents. And political opponents are dealt with politically. They should not cry, for they have re-defined the rules of engagement .... Money continues to pour in variously: through individuals, through Trojan horses, among them NGOs, trade unions, select private media ... all to be used against us. (Mugabe 2001)

These were clearly exaggerated claims on the part of government and reflective of a growing paranoia and 'siege mentality'. There were no CSOs seeking governmental power. The CSO community was not homogeneous by any means, but there was no mistaking the deep suspicion and rancour on the part of government towards them. The hostility towards NGOs was also reflected in bitter attacks on them by government ministers such as Jonathan Moyo during the period 2000 to 2005.

The most serious potential threat to the survival of CSOs during the lost decades was a piece of draft legislation presented to Parliament in 2004. The proposed bill on NGOs was the culmination of warnings issued by government leaders to NGOs from 2000 onwards. The orchestration of the legislation fitted into a pattern of earlier authoritarian laws, namely, the aforementioned POSA and AIPPA. Had the bill had been given assent by the President, this trinity of legislation would have confirmed beyond any reasonable doubt the 'police state' character of the Zimbabwean state.

What, then, were the main provisions of the NGO bill? First, it sought to monitor and regulate all NGOs, including the funding of local CSOs. One of its prohibitive stipulations was that no local CSO should receive any foreign funding or donation to carry out activities related to governance issues (Draft NGO Bill 2004). Second, an NGO Council would be established that consisted of five members whom the Minister considered representative of NGOs, an appointee from each of the eight ministries as well as a representative from the Office of the President and Cabinet. Some of the functions of the proposed Council would be 'to promote and encourage the co-ordination of the activities of registered NGOs having similar or related objects; to formulate rules for registration or deregistration of NGOs and to formulate a Code of Conduct for NGOs' (Ibid.).

Clearly, one of the aims of the bill was to clamp down on CSOs engaged in governance and human rights work. The denial of their access to external funding and the hanging threat of deregistration created a very uncertain and insecure environment for this coterie of CSOs. As it was argued:

> the Bill was going to give the Government the power to run all NGOs by allowing it unfettered powers to inspect, monitor, invade, split and dictate what happens in NGOs. This is similar to the powers of the Minister of Local Government to remove elected councillors and replace them with his own appointees. (Ibid.)

What was the response of NGOs to the proposed legislation? First, NGOs organised public meetings under the auspices of umbrella organisations, namely, the CZC and NCA, to discuss the contents and repercussions of the bill. Second, the apex body of NGOs, the National Association of NGOs (NANGO), played a pivotal part in co-ordinating the response to the bill. NANGO argued that any legislation should ensure social stability and the rule of law, efficient and accountable operations of NGOs, regulation on mergers and split-ups in the sector and spell out a Code of Conduct (NANGO 2002; McCandless and Pajibo 2003). However, once the bill had been debated and passed by Parliament (with ZANU-PF exploiting its advantage of a built-in majority of 30 non-constituency Members of Parliament), NANGO's task became one of lobbying those with influence over President Mugabe to persuade him not to give it assent and transform it into law.

The lobbying against the signing of the bill was intense. NANGO appealed to members of the ZANU-PF politburo and to church figures to dissuade the President from signing it. The political alliances for and against the bill were secretive and intriguing. However, it emerged that some of the ZANU-PF figures involved in the Tsholotsho Declaration of November 2004 had been prime movers behind the Bill for their own narrow ends. At the same time, the bill would have undermined those ministers who were close to certain NGOs and who derived patronage leverage from NGOs that would be affected. In short, there were divisions even in the Cabinet over the contents of the Bill, divisions that President Mugabe was aware of. In addition, another compelling reason for not signing the bill was that it would have further confirmed the country's 'pariah status' as being in the same league as apartheid South Africa and Myanmar. Had it been made into law, the bill would have violated the international treaties to which Zimbabwe is signatory and contravened the *SADC Guidelines and Principles Governing Democratic Elections*. In some quarters, the issue became whether the intended NGO law should be deliberately contravened, as was apartheid-related legislation in South Africa (Sachikonye 2006). If anything, the moral base of the intended law was very shaky.

It is more than five years since the NGO bill was shelved. Ironically, there developed a consensus that the unsigned bill has nevertheless had almost the same effect:

> the mere threat of its existence has forced NGOs to regulate themselves. Its mere existence sends a powerful signal. (Ibid.:29)

Thus there exists an unusual situation where a draft law has the same effect as real law on the behaviour of those that it was intended to regulate. However, one positive aspect of the lobbying process against the bill was that it brought the NGOs closer to each other. Like the opposition parties and the independent media, NGOs have been operating under the shadow of an authoritarian state that does not respect individual and organisational autonomy. There are no signals that this shadow will pass in the short and medium term as long as the present authoritarian state survives intact.

In addition to the legislative framework, there have been other aspects to the state strategies against CSOs. Coercive measures against them have become increasingly common. Intimidation and intrusion have been amongst the tactics that have been used. As it was observed:

> in 2004, about 30 NGOs were searched, interrogated and forced to disclose confidential information …. The manner in which it was done, not mentioning its failure to pass the constitutionality test, is evidence that one of the intrusive tendencies of government and the sweeping powers that render all NGOs vulnerable to abuse by the state. This clearly underscores the point that the NGO sector is really under siege. (ZHR NGO Forum 2005:55)

This trend of repression continued through to 2008 when abductions and torture of CSO leaders and activists reached a climax. Perhaps the most symbolic of the wave of repression in 2008 was the abduction and prolonged torture of Jestina Mukoko and other staff of the Zimbabwe Peace Project (ZPP). Other notorious instances of torture were those of Wellington Chibebe and Lovemore Matombo, the ZCTU leaders, in 2006, and the beatings of civil society leaders such as Lovemore Madhuku in March 2007.

State authorities also mounted a 'soft strategy', that of a propaganda offensive in its media such as the *Herald* against CSOs. This has included exposés ostensibly about their sources of funding from the West, with reference made to agencies such as the Central Intelligence Agency (CIA) and others as sources of their funding. For instance, a report about British Embassy funding for CSOs was prominently displayed on the front page of a daily with the statement that:

> Britain has increased funding for its regime change agenda in Zimbabwe by pouring in 3.3 million pounds to support NGOs, anti-government lawyers, doctors and other opposition elements to step up their demonisation campaigns. (Herald, 20 February 2008)

CSOs are often at the receiving end of this sort of judgemental and/ or biased reporting by the state media. Another strategy used by state institutions has been to tighten the monitoring of flows of funds to CSOs and their use. The Reserve Bank of Zimbabwe, for example, introduced a monitoring mechanism by putting the foreign currency accounts of CSOs under its ambit. This resulted in orchestrated delays to their access to funds and thus a chain of delay in their advocacy and lobbying activities, research and civic education as well as election monitoring. This form of state control has adversely affected the effectiveness of CSOs.

This discussion of state strategies would be incomplete without reference to government creation and co-optation of some CSOs. These include the Zimbabwe Federation of Trade Unions (ZFTU), which receives state financial and administrative support. The ZFTU has served as an opponent and critic of the ZCTU as well as acted as a spoiler during stay-aways and May Day celebrations. Another state-sponsored CSO is the Zimbabwe Congress of Students, which played an active role in the celebration of Mugabe's 84th birthday in 2008. This trend towards state penetration of CSOs or their creation also extends to the formation and support of churches such as that of Reverend Msindo. Thus some bogus CSOs have been created or supported to buttress Mugabe's authoritarian project. However, this is not wholly unusual in a world in which governments can create their own government NGOs (GONGOs) to use as conduits of patronage in various sectors in return for political support and legitimation.

The Quest for Justice, Restitution and Healing

Zimbabwe is a society that has experienced both political violence between rival parties and state violence against civilians for at least half a century. It is thus deeply traumatised. The colonial state and post-colonial government were accomplices in some of that violence and trauma. It was left largely to CSOs to raise the alarm and undertake extensive documentation of human rights abuses such as detention without trial, torture and extra-judicial killings. In the last decade of colonial rule in the 1970s, the Catholic Commission for Peace and Justice in Rhodesia (CCJPR, now CCJPZ) was pivotal in collecting and disseminating information about human rights violations and atrocities against civilians during the civil war. During the 1982–1987 *Gukurahundi* conflict in Matabeleland, it found itself playing a similar role of conducting research and disseminating information about the brutalities perpetrated against thousands of civilians. The resultant report, *Breaking the Silence*, was co-published with the Legal Resources Foundation (LRF) and has become an important reference point for the discourse on transitional justice in the country (CCJPZ and LRF 1997). The report was the outcome of meticulous investigations of how the state's armed forces trampled on basic human rights and tortured, maimed and killed thousands of civilians in their war against 'dissidents'. Close co-operation between local community and church-related organisations made possible grassroots research that enabled a full picture of the patterns of violence to emerge.

For more than a decade after the Gukurahundi conflict, most people nationally and internationally remained in ignorance of its true scale and devastating impact (Eppel 2004). In contrast, however, scarcely a family in Matabeleland:

> escaped the violence of those years, and the people of those provinces were forced to live with their silenced memories of horror and fear. (Ibid.:46.)

In the affected areas, about 75 per cent of rural civilians interviewed were survivors of Gukurahundi, of whom 80 per cent had suffered violence in the 1980s.

The role of CSOs in collecting material on human rights violations was extended to the situation of food riots in urban centres in 1998, and to the years of violence that accompanied land reform and the post-2000 elections. State institutions could not be relied upon to carry out the documentation of those arrested, injured, killed and displaced during those tumultuous years (1998–2008). This vacuum was filled by CSOs that pooled their resources and formed formal coalitions to collect and periodically disseminate data on trends in political violence, intimidation, arrests and torture. CSOs such as the ZHR NGO Forum and the ZPP played a prominent role in the collection of data from grassroots organisations. Their databases have such extensive data that they may be superior to those held by state agencies. As we have already observed above, the documentation by CSOs on the effects of Operation *Murambatsvina/ Restore Order* was so extensive and credible that the UN mission led by Anna Tibaijuka drew a great deal from it for its analysis and recommendations (ActionAid 2005; ZHR NGO Forum 2006a).

However, CSOs have not restricted their role to research, dissemination and advocacy. They have also been involved in the counselling and rehabilitation of the victims of displacements, intimidation and violence. While some of them have sought to rehabilitate and provide housing to ex-farm workers, others have provided psychological counselling and treatment to victims of torture. The work of organisations such as the Amani Trust, the Counselling Services Unit and Research and Advocacy Unit has also revolved around this provision of psychological counselling and treatment. In other instances, CSOs have provided food aid, shelter and medical assistance to victims of *Operation Murambatsvina*/Restore Order where state institutions were reluctant so to do. Groups such as tertiary students who have experienced arrest and torture have also sought succour from CSOs. In other words, CSOs have found themselves at the frontline, providing relief and emergency assistance at clinics and hospitals. Clashes with state authorities have been unavoidable in such situations.

Another significant intervention by CSOs relates to the process of defining the discourse and sequencing of transitional justice and healing. Several major conferences were organised to this effect (ZHR NGO Forum 2006b). In 2001, the Amani Trust convened a 'Truth and Justice' conference that specifically focused on the experiences of the Matabeleland provinces. However, it was the symposium 'Civil Society and Justice in Zimbabwe' that was convened in 2003 in Johannesburg that for the first time provided a relatively comprehensive framework of transitional justice issues that needed to be addressed (Ibid.). The principal outcome of the symposium was a formal declaration which stated that:

> *victims of all past human rights abuses have the right to redress and to be consulted about the nature of the mechanisms that will be established to address their needs. The mechanisms that are established must be victim-centred and must be capable of addressing the needs of victims in a meaningful way. Prior to the establishment of these mechanisms there must be an extensive process of consultation with the victims and the broader community about the mechanisms and the sort of persons who should be made responsible for operating them. Civic organisations and the churches should assist in this process. The main mechanism of dealing with past human rights abuses will be a Truth, Justice and Reconciliation Commission (Ibid.:43).*

Specific suggestions were also made on how violations post-1960 could be dealt with by that Commission.

The idea of a truth, justice and reconciliation commission was rekindled

Box 7.1 – Recommendations on transitional justice

- *Participants noted the need for a formal and comprehensive process of national healing, reconciliation and transitional justice to begin in Zimbabwe.*
- *For transitional justice to be effective, local communities needed to be involved and take ownership of the process.*
- *Decentralisation and restructuring of judicial processes in the event of massive prosecutions of many offenders was also recommended.*
- *The capacity of the Zimbabwe judicial system and its past record in dealing with political cases needs innovative and immediate reforms and decentralisation, particularly the court system, in order to deal expeditiously and conclusively with cases of violence.*
- *Participants noted challenges that faced victims and witnesses, such as long distances to the courts and resistance by some perpetrators before the courts and traditional leaders. Victim-friendly processes that would be accessible need to be established.*
- *Women and men of integrity should constitute any body that might be created to deal with transitional justice issues such as truth-seeking or prosecutions, and on an equal basis to ensure that interests of both sexes are equally and fairly heard.*
- *Participants voiced concern of actors in the former regime being part of any bodies that might be created and recommended victim-centred processes more than anything else.*

Source: ZHR NGO Forum (2009: 31)

with the formation of the Inclusive Government in 2009 after the signing of a Global Political Agreement (GPA) in 2008. However, it was watered down considerably to the structure of an Organ of National Healing, Reconciliation and Integration (ONHRI) that would advise on what 'measures might be necessary and practicable to achieve national healing, cohesion and unity in respect of victims of pre- and post-independence political conflicts' (GPA 2008). This formulation devalued the idea of truth, justice and reconciliation (TJR). Indeed, the subsequent terms of reference of the Organ itself were considerably ambiguous, resulting in lack of clarity of its mission and role as well as diminished credibility.

Nevertheless, CSOs continued to pursue the concept of a TJR commission and took advantage of the small window opened by the GPA to conduct field consultations on what form and depth the process should take. The outcome of those consultations in 2009 was published in a report by a consortium of human rights CSOs and the ZHR NGO Forum (2009). The findings were much more explicit than those envisaged under the Organ's own consultations that were carried out in 2009 and 2010. The CSOs programme was termed 'Taking Transitional Justice to the People' and focused on truth-seeking, prosecutions, reparations and institutional reforms (ZHR NGO Forum, 2009). The overall recommendations that were made during the consultations are instructive (Box 7.1).

Clearly, there will remain a major role for CSOs in shaping the discourse on transitional justice and the processes of seeking to achieve it. While obstacles from state institutions implicated in human rights violations will remain, CSOs need to continue to apply pressure to ensure transparency and accountability in the eventual transitional justice process. The CSOs have the requisite data, skills and institutional memory to enable them to play a meaningful role in the process.

Conclusion

This chapter has explored the usefulness and relevance of the concepts of civil society and the social contract to examine the changing balance in relations between the state and society during Zimbabwe's lost decades. While the relative autonomy of civil society organisations is an important if contingent asset, their relations with the state are not necessarily or always dichotomised. In reality, since 2000, the relationship between the two has undergone phases of paternalism and partnership and then estrangement and conflict. Even so, as this chapter has demonstrated, with CSOs being heterogeneous, the different forms of relationships have affected CSOs differently. Those CSOs involved in the 'soft' areas of development, health and gender tended to have a non-antagonistic relationship with the state, while those in 'hard areas' of governance and human rights experienced relations of mutual suspicion and conflict on political and operational grounds.

This chapter has also suggested that the social contract that underpinned state–society relations in the first decade of independence began to experience multiple economic and political pressures in the 1990s. The social contract broke down in 2000 and attempts to resuscitate it proved difficult in conditions of authoritarianism. A coercive social contract was in the ascendant but proved fragile as efforts to literally draw up a conciliatory alternative floundered for many years.

The growth of civil society, and its strengths and weaknesses during the three decades of independence were also assessed. While it was weakly developed in the 1980s, it became stronger and more diverse in the 1990s. Civil society came under the onslaught of the state in the post-2000 period, especially in the sector of governance and human rights. However, despite the formidable obstacles such as funding constraints, repression and burnout, CSOs proved resilient. Their lobbying and advocacy achievements were notable during the particularly difficult decade of economic and political crisis (1998–2008). They will continue to play a key role in Zimbabwe's long, drawn-out democratic transition from the 1990s to the present.

8
Society, Livelihoods & Migration

Introduction

The impact of the political developments assessed in the first part of this book, and the economic disruptions described in Chapters 5 and 6, have been very profound for Zimbabwean society. The severe repercussions have included the spread and deepening of poverty, a relentlessly tight squeeze on livelihoods and one of the largest peacetime migrations in recent history. Although estimates vary, it has been asserted that up to three million Zimbabweans (about a quarter of the population) have migrated to other countries for economic and political reasons (UNDP 2008; Crush and Tevera 2010). Migration on such a massive scale is an eloquent indictment of the policies that the Mugabe government implemented during the lost decades. There is a deep sense in which 'things will never be the same again' after the unravelling of the country's political social fabric over the last 30 years. However, it was during the third decade of independence that this unravelling reached crisis proportions, as Chapters 5 and 6 illustrated. It is no coincidence that most livelihoods received their sternest test and shocks, and that out-migration reached its peak in the period 2000–2008.

In this chapter we explore the links between patterns of inequalities and pressures on livelihoods of both the middle and working classes, pressures which created a large momentum for migration. It then examines the implications of the growth of the Zimbabwean diaspora and whether its remittances have had a positive impact on livelihoods and economic development. Finally, the chapter explores the effects of the crisis on culture, values and ideas about society and development.

Classes, Wealth and Poverty

The state of livelihoods is conditioned by class and patterns of wealth and poverty in society. Zimbabwe's inheritance at independence consisted of a skewed class system with most of the wealth concentrated in the white minority, a small African middle class and a growing working class. Numerically, the peasant class was the largest although it had connections with the working class, to the extent that the latter retained strong links with the former. However, one clear trend during the following three decades was the steady decline in the size of the white population, which fell from about 200,000 in 1980 to less than 50,000 in 2010. During the first 15 years of independence, the growth of the working and middle classes was notable as public sector employment expanded together with the education and health systems. As the manufacturing, services and financial sectors grew, so did the numbers of workers, who reached the 1.5 million mark in the 1990s. Amongst them was an African middle class which not only occupied senior positions in government ministries, parastatals and uniformed forces but also the higher echelons in the private sector. Another fraction of the middle class was beginning to root itself in the small and medium-sized business sectors. The growth in the size of these classes would have been more dynamic and faster had the economy had been robust.

The post-independence state created opportunities for class formation and mobility as the education and economic sectors expanded. However, the inroads into inequalities were limited. For instance, one report in 1998 observed that:

> *inequality in income distribution is indicated by a high Gini coefficient of 0.63. Some 41 per cent of the population lived below the poverty line. The richest ten per cent earns 47 per cent of national income while the poorest ten per cent earns only two per cent. The richest 20 per cent earns 62 per cent compared to only four per cent earned by the poorest 20 per cent. (SADC RHDR 1998:47)*

Thus the country experienced some of the sharpest levels of inequality on the continent together with Namibia and South Africa, also former white settler societies. Of the 24 sub-Saharan countries listed in Deininger and Squire (1996), only South Africa, Gabon and Sierra Leone had a more unequal pattern of income distribution. The United Nations Conference on Trade and Development (UNCTAD) classified Zimbabwe as a 'highly unequal society' in which the richest 20 per cent of the population received 60 per cent of the income (UNCTAD 1997). Nearly two decades of independence failed to address the sharp inequalities in Zimbabwean society.

Poverty levels steadily deepened after the first decade of independence. A government-sponsored survey that was undertaken in 1995 found that 61 per cent of Zimbabwean households were 'poor', and of these 45 per cent were 'very poor' (MPSLSW 1997). Poor households were defined as those with incomes below the national total consumption poverty line (TCPL), and very poor households as those below the national food poverty line (ZHDR 1998). The survey also found out that poverty was more prevalent in rural areas, with 75 per cent of households in the total poor category compared to 39 per cent of urban households. Another important finding was that about 72 per cent of female-headed households fell into the combined poor and very poor category compared to 58 per cent of male-headed households. The proportion of the population living below the TCPL increased to 80 per cent in 2002 (Zimbabwe Government and UNDP, 2004). The onset of the economic crisis in 1998 certainly exacerbated the situation, as we saw in Chapter 5. The decline in the population employed in the formal sector from 14 per cent in 1980 to ten per cent in 2004, and then to six per cent by 2007, was another contributory factor to the surge in poverty levels.

No comparable surveys have been conducted on patterns in the growth or otherwise of wealth in Zimbabwean society. Circumstantial evidence points to growth in wealth amongst the political class concentrated in ZANU-PF as well as those connected to its extensive patronage system. Proximity to the state as well as exploitation of state-centred accumulation opportunities made the top echelons of the political class, the senior government bureaucrats and senior officers in the military-security establishment wealthy. Opportunities to accumulate wealth also existed during the intervention into the DRC in 1998–2002 and during the land reform exercise in 2000–2003 (Zimbabwe Institute 2008). The discovery of diamonds in Marange in 2007 and the spread of gold mining in various regions of the country also sparked a wave of accumulation from which these groups benefited (Moore and Mawowa 2008). However, precise information on the resources exploited, fortunes made and monetary value of assets acquired or stripped remains a grey area, making it difficult to make quantitative estimates of wealth accumulated during the lost decades. The epitome of this new wealth includes and is flaunted by such flamboyant figures as Philip Chiyangwa and Gideon Gono, amongst others, and by quieter figures like Solomon Mujuru and Ignatius Chombo. The conception and implementation of legislation such as the Indigenisation and Economic Empowerment Act was meant to facilitate the growth of a new African business class that draws a great deal from its access to the state, but in fact only a minority have actually benefitted.

Education, Health and Epidemics

The deepening of poverty was reflected in and indeed reinforced by declining access to basic education and health, especially during the third decade of independence. Diminishing access to these basic social services and assets was compounded by the HIV/AIDS pandemic and by tuberculosis and cholera, with the cholera outbreak in 2008–09 being one of the worst in Africa in recent years.

During the first two decades of independence, considerable strides were made in the provision of both primary and secondary education, with the result that literacy and education attainments ranked amongst the highest on the continent. However, by 2008 and 2009, the education sector was almost collapsing. According to UNICEF:

> now on the brink of collapse, Zimbabwe's education system was once the best in Africa …. Past successes have been reversed by a raft of problems hinging on the lack of financing, which led to a marked decline in the pay envelope of teachers and school improvement grants. (UNICEF, 10 February 2009:1)

The crisis in the education sector spread in 2007, with a marked depletion of teachers in schools and plummeting school attendance; this fell from over 80 per cent to 20 per cent. In 2008, 94 per cent of schools in rural Zimbabwe were closed (Ibid.). When the Inclusive Government entered office in February 2009, conditions in this sector were dire. There were serious shortages of learning materials, textbooks and supplies in schools. One assessment showed that there was:

> a ratio of ten pupils per every textbook across Zimbabwe … and a staggering 20 per cent of primary schools had no textbooks for English, Maths or an African language. (Ibid.)

The impact of the deteriorating quality in education was stark, with Grade 7 examination pass rates declining from 53 per cent (1999) to 33 per cent (2007). In addition, statistics showed that almost 50 per cent of children graduating from primary school were not proceeding to secondary school (Ibid.).

The major cause of the crisis was an economic one: state spending on education declined significantly during the decade 1998–2008. The government of Zimbabwe itself acknowledged that low teacher morale was one of the many consequences of diminishing state spending on salaries and on education infrastructure. Admitting that low salaries, poor staff accommodation and increased working loads were major challenges, the government stated that 'these factors have partly contributed to the massive brain drain of qualified teachers' (Government of Zimbabwe and UN, 2004). In 2009 and 2010, some of the decline was arrested with the setting up of an Education Transition Fund (ETF) and some improvement in teachers' remuneration. Even so, remuneration was still relatively low, at between USD150 and USD200 per month. Although low salaries sparked several countrywide strikes by the teachers, most schools reopened in the course of 2009. However, the recovery in the education sector will take years given the damage done during the lost decades.

The health sector took a major battering from the economic crisis of 1998 to 2008. As a reflection of a deepening crisis, state spending on health declined significantly. Statistics on the under-five mortality rate as well as the rate of infant mortality (less than one year old) illustrate a worrying decline in the health sector. In 1990, the under-five mortality rate was 79 per 100,000; it had climbed to 96 by 2008 (UNICEF, 24 November 2009). Infant mortality increased from 51 per 100,000 in 1990 to 62 in 2008. While life expectancy declined from 61 years in 1990 to 44 in 2008, the crude death rate increased from nine per 100,000 in 1990 to 16 in 2008 (Ibid.). These indicators strongly suggested a worsening of health conditions and a rise in infant mortality and adult mortality.

In its own diagnosis of the health sector, the government of Zimbabwe acknowledged that the decrease in the health budget:

> made the procurement of essential drugs and equipment, as well as the retention of staff difficult. In addition, the impact of HIV/AIDS and brain drain on human resources in the health sector has been particularly severe. The challenge, therefore, is to protect social sector expenditure within the national budget in order to support strengthening and transformation of the health delivery system. (Government of Zimbabwe and UN 2004:36)

Illustrating more dramatically the depth of the health sector crisis was the fact that the major referral hospitals in Harare were closed towards the end of 2008. This coincided with the outbreak of cholera that claimed about 4,300 lives and saw around 98,000 people being treated for the disease. The principal cause of cholera is lack of access to safe water supply, sanitation and garbage collection systems. The nationwide breakdown of the water supply system due to shortage of purification chemicals resulted in the collapse of sanitation procedures. The outbreak was declared a national emergency by the government of Zimbabwe, and foreign assistance became the principal lifeline that contributed to the containment of the epidemic.

Another major indicator of the crisis in the health sector was the significant spread of HIV/AIDS during the lost decades. With a prevalence rate of 34 per cent at the peak of the epidemic in 2002, Zimbabwe was among the top five countries in Africa worst hit by the pandemic. The first case of HIV/AIDS in Zimbabwe was diagnosed in 1985. The United Nations Programme on HIV/AIDS (UNAIDS) estimated that 2.3 million people (slightly less than 20 per cent of the population) had been affected with HIV/AIDS by the end of 2002. The spread of HIV/AIDS has had multiple consequences, ranging from absenteeism at work and frequent illness resulting in lowered productivity and the rise of HIV/AIDS-related diseases such as tuberculosis. Another consequence has been a significant increase in the number of orphans. In 2007, there were about one million AIDS orphans (eight per cent of the total population) (UNICEF, November 2009). A major report on HIV/AIDS in the early 2000s observed and predicted that:

> the precious and hard-won infant and child survival gains in Zimbabwe during the 1980s have been severely eroded by HIV/AIDS. The infant mortality rate is now 72 per cent higher than it would have been without the pandemic .... By 2010, the mortality rate among children under five will be three and half times higher than it would be without AIDS. (ZHDR 2003:87-8)

When the significant economic and social damage of HIV/AIDS to society became all too obvious, government, donors, NGOs and communities mounted a major effort to contain the epidemic. It included campaigns for behavioural change, use of condoms and voluntary testing. The effort began to yield fruit with the drop of the prevalence rate to 14 per cent in 2009. However, even this lower prevalence rate remains worrying, for it needs to be lowered into single digits. In 2007, there were between 1.2 million and 1.4 million people living with HIV/AIDS (UNICEF 2010). Access to anti-retroviral therapy by those in need of treatment has been growing in the past few years, but demand far outstrips supply (in 2009, some 389,895 adults and children needed such therapy urgently). As we explain below, the impact of HIV/AIDS on Zimbabwean society has been profound, ranging from the dramatic drop in life expectancy and the traumatic experiences of orphan-led families to the disruptions of families and dislocation of culture and values.

The Mugabe government admitted that its response to the cholera epidemic and to HIV/AIDS was slow, weak and poorly co-ordinated. Had the response been as decisive as in countries such as Uganda and Senegal, it is possible that Zimbabwe might have been spared the worst effects of the HIV/AIDS pandemic. The strong element of official 'denialism' for almost a decade contributed to the slow and lukewarm response by government leadership. But the social, economic and cultural consequences of the epidemics will be felt for many decades to come.

Displacement and its Consequences

It was not only the crisis in the education and health sectors that, combined with the cholera and HIV/AIDS, caused a great deal of suffering and hardship. Other decisions and processes instigated by the Mugabe government exacerbated the already difficult economic and social conditions. In Chapter 6 we saw how the chaotic land reform programme uprooted and displaced almost 200,000 farm workers' households. While some remained in the farming sector as itinerant, casual workers, others drifted into the urban informal economy and survived on the margins of society. Other displaced farm workers sought employment on farms in the northern province of Limpopo, South Africa, and elsewhere in that country.

However, the most serious large-scale displacement was *Operation Murambatsvina*/Restore Order (hereafter OM) which was instigated by the Mugabe government in 2005. It implemented a sweeping operation in urban and rural areas to 'clean them up' ostensibly of dirt, crime and subversion. Some of the farm workers who had migrated into towns and cities and lived in poor housing were caught up in the exercise and subjected to further displacement. OM was a sweeping, military-style programme purportedly designed to solve the simultaneous social, economic and political problems facing the country. An estimated 700,000 people were directly affected and 2.5 million people indirectly affected. Launched in 2005, OM engulfed the country's cities, towns and 'growth points' as well as some rural areas from May until the end of July. Shortly thereafter UN Special Envoy Anna Tibaijuka visited Zimbabwe and compiled a critical report. Although there were extensive preliminary surveys, the full social, economic and psychological impact of OM would not be felt for years to come.

OM was an example of post-election retribution by the Mugabe regime, mainly against an opposition movement that had become strongly rooted in urban centres. As we observed elsewhere, no government since the founding of the modern state of Zimbabwe 120 years ago had ever attempted such an ambitious project (Sachikonye 2005). Its scale, in terms of numbers affected and resources destroyed, was unprecedented, and not only in the country's history. It was also unheard of in contemporary Africa. It was not surprising that when news and images of the project were broadcast around the globe the response was swift and damning. Coming not long after Asia's tsunami of 2004, it was not long before the earier natural and the later man-made Zimbabwean 'tsunami' were compared and contrasted.

What was the official explanation for this project of social displacement against predominantly poor urban Zimbabweans? It was claimed that it was intended to:

> deal with crime, squalor and lawlessness, and rebuild and reorganise urban settlements and small and medium enterprises (SMEs). (Government of Zimbabwe 2005:15)

More broadly, OM was intended to address what was termed 'a cocktail of social, economic and security challenges that had come to negatively impact upon the economy and the populace' (Ibid.). OM was specifically justified on the grounds that it sought to:

- *Stem disorderly and chaotic urbanisation and attendant problems that hinder government and local authorities from enforcing national and local authority by-laws and providing service*
- *Stop economic crimes especially black market transactions in foreign currency*
- *Eliminate the parallel market and fight economic sabotage*
- *Stop the hoarding of consumer commodities, and other commodities in short supply*
- *Reduce high crime levels by targeting organised crime syndicates*
- *Minimise the threat of major disease outbreaks due to overcrowding and squalor. (Government of Zimbabwe 2005:5-6)*

However, the real motivation of OM was *political retribution* in the aftermath of the 2005 election. Having gained 26 of the 30 parliamentary seats in major cities and towns, and continuing to control local government in urban centres, the MDC was viewed as a persistent threat to ZANU-PF. The Mugabe regime thus sought to weaken the MDC, punish its urban supporters and 'lance the boil of dissatisfaction in heavily populated urban areas before it could reach explosive levels' (ICG 2005:4). The then Minister of State Security, Didymus Mutasa, had warned of the possibility of spontaneous uprisings in urban areas as a result of food shortages and economic crisis. Just prior to OM, over 100 opposition supporters had been arrested by the regime, ostensibly to break up pockets of urban resistance. Indeed, the simmering anger in urban areas was also apparent when armed police beat up and forcibly dispersed residents of Harare's low-income suburb of Mabvuku in 2005. They had been protesting against having gone for three days without water. Viewed from this perspective, OM was both retribution against opposition supporters and a pre-emptive strike against urban discontents. The UN mission led by Anna Tibaijuka was highly critical of OM, condemning the violence and violation of social and economic rights that accompanied it (Tibaijuka 2005). It recommended measures to be taken against the perpetrators of the operation.

In economic and social terms, the impact of OM was massive. The loss of jobs and livelihoods by those it affected in the informal economy meant that demand for goods and services plummeted. Their capacity to purchase goods, including basic commodities, also diminished. This was immediately felt by the formal sector. While there might now have been 'cleaner surroundings' in cities and towns, these came at the expense of the flow of business and purchasing power. One conservative estimate was that OM put about one million people (and their dependents) out of work (ZHR NGO Forum 2005). If one accepted that about half of business activity at that time in 2005 was in the informal economy, then the direct impact on GDP would have been a reduction of 25 per cent.

However, the consequences of displacement from the farms under *jambanja*, and from urban centres under OM, went beyond the economic and social. There remained a considerable residue of trauma and fear within the displaced communities. As one report explained:

> *Operation Murambatsvina has had devastating consequences on the mental health of those affected. It is clear that this is not due to the operation alone, but that the organised violence and torture of the past five years or so has had the cumulative effect seen in the consequences of OM. The overall morbidity is*

enormous – conservatively estimated at about 800,000 persons – and reflec-tive of a situation in a 'complex emergency' …. It is important here to point out that we are talking about 'clinically significant disorders'; that is, psycho-logical disorders that ordinarily would require the attention of mental health professionals and that are unlikely to heal without such attention. (ActionAid, CSU, CHRA and ZPP 2005:39)

OM acted as a rehearsal for later operations such as orchestrated elec-tion-related violence of June 2008 aimed at subduing the opposition movement. The rehearsal witnessed close co-ordination in repression by the police, local authorities and the Joint Operations Command, which was believed to be one of the architects of the Operation. The show of force was intended to cow the population to the extent that it was forced to undertake the physical destruction of their own property and out-buildings for fear of beatings and detention if they refused to co-operate. The compliance with orders was fear-induced and involuntary. And this widespread anguish and trauma has persisted. The combination of deteri-orating economic and social conditions, education and health standards, epidemics and state-induced displacement provided the stimulus for large-scale migration to which we turn in the next section.

Livelihoods and Pressures for Migration

In the late 1990s, the foundations of a deep-rooted crisis had been laid through unorthodox and reckless state expenditure that led directly to currency depreciation and spiralling inflation. As we explained in Chapter 5, the award of non-budgeted gratuities and pensions to about 50,000 war veterans had a permanent impact on the value of the Zimbabwe dollar, on levels of balance of payments and on inflation. In 2000, the intersection of political violence, haphazard land reform and economic deprivation produced a cocktail of discontent and alienation within the population. Endemic shortages of basic commodities such as food and fuel, and of basic services like water and electricity supplies, significant-ly undermined living standards. Salaries and wages were substantially eroded by inflation, making it difficult, if not impossible, for most mem-bers of the working and middle classes to 'make ends meet' month after month. Most of them now found themselves earning less than the nomi-nal living wage. Their economic insecurity was compounded by political insecurity as the election and land reform processes were characterised by violence which was graphically reported in the independent media. Rising crime levels also threatened human security.

It was against this background, which included the aforementioned problems of cholera, TB and HIV/AIDS and the collapse of the health and education sectors, that migration became a major option for many of those affected.

Although economic migration was underway in the 1990s, it was on a modest scale and confined to sections of highly skilled professionals (Gaidzanwa 1999). This changed after 2000 when the 'migration option' became compelling to the working and middle classes, traders, unskilled workers, the poor and the politically persecuted. The post-2000 Zimbabwean out-migration is outstanding in its confluence of economic and political grievances and insecurity, its size (about a quarter of the total population) and its multi-class composition. In one sense, migration was an act of despair as the political and economic crises combined to make decent livelihoods impossible and hope for reform and change a distant possibility. It was partly an act of defiance and protest against the policies and measures of the Mugabe government. In another sense, it symbolised an abrogation of a social contract between the state and its citizens. Most migrants were bitter towards the Mugabe government for its repression, economic mismanagement and corruption.

Most accounts of Zimbabwean migration tend to steer clear of the political dynamics of the process, preferring to dwell more on the economic imperatives (Chetsanga and Muchenje 2003; Bloch 2005; Crush and Tevera 2010). If migration is partly a politically motivated act, then the Zimbabwean 'exodus' is more complicated than the 'economic reading' that is often given to it. At the same time, it raises a question about the political utility of migration. Is migrating out of an authoritarian state the most effective response to a situation that requires collective political change? Does migrating in fact contribute to the longevity of the incumbent authoritarian regime? These are uncomfortable questions that are avoided by focusing mainly on the economic imperatives of migration. The Zimbabwe exodus should have inspired a more searching debate on the meaning and consequences of a migration process in which up to a quarter of the population of a modern state has voted with its feet. But the silence is partly due to various interested parties ranging from receiving countries that have benefitted from skilled migrants, insecure migrant workers who are exploitable and a sending country that does not own up to the fact that its policies have driven citizens away.

Let us explore the patterns of migration, in particular from 2000 onwards. Fortunately, there are many scholarly surveys that have been conducted on Zimbabwean migrants in southern Africa and elsewhere, including the United Kingdom (Zinyama and Tevera 2002; Chestanga and Muchenje 2003; Makina 2007). A survey in 2003 estimated that nearly 500,000 skilled Zimbabweans had migrated and that of these 24 per cent were trained doctors, nurses or pharmacists, 23 per cent were engineers or scientists, 20 per cent were teachers and about 17 per cent were accountants (Chetsanga and Muchenje 2003). Another study stated that more than 80 per cent of the doctors, nurses, pharmacists, radiologists and therapists trained in Zimbabwe since 1980 had migrated, with over 2,100 doctors spread between South Africa, Botswana, Namibia, the UK and Australia by 2003 as a result (Chikanda 2005). In 2009, it was estimated that the country was losing an average of 20 per cent of its health care professionals annually to emigration (Makina and Kanyenze 2010). Skilled professionals, especially health and teaching professionals, appeared to be in considerable demand in southern Africa, Europe and America. Artisans and service workers were also sought after.

However, a substantial proportion of Zimbabwean migrants found themselves in lowly-skilled and poorly paid positions that were not commensurate with their qualifications and experience. For instance, in a survey in Johannesburg, South Africa, 35 per cent of respondents reported that they did work that was not equal to their qualifications (Makina 2007). A survey that covered both South Africa and the UK revealed significant unused skills of teachers (17 per cent) and of staff experienced in finance, banking and sales (16 per cent) (Bloch 2005). Many others do not or cannot work in the professions in which they were trained (Makina and Kanyenze 2010). This process of deskilling is a loss for Zimbabwe and the destination country, not to mention the migrants themselves. As one study observed with respect to the UK care industry:

> most Zimbabweans working as carers are stressed and frustrated because they have experienced de-skilling and a loss of status, and feel trapped in care work, with little prospect of using their qualifications in the UK. Some feel ashamed by the nature of the work. For men who have gone into caring, these feelings can be heightened by the humiliation of having to do dirty and demeaning 'women's work'. (McGregor 2010:180)

The phenomenon of de-skilling is exacerbated by the stringent conditions relating to visa and work permits and professional registration in most countries, including the UK.

In South Africa, it would appear that there is wide diversity for Zimbabwean migrants, ranging from farm and domestic work to security and services jobs, among others. Unskilled migrants have successfully entered these forms of employment, but at lower rates of pay and working conditions than local workers. An above-mentioned survey observed that almost a third of the sampled migrants were unemployed when they left Zimbabwe but soon found some form of employment thereafter:

> in Johannesburg, around 90 per cent have jobs and the remaining ten per cent work in the informal economy .... However, there does appear to be some de-skilling, with migrants working in positions below their level of training and experience. In Zimbabwe, for example, 16 per cent had worked as teachers. In Johannesburg, only seven per cent were working in that field. (Makina 2010:236)

Conditions in agricultural and domestic work are quite difficult for and exploitative of Zimbabwean migrants. Their earnings and other conditions of work are often subject to the whims of the individual employer, who can take advantage of their lack of papers and permits. This category of lowly-skilled workers will likely encounter problems in obtaining jobs if they return to Zimbabwe in the near future given the high unemployment rate of about 80 per cent. Another category of Zimbabwean migrants comprises those who cannot find work in the destination country for one reason or another. Some resort to grey activities, such as prostitution and crime.

It would be an advance in migration studies if a fuller profile and more precise numbers of Zimbabwean migrants were established. For the moment, there is a tendency to view them as a monolithic group. This is misleading and unhelpful in policy planning relating to the Zimbabwean diaspora.

The Zimbabwe Diaspora, Remittances and Livelihoods

The size of the Zimbabwean diaspora exploded after 2000. Although the largest concentration is found within southern Africa, it has also spread to the UK, mainland Europe (chiefly Germany), North America, Australia and New Zealand. Perhaps the most comprehensive attempts to assess the

Table 8.1 – The estimated number of Zimbabweans in the diaspora by location

Country/Region	Estimated Population
South Africa	2,120,000
UK	400,000
Botswana	200,000
Elsewhere in Africa	200,000
US and Canada	50,000
Australia and New Zealand	20,000
Elsewhere in the world	50,000
TOTAL	3,040,000

Source: Makina and Kanyenze (2010)

size and location of the Zimbabwean diaspora are the detailed paper by Makina and Kanyenze (2010) and the collection of case studies by Crush and Tevera (2010). In their calculation of the size of the diaspora, Makina and Kanyenze observe that:

> the Zimbabwean migrant population in South Africa is estimated to be 2,12 million at the end of 2009 .... In the UK, the Zimbabwean population has been estimated at between 300,000 and 500,000, while in Botswana it is in the range of 200,000 to 300,000. Globally, we estimate the number of Zimbabweans living outside the country to be between 3-4 million, about a quarter of the country's population. (Makina and Kanyenze 2010:9)

Several observations may be made about the location and numerical size of the Zimbabwean diaspora (Table 8.1). According to Makina and Kanyenze (2010), two-thirds of the Zimbabwean diaspora lives in neighbouring South Africa, and 83 per cent of the total is located in Africa. This means that about 17 per cent of the diaspora is spread between Europe, North America and Australia/New Zealand. However, Crush and Tevera (2010) suggest that about 70 per cent have remained in Africa and that Western Europe, North America, Australasia and the Pacific have a combined proportion of 27 per cent.

There are, however, questions pertaining to methodology that arise from the different estimates arrived. It is not clear whether different studies have used similar or different methodologies and sources, or whether these have been rigorous enough. To what extent have official sources such as national immigration and border agencies been used? To what degree have other sources been used to compare with such official data? One weakness in studies on Zimbabwean migration is the wide variation in the figures arrived at. For instance, former President Mbeki was once quoted as stating that there were three million Zimbabweans in South Africa, 400,000 in Mozambique and 200,000 in Botswana, which is a stark contrast to the numbers published in other studies (Solidarity Peace Trust 2004). There is an absolute need to refine the methodology of estimating the size of the diaspora. Whatever the actual numbers, the significance of the size of the Zimbabwean diaspora becomes clear when it is illustrated as amounting to the combined populations of Botswana and Swaziland (about three million). The geographic concentration of the diaspora has economic and political implications in relation to remittances and possible bilateral state programmes of repatriation of migrants at the opportune time in the future.

The importance of the diaspora has risen in tandem with its capacity to send remittances back to Zimbabwe in a context of a deep economic and humanitarian crisis, especially between 2000 and 2008. Remittances became a significant lifeline for many households in Zimbabwe during this period. As it was observed:

> the vast majority of Zimbabwean households with a migrant member in the region or abroad regularly receive remittances. Indeed, remittances from the Zimbabwean diaspora have reached such volumes that they kept the economy grinding along for a number of years .... The proportion of migrant remittances spent on food is among the highest in the world. (Crush and Tevera 2010:14)

The pivotal importance of remittances for livelihoods of Zimbabwean households was corroborated in our own field studies in 2005 and 2006 (Sachikonye and Bracking 2006, 2008). The field studies that covered 300 urban households in Harare and Bulawayo sought to assess the patterns of receipt and use of remittances by receiving households. The findings were both interesting and revealing.

First, a significant proportion of randomly sampled urban households

(about 50 per cent) in both cities received remittances. In 2005, the proportion of households that received remittances varied from 28 per cent
in low-density suburbs in Bulawayo to 78 per cent in low-density Harare
(Sachikonye and Bracking 2010). Some 57 per cent of households spent
remittances on food in 2006, up from 50 per cent in 2005, with a constant
95 per cent stating that they 'could now not be hungry' in both years.

Second, the field studies indicated that 90 per cent of the sampled
households were living below the poverty line, suggesting that middle-
class incomes had collapsed, thus reflecting the shrinking of the formal
and professional sectors (Sachikonye and Bracking 2006). Hence, remittances had become the principal catalyst of reproduction in traditionally
middle-class suburbs in Harare and Bulawayo.

Third, it was of interest that of the 149 households that received remittances, in only 38 of them were they in the form of cash. For the majority,
remittances came in the form of goods. Thus, perceiving remittance economies as principally money transfer economies can be misleading (Ibid. 22).

Fourth, the most common types of remitted goods were also the most
basic: food, medical and school fees, clothes and footwear, bearing testimony to the wider household reproduction crisis. Finally, it was significant
that of those who received cash remittances, about 60 per cent did so
through informal channels, while the remainder did so through banks,
money transfer agencies and private agents.

These findings led us to several broad conclusions. The first was that
there was:

> *a high proportion of the respondents whose household economic exchanges
> are outside the formal sector, in terms of receipt, use and storage thus indi-
> cating a critical role for the informal and personal sector in the reproduction
> of these households. Indeed, household reproduction in these two cities is
> underwritten by an internationalised, informalised system based in personal-
> ised migrant remittances. (Ibid.: 41)*

Second, it was clear from our research that a complex web of money and
goods transactions within the informal economy supported the Zimbabwean economy in myriad unrecorded ways. The country's economic
collapse between 2000 and 2008 was being offset by this informal, inter-
nationalised economy. In practical terms, it was difficult to see how some
of the households would survive without the informal remittance transfers.

Studies on remittances to rural Zimbabwe have also reached interesting and related findings. In one, about 80 per cent of sampled households in Matabeleland South received regular remittances which were used primarily for their livelihood needs (Maphosa 2010). Although some of the remittances (by 31 per cent of senders) were invested in small-scale agriculture (through stock purchase, scotch-carts, seeds and fertiliser), there was no significant investment in other income-generating ventures. As in urban households, food was the major item sent by remitters:

> almost all the remittance-receiving households mentioned food as one kind of remittance. This indicates the precarious food security situation in the area where most household income is spent on food because harvests are very low and barely last to the next harvest season. (Maphosa 2010:351).

This is another instance where remittances made a difference to chronic hunger and access to food. Their basic role in household reproduction is again highlighted but this time in the rural context.

Of course, there is a specific interest in estimates of the total annual cash remittances to Zimbabwe. As with estimating the actual size of the Zimbabwean diaspora, this has proved methodologically difficult, although this has not deterred the production of figures that vary widely from USD361 million per year in 2007 to between USD940 million and USD1.4 billion in 2009 (IFAD 2007; Magunha et al. 2009; Makina and Kanyenze 2010). A survey of Zimbabwean migrants in South Africa estimated that the average annual remittance was about R3,700 (about USD550) per annum. From the UK, remittances were between USD150 and USD300, and were sent more regularly. On the whole, the average remittance sent by a working migrant was estimated to be USD500 per year (Makina and Kanyenze 2010).

There is need for a more rigorous methodology to be used in calculating the size of remittances, and against excessive enthusiasm about remittances as a new development mantra. Despite the euphoria expressed by international financial institutions and multilateral development agencies, remittances are too diffuse, diverse and largely informalised in their reach to act as a major stimulant of development. For instance, major remittance economies such as Lesotho and Cape Verde in Africa and the Philippines in Asia are not outstanding models of remittance-powered development. We would largely concur with the observation that:

> the Zimbabwean ruling elite views remittances as somehow belonging to

them, and punitive taxation regimes and spurious taxes are often devised to capture some of the income sent by migrants. The government's 'Home Link' scheme failed because the indirect tax built into the scheme was built in relation to the value of money …. Spoils politics undermines the pecuniary value of remittances, by reproducing chronic scarcity in the goods markets, and by failing the citizens in terms of the welfare obligations of the government to the poor. (Crush and Tevera 2010:38)

These specific conditions prevailed prior to the inauguration of the Inclusive Government in 2009, but it is still too early to conclude that the more stable conditions since then have resulted in most remittances going through formal channels. The more remittances enter through formal channels, the greater their positive effect on the financial sector and the wider economy.

Those who will design a policy to encourage the developmental value of remittances would do well to take into account the critique that has been mounted against remittances as a major growth stimulant. The critique argues that in many countries it is difficult to convert remittances into sustainable productive capacity; that remittance income is rarely used for productive purposes but for direct consumption; and that very little is directed to income-earning job-creating investment (Hamilton 2003). Furthermore, remittances tend to encourage import consumption and create dependency. In sum, while remittances were extremely useful at the height of Zimbabwe's economic crisis, when the state was almost bankrupt, by providing food and other basic necessities for survival, their development value tends to be exaggerated. It is unlikely that in the long term they can compensate for lost scarce skills and the erosion of the tax base created by the brain drain. Moreover, the frequent deportations of remittance senders without necessary papers and permits from South Africa, Botswana and the UK make flows insecure and volatile.

Culture, Values and Ideas

The extreme changes in politics, economics and society during the lost decades could not fail to produce shifts in the spheres of culture, values and ideas. Things could not remain the same (Bourdillon 1997). For instance, HIV/AIDS and large-scale migration acutely affected these various spheres. The seismic pandemic that is HIV/AIDS, which has resulted in the infection of millions of adults and created over one million orphans, could not fail to have a profound effect on the family as an institution. First, the social fabric of the extended family system showed signs of erosion as the close bonds that held family members together weakened and disappeared (ZHDR 2003). In some instances, sick parents or stepparents were forced to send their children to work or take them out of school. Traditional roles, duties and responsibilities of family members became blurred as HIV/AIDS placed additional demands and pressures on orphans, particularly economic uncertainty, stigmatisation and emotional insecurity (Ibid.). Youth were being deprived of life skills and sex education, which are instrumental in establishing a code of conduct between men and women and husbands and wives. In various surveys, the majority of parents attributed early sexual activity and multiple or casual partners to the disappearance of family life education, the direct result of parents dying in their 30s and 40s. Grandparents often found themselves unable to control or discipline adolescents. Since the welfare system was under extreme pressure, the elderly found themselves doing care work under conditions of poverty, stigma, abuse and lack of support, resulting from witchcraft accusations and other challenges faced in old age (Ibid.).

According to estimates, the total number of orphans – as a result of HIV/AIDS and other causes – in Zimbabwean society is about 1.3 million, or nearly ten per cent of the total population. This would be an enormous social and economic burden on any society. But this particular burden exists in a society in which the young (the under-18s) constitute 6.02 million, which is slightly less than 50 per cent of the total population. This double dependence of orphans and the young is very burdensome in an economy that has experienced such a deep crisis as Zimbabwe's has done. Furthermore, orphans are particularly vulnerable to a number of ill-effects, including:

> poor socialisation through transfer to various relatives who offer diverse care and support, poor nutrition, inadequate schooling through poor school performance and dropout, psychological scarring from the loss of parents resulting in delinquent and criminal behaviours and physical, psychological and sexual abuse. (ZHDR 2003:88)

For its part, migration can affect cohesion in families if spouses and children live, work and study in different countries. Lack of parental care due to one or both parents having to work in a different country can cause some of the emotional and psychological problems mentioned above.

Marriage problems and break-ups have also been caused by absence of spouses working for prolonged periods in different countries, or as a result of stress from the redefinition and application of different gender roles in the adopted cultural environment (Pasura 2010).

One reflection of the mounting pressures on the family as a unit and the despair due to the increase in adult and infant mortality has been the swelling of numbers of those who have sought solace in religion. Countless new churches have mushroomed in the last decade, ostensibly to offer protection to followers from epidemics, witchcraft and 'bad luck'. They include evangelical churches, *Vapostori* or 'Apostolic' churches which draw on charismatic approaches to worship, the use of prophecy and healing by prayer and water. This introspective approach to religion and life may have inadvertently disempowered worshippers and communities through their withdrawal from active community life and from political action that could bring change to the authoritarianism that originally triggered the multiple socio-economic crises under which Zimbabwean society labours.

The strengthening of patriarchy and traditional authority is another consequence of the shifts in culture. Political and traditional elites have deliberately cultivated what has been termed 'dodaism' which extols 'virtues' of manhood or masculinity. 'Dodaism' is a term used in southern Africa to capture the combination of patriarchal anxiety and deformed masculinity (Campbell 2003). President Mugabe described as real men *'amadoda sibili'* those who he chose to constitute his Cabinet in 2002; they were to be tested in the contests with Western powers led by Tony Blair and George Bush. The ideology of dodaism was also aimed against homosexuals, who became the objects of some of Mugabe's harshest criticism. Traditional authorities were consciously cultivated so that they would deliver the rural vote at election time. Chiefs were not encouraged to be apolitical or credible custodians of culture in their communities; they were instead required to be actively partisan in politics, food distribution and local development projects. There was a resurgence of interest in traditional practices, including polygamy, which was given the trendy urban term of 'small house'. As it was observed:

> in the media, and in popular culture, there were numerous displays of the symbols of male bravery and victory in liberation. Annual celebrations and tributes to the 'freedom fighters' dominated the discourse on African nationalism. (Ibid.:131)

The widespread use of coercion and violence during land reform and elections was conducted within the context of aggressive dodaism.

Finally, there was growing politicisation of public culture and rituals such as those of weddings, funerals and commemorations. Politicians exploited opportunities of weddings and funerals to make political speeches and mobilise support. At funerals at Heroes' Acre, President Mugabe perfected the art of criticising what he termed 'sell-outs and stooges' of Western imperialists who themselves were often instructed 'to go to hell'. Occasions that should have been marked by sorrow and respect, or celebration, were transformed into political rallies. In addition, ZANU-PF consciously used celebrations such as musical galas to recreate the wartime *pungwe* strategy of politicisation.

As it was pointed out:

> the musical gala formed a key part of the revival of cultural nationalism, and aimed to popularise the commemoration of national days and 'national heroes' that had long been part of the elite memorialism of 1980s and 1990s.... Like the pungwe, galas sought to instil 'patriotism' into those most likely to vote for the opposition MDC, such as youths and urbanites. Through the mixture of new 'urban grooves' tunes and old Chimurenga songs, the gala sought to seduce the 'born-frees' into the nationalist project. The televised nature of all music galas ensured that urban residents were reached .... The national imaginary that was promoted through music galas was by no means an inclusive definition of the 'nation', but should rather be seen as the mediation of the 'party-nation'. (Ndlovu-Gatsheni and Willem 2009:943-65)

We cannot exhaust here the various ways in which culture was affected and shaped during the lost decades. What is clear is that the ruling elite pursued an agenda to shape the consciousness of the population, even if this resulted in the distortion of traditional and modern culture.

Our discussion of political culture would not be complete without reference to the growth of the personality cult of Robert Mugabe, and the debate about criteria for choosing 'National Heroes'. The present decade has witnessed significant emphasis on the qualities and indispensable leadership of Mugabe. Not only is his birthday (20 February) celebrated in a high-profile manner, but his image emblazons T-shirts, dresses, shirts, wrappers and caps of his supporters. The 20th February movement is the epitome of the Mugabe personality cult. However, other manifestations include the lobby for him to be made a 'Life President'.

The debate about who should be designated as a 'National Hero' intensified during the tenure of the Inclusive Government in 2009–2010. For the first time, ZANU-PF admitted that only those chosen by its party would be designated 'National Heroes' and buried at the shrine that is Heroes' Acre in Harare. The qualifications of involvement in the nationalist struggle and liberation war were not sufficient according to these criteria. This explained, in retrospect, why nationalist leaders like Ndabaningi Sithole and Noel Mukono of Zanu-Ndonga, and Gibson Sibanda of MDC-M had been denied 'National Hero' status. However, another dimension to the debate was added when Welshman Mabena indicated that were he designated a 'National Hero' he would not like to be buried at Heroes' Acre. When his wish was respected by his family after death from natural causes in early 2011, it caused much embarrassment and anger within the ZANU-PF leadership, adding another twist to the controversy over 'National Hero' status.

Shifts in culture inherently involve changes in values in society. During the lost decades there was a steady growth in individualism as against collective community spirit, and towards instant gratification instead of sustained efforts at transparent accumulation process. As civic values have weakened and collective attempts at protest have been ruthlessly crushed, political culture has been distinguished by high levels of mistrust, fear and individualism (Masunungure 2000; Sachikonye 2011). Voter apathy and migration are some of the expressions of individualism in a context of decreased faith in the efficacy of collective movements and strategies for change. Although civil society organisations and political parties have not faltered in their mobilisation campaigns, it has been difficult to address the often termed 'docility' of Zimbabwean citizens under authoritarian conditions. 'Instant gratification' is visible in increasing levels of corruption at all layers of society, from the average worker to the police, business leaders and politicians. In an economy that experienced many endemic shortages, shortcuts to access goods and services became a matter of survival at all layers of society. Both 'small-time' and 'grand' corruption co-existed as citizens entered thousands of corrupt 'deals' to access basic goods or create profiteering opportunities. During the lost decades, the media was often awash with reports of corruption in government departments, parastatals, private sector companies, local authorities, NGOs and even in churches. In international corruption rankings, Zimbabwe scored poorly (Transparency International 2010).

The role models for many became business tycoons. Employing

'get-rich-quick' methods, they amassed considerable wealth using questionable means. They spent lavishly, building expensive mansions in exclusive suburbs and purchasing luxury vehicles. This new, rich elite also donated lavishly to sports teams and other beneficiaries to raise their public relations profiles. The new values extolled were wealth, opulence and deal-making by hook or crook. Brashness, ruthlessness and opaqueness replaced decency, probity and transparency in social and business relationships. Community spirit and welfarist values were downgraded. For many, life became 'nasty, brutish and short' during the decade 2000 to 2008. Levels of public morality declined considerably, and social cohesion was threatened.

Ideas

The crisis and contestation in the economic and political realms during the difficult decade of 1998–2008 sparked intense debates between different schools of intellectuals. Unlike the earlier decades, when debates were civil and conducted in the same framework as we saw in Chapter 4, those during this latter period were marked by rancour and polarising rhetoric (Mandaza and Sachikonye 1991; Raftopoulos 2002; Tendi 2008). The broad schools of intellectuals can loosely be defined by their political bearings: those that supported the ZANU-PF party and state, and those who opposed them. This division was also reflected in the editorial stances of the media. The intellectuals who were provided space in state papers such as the *Herald*, *Chronicle* and the *Sunday Mail* and on state radio and television were mostly state-aligned, while those who contributed to independent papers such as the *Independent*, *Standard* and *Daily News* were exponents of democracy, human rights and greater space for civil society and opposition parties. External radio stations such as Studio 7 and SWR Africa drew largely on the latter school for analysis of developments inside the country. Unfortunately, the two sets of intellectuals did not use the same papers and electronic media to debate directly. Instead, they debated indirectly through media of their preference. In part, this was also due to restrictions imposed by the media. For instance, intellectuals who opposed the authoritarian state were shut out of state radio and television, while those extolled it were not given space in the independent media. This diminished the freshness and directness of the debate as each set of intellectuals found refuge in a favourable habitat.

In spite of this defect, the debates were nevertheless robust. They ranged from how to interpret Zimbabwe's history since colonization, to how to assess land reform and to issues of democracy, human rights, relations with the West, sanctions and gay and lesbian rights. With speakers drawn mainly from the University of Zimbabwe (UZ), but also from the newer universities of NUST and Midlands State University, Harare Polytechnic and Zimbabwean lecturers at several foreign universities, the debates were marked by considerable vitriol. One of the most prolific backers of the Mugabe government after an early period of lampooning it was Jonathan Moyo, who had taught political science at UZ. His reward was the post of Minister of Information and Publicity, a position which he used effectively to aggressively project messages of the government and to introduce legislation to emasculate both local independent media and foreign journalists. Other prominent intellectuals who wrote in favour of the Mugabe government included Joseph Kurebwa, a political scientist, and Claude Mararike, a sociologist. Others who were provided a great of space in the print and electronic media were Tafataona Mahoso, a media specialist, Sheunesu Mupepereki, a crop expert, and Godfrey Chikowore, a development studies specialist. Among foreign universities, George Shire at the Open University in the UK could be relied upon by the Mugabe government to project its decisions and policies in a more favourable light. Independent scholars who were given space in the state media included Sam Moyo, especially on land reform, and, on governance and foreign affairs, Ibbo Mandaza, until he joined a new party called *Mavambo* in 2008. Together with a number of columnists such as Caesar Zvayi and others from the *Herald* and the *Sunday Mail*, the Mugabe government had a phalanx of intellectuals who provided a conceptual and ideological defence of its policies during a decade of crisis.

Prominent opposition intellectuals included UZ political scientists John Makumbe, Elphas Mukonoweshuro and the late Masipula Sithole; law lecturers Lovemore Madhuku, Welshman Ncube and Munyaradzi Gwisai; the mathematician Heneri Dzinotyiwei; and development studies expert Brian Raftopoulos. Censored by the state media, they mainly published in the independent papers and scholarly journals. This group of intellectuals was relatively small, and with time it suffered attrition through migration. However, Mukonoweshuro and Dzinotyiwei would later become ministers in the MDC-T team and Welshman Ncube in the MDC-M team in the Inclusive Government. However, what might have been engaging debates between the two broad schools of thought on patriotic history, democracy and land reform:

> degenerated into crude labelling on both sides. ZANU-PF-aligned intellec-
> tuals thought critical public intellectuals were western-trained intellectual
> sell-outs whose 'African-ness' was questionable, 'unpatriotic' and 'middle-
> class' with a peasant background but without rural homes because they suffer
> from an identity crisis. Some ZANU-PF aligned intellectuals were in fact Ameri-
> can trained, highlighting that 'western trained intellectuals are sell-outs' was
> simply a construction. Critical public intellectuals, for their part, labelled
> ZANU-PF intellectuals as an irrational and hate-mongering assemblage of
> history distorters hired by the Mugabe government. (Tendi 2008:379-96)

The debate will continue but it would have been more invaluable if it had been able to be conducted directly, in the same forums and media. It is a sad commentary of the state of censorship under the authoritarian state that the two schools of policy intellectuals cannot engage each other directly for the benefit of the public and development of ideas.

Conclusion

Most analyses of the Zimbabwean crisis do not attempt the Herculean task of integrating an examination of the inter-linkages between politi-cal and economic developments and the deeper changes in society. This is a difficult task. In this chapter, however, we have not shied away from making an attempt to reflect on those linkages. It was our overall argu-ment that the state of livelihoods during the lost decades, especially between 1998 and 2008, and the subsequent flows of migration cannot be fully understood in isolation from the governance and economic con-ditions explored in early chapters of this book. Similarly, shifts in culture and values, although less visible and dramatic, cannot be explained per-ceptively without an understanding of the structural and social changes in state–society relations, which we assessed in Chapters 7 and 8.

This chapter began by providing a narrative of trends in patterns of wealth and poverty and their effects on class formation and dismember-ment due to the crisis; prominent in the latter process was the drastic decline of the middle class in the period 1998–2008. This was the con-sequence of the economic crisis and out-migration, and also of the entrenchment of authoritarianism. Other effects of the crisis were dimin-ished access to basic social services of education and health, marking a significant reversal of gains that had been made during the first 15 years of independence. Even more dramatic – and tragic – were the effects of the cholera epidemic, which illustrated the virtual breakdown of basic infrastructure of water and sanitation, and of HIV/AIDS, to which the state initially responded in lukewarm fashion for a decade, and thus let its prevalence go unchecked until levels reached epidemic proportions. In our assessment of the dynamics of migration, we have argued the need to pay equal attention to the economic and political factors behind it. The methodologies for estimating the numbers involved in migration require greater rigour, as do those that calculate remittance flows, if the discourse is to go beyond guesswork. Finally, we examined how Zimbabwean culture, values and intellectual discourse have undergone change as a result of domestic and external developments in the spheres of economics, politics and ideas.

9

Punching above its Weight in Foreign Relations

Introduction

How did Zimbabwe manage its foreign policy and relations during the lost decades, especially during the turbulence of 1998 to 2008? Given its systemic decline, the country has failed to punch above its weight, despite the bellicose rhetoric and expansive worldview of Robert Mugabe that posited the contrary. Were there missed opportunities for Zimbabwean diplomacy, particularly in what has been termed 'economic diplomacy', during these decades? This last chapter of the book explores these issues in a broad critique of the Mugabe government's foreign policy and external relations.

Several factors determine a country's capacity to wield power and influence in international relations as well as its strategic standing in the eyes of global powers and other countries. These include its geographical location, population size, and economic weight, possession of strategic resources such as oil, defence capability and track record in dealing with challenges such as terrorism.

By African standards, Zimbabwe is a medium-sized power of 12 million people with a relatively weak economy compared to bigger African powers such as South Africa, Kenya, Egypt and Nigeria. In terms of its importance as a developing country, Zimbabwe is of limited strategic advantage to a unipolar world in which the possession of valuable assets such as oil and uranium and having a key role in the campaign against terrorism and Islamic fundamentalism confer geopolitical advantage. From this perspective, Zimbabwe would not score as highly as would South Africa, Angola, Kenya, Ethiopia, Nigeria or Egypt, for example. Yet Zimbabwe has been distinguished by the fiery rhetoric and aggressiveness of its foreign policy, especially with respect to Western powers. In this chapter we will explore the basis and consequences of this ambitious grandstanding in Zimbabwe's foreign policy.

Zimbabwe's Foreign Policy and National Interests

Historical experience has been a major determinant in Zimbabwe's foreign policy. The overall experience of its struggle for liberation in the 1960s and 1970s was a formative influence on its foreign relations. Achieving independence on the back of military and political support from socialist powers, principally China and the Soviet Union, and in a regional neighbourhood of apartheid South Africa and colonial Namibia, the major element in Zimbabwe's foreign policy was support for liberation movements. This was not limited to southern Africa; it extended to movements in Western Sahara, Palestine and East Timor. Although it became more or less anachronistic in the post-Cold War context, another feature of Zimbabwe's foreign policy was an expressed commitment to non-alignment. In summing up the guiding principles of Zimbabwe's foreign policy, the Ministry of Foreign Affairs stated that:

> *Zimbabwe is guided by its belief in self-determination and support for liberation movements, adherence to the principle of national sovereignty; respect for territorial integrity of all countries; promotion of the principle of equality among nations; belief in non-discrimination, whether based on colour, creed, religion or other forms; and the promotion of peaceful settlement of disputes and non-interference in the internal affairs of other states. (Ministry of Foreign Affairs, November 2010)*

Possessing a creed-like status is the emphasis on the triad of 'national sovereignty', 'territorial integrity' and 'non-interference in internal affairs'. These are principles that Zimbabwe deployed to maximum effect in a defensive sense during the lost decades to deflect criticism of its authoritarian domestic policies.

Historically, therefore, there has been a radical kernel in the framework and content of the country's foreign policy. Soon after independence, it was Robert Mugabe, then Prime Minister, who reiterated these principles at the United Nations (UN) in New York in 1980. He identified them as:

1. *National sovereignty and equality among nations*
2. *Positive non-alignment and peaceful co-existence among nations*
3. *Non-racialism at home and abroad*
4. *The attainment of a socialist, egalitarian and democratic society*
5. *The right of all peoples to self-determination and independence.*

The ideological content in some of these principles is clear: the emphasis on non-racialism and socialism has the unmistakable context of the anti-apartheid struggle and the Cold War contest between socialism and capitalism, respectively. However, as we will observe below, the ideological content in present-day foreign policy remains significant.

There are also pragmatic considerations that are taken into consideration in foreign policy-making. It is recognised that foreign policy is an extension of domestic policy 'since it is the supreme national interest that drives the conception of a country's foreign policy' (Ministry of Foreign Affairs November 2010). Furthermore, the fundamental principles of national security, national economic wellbeing and international image that transcend the government of the day formed the foundation of Zimbabwe's foreign policy (Ibid.). The pragmatic focus on national interest is illustrated in the emphasis on political, economic and cultural co-operation with its neighbours, and in the importance attached to membership and activities in Southern African Development Cooperation (SADC), Common Market for Eastern and Southern Africa (COMESA) and the African Union (AU). In addition, Zimbabwe uses its membership of the G15 and G77 groups of countries as well as the Non-Aligned Movement, together with its participation in other organisations promoting international peace, security and co-operation through the UN, to pursue its national interests (Ibid.).

The concept of 'national interest' itself has not only been used as an analytical tool to identify objectives of foreign policy but also as an all-embracing concept of political discourse to justify particular policy preferences of government (Badza 2005). It refers to the basic determinants that guide government policy in relation to the external environment. At the root of the idea of 'national interest' is the principle of national security and socio-economic wellbeing. However, the concept can lend itself to abuse. As it was argued:

> Despite its centrality in inter-state interactions, the concept of national interest, like that of national security, has occasionally been rendered vulnerable to abuse by the elites especially in less developed countries. The situation becomes worse in less democratic societies where foreign policy is generally perceived as a sole preserve of the ruling party in general and of the Executive head of state in particular. (Ibid.:54)

In such a context, there is no transparency in foreign policy-making and administration, as parliament's and civil society's roles are negligible. During the lost decades, foreign policy was centralised in the Presidency, with the Ministry of Foreign Affairs playing a largely administrative role. This was acknowledged by the Ministry, which stated that the Head of State set the parameters of foreign policy while ministries moulded and refined it (Ministry of Foreign Affairs, November 2010). Although reference is made to Parliament's involvement, its role is clearly marginal.

As a medium-sized African power, there are clear limits to the leverage Zimbabwe can bring to bear on regional and international affairs. Early analysis of the external environment soon after independence in 1980 argued that the dominance of international finance capital and the imperatives of imperialist policy in southern Africa defined the broad parameters of state action on the external front (Mandaza 1986). Although it was in foreign policy that the government was most keen to project the impression of independent action, international relations by definition prescribed and proscribed the limits of that 'independent action' on the part of the state. This conception of international relations:

> *raises the question of hierarchy in global politics, with the major powers not only defining the arena of international politics but also controlling it; and the small states, in their 'foreign policies', merely reflecting or at best singing to the music of these giants. (Ibid.: 63)*

For its part, Zimbabwe has not been modest in the conception of its foreign policy. Instead, it has been ambitious and somewhat confrontational where prudence and nuanced diplomacy might have achieved better results during the lost decades. Let us now turn to specific regional arenas of its foreign policy to examine its orientation and limitations.

Foreign Relations and Interventions in Southern Africa

Perhaps inevitably, Zimbabwe's foreign policy during the lost decades had southern Africa as its centrepiece. This was primarily due to the exigencies of liberation struggles in the 1980s in Namibia and South Africa and the destabilisation campaigns of the apartheid regime, particularly in Mozambique and Angola. Zimbabwe's primary national interests were the safeguarding of its national security and the provision of diplomatic and material support to liberation movements. In addition, key areas of its foreign policy revolved around economic co-operation in the Southern African Development Coordination Conference (SADCC) that was formed in 1980 and its successor organisation, SADC, which was founded in 1992. Finally, in order to protect its interests, Zimbabwe executed military intervention in Mozambique against RENAMO guerrillas between 1985 and 1992. This was not the last military intervention, as the conflict in the Democratic Republic of the Congo (DRC) would later suck in Zimbabwe's forces in a more controversial way.

Zimbabwe's own attainment of independence brought with it admission into the club of Frontline States (FLS) of southern Africa, whose primary objective was provision of moral and material support to liberation movements in the region. This exclusive club consisted of founding members Angola, Botswana, Lesotho, Mozambique, Tanzania and Zambia; Zimbabwe was admitted in 1980. In response to changing dynamics, a wider economic grouping was founded as SADCC, as we saw above, ostensibly to 'reduce dependence on apartheid South Africa'. (Lusaka Declaration of 1980). Zimbabwe's membership and role in the FLS and SADCC were consistent with its principles of supporting rights to self-determination and national interest in regional economic co-operation. At the same time, pragmatism in foreign policy was expressed through refraining from providing rear military bases for liberation forces in Namibia and South Africa. This did not, however, protect Zimbabwe from sabotage attacks by South Africa in 1986.

Military intervention in Mozambique was an expression of political support to the Frelimo government that had been active in supporting Zimbabwe's own liberation struggle in the 1970s. Another key objective was the protection of its major transport artery to the sea through the Beira Corridor. From an original contingent of 5,000, the Zimbabwean forces swelled to about 10,000 at the height of the conflict. Zimbabwe's role was not confined to the military containment of RENAMO, which received the bulk of its support from the apartheid regime. It was scarcely surprising that Zimbabwe was a central player in peace negotiations between Frelimo and RENAMO. On the whole, Zimbabwe's foreign policy in southern Africa during the first 15 years of independence was judged successful by one analyst, who said that:

> by 1989, the Beira Corridor was safe … and South Africa had been dragged to the conference table over Angola and Namibia …. There were, altogether, 12 rounds of talks in Rome beginning in July 1990 and ending in October 1992. It was Mugabe who suggested Rome as the venue for the signing of the Frelimo–Renamo accord. (Chan 2003:39)

In retrospect, this Accord was viewed as a major triumph for Zimbabwean diplomacy.

Zimbabwe's other major foreign policy challenge and military intervention was in the DRC, where it attempted to shore up the regime of Laurent Kabila in 1998. This was a more ambitious intervention underpinned by motives of accumulation and unrealistic projections of its military power. The intervention caused divisions in SADC and among countries such as Rwanda and Uganda in the Great Lakes region and drew condemnation from domestic and external sources. The motives of intervention by a medium-sized power far away from its own borders were questioned by civil society and opposition groups in Zimbabwe and by external powers, including the European Union and multilateral institutions such as the International Monetary Fund (IMF). In one of the more authoritative assessments of the intervention it was recalled that Carl Von Clausewitz, an esteemed nineteenth-century Prussian military theorist, had argued that no one starts a war without being clear as to its political purpose. Hence:

> In the case of Zimbabwe, there were both economic and political objectives in the deployment to assist Kabila. The economic objective was to secure Inga Dam, from which Zimbabwe received a third of its electricity. The political objective was to defend the territorial integrity of a SADC member state. The political objective of the Kabila regime was to stay in power, irrespective of the democratic claims by the Congolese people. The political objective of the Angolans was to deny a rear base and military support to UNITA .... Thus Zimbabwe was being drawn into a war in which, among the 'allies', the political objectives were different. (Campbell 2003:206)

In this first African 'world war', the motives of the belligerent states, Uganda and Rwanda, were also different, but nevertheless poised to profit from the rich natural resources of DRC. The motives of the various forces were thus complex and competitive.

What the DRC campaign exposed was Zimbabwe's limited capacity to prosecute an intervention far removed from its geographical borders, and for mixed motives of personal accumulation by senior army officers and for the conventional safeguarding of territorial integrity in a sprawling, underdeveloped state with weak infrastructure. The military reverses sustained by Zimbabwe were considerable during the fall of Kindu in 1998, the siege of Ikela and the battle of Pweto in 1999. Not only did the intervention prove expensive at about USD300 million per year, but the Zimbabwean casualties were also significant. After the battle at Kabalo in December 1998, in which 47 troops lost their lives, Zimbabwean authorities reportedly stopped disclosing casualty figures (Ibid.). Zimbabwe started its intervention with 3,000 troops, but by the time of the siege of Ikela the deployment had increased to 12,000. There were other contradictions that stoked the criticism of the intervention in the DRC, namely:

> the DRC deployment gave the government another opportunity to represent itself as a regional political and military power, at a time when its leaders were begging for international aid for resettlement of small farmers. The government could find resources to equip the army and air force but begged for money for health and education. (Ibid.: 206)

The DRC intervention demonstrated an instance of over-reach by a medium-sized power. The capacity of Zimbabwe's air force was found wanting in the sprawling DRC territory. Promises of 'war self-financing' proved largely a mirage. The devotion of scarce national resources to a distant conflict generated domestic criticism of the intervention and foreign policy associated with it. To critics, there was no national interest being pursued in the DRC conflict. Instead, according to some analysts, sectional interests were involved:

> What the Zimbabweans did was to enter the struggle on the side of one of the factions and, in the process, to secure control of a vast swathe of mineral deposits with which Mugabe has been able to buy off military dissent – or buy in a guarantee of senior military support for his own government during the farm invasions and the resulting economic meltdown. (Chan 2006:180)

Following the DRC debacle, one looks hard but in vain for any outstanding foreign policy success by the Mugabe government as it slid into a decade-long political and economic crisis. Punching above its weight had created enormous challenges on the domestic and external fronts.

Zimbabwe's Relations with South Africa and the Wider Continent

As the political and economic crisis deepened, especially after 2000, perhaps no comparable topic evoked as intense a debate as how Zimbabwe–South African relations were being conducted. The key protagonists in that relationship were Thabo Mbeki, Robert Mugabe and Morgan Tsvangirai. Clearly, other major players on the 'Zimbabwe Question' included SADC, and, to a lesser extent, the AU and the UN. Most focus was on Thabo Mbeki in relation to the question of whether he would deploy South African power and influence to usher a process of change in Zimbabwe. Did Mbeki live up to international expectations, or to Zimbabwean aspirations for that change? There has been an intense debate on this issue (Lodge 2004; McKinley 2004; SPT 2007; SALO 2010).

Several developments beginning in March 2002 put South Africa's mediation efforts to severe test. The first related to the Mbeki government's assessment of the 2002 presidential election and the second to its response to the position taken by the Commonwealth on Zimbabwe, namely, its suspension in 2002 and the extension of suspension in 2003. South Africa's election assessment and response were widely perceived as tacitly siding with the Mugabe government. Hence, there began sustained criticism of the 'quiet diplomacy' approach, within both South Africa and Zimbabwe (Sachikonye 2004).

Prior to the 2002 election, South Africa's approach to the Zimbabwe Question had appeared even-handed, befitting its potential role of mediator between ZANU-PF and the MDC. However, a puzzling development was the endorsement of the conduct and outcome of the 2002 election by a government-sponsored South African observer mission headed by Sam Motsuenyane. Its verdict that the result was 'legitimate' came fairly soon after the publication of the election outcome. (The Mbeki government subsequently received a great deal of flak for the mission's somewhat enthusiastic endorsement). This view was contradicted by the assessments of the SADC Parliamentary Forum, the Zimbabwe Election Support Network and the Commonwealth Observer Group, all of which concluded that the election conduct and outcome were deeply flawed. Significantly, an examination of SADC's norms and standards for elections indicated that 11 of the most significant standards were flouted during the 2002 election. These included standards relating to voter registration, election monitoring, conduct of the election process itself in the cities of Harare and Chitungwiza and access to the public media.

The readiness of the South Africans to whitewash the election's conduct and outcome was quickly followed by the undertaking (together with Nigeria) of a rapid initiative to persuade ZANU-PF and the MDC to enter negotiations for a government of national unity.

A similarly puzzling position that South Africa took on the Zimbabwe Question emerged during the Commonwealth summit in Abuja in December 2003. It would appear that the Mbeki government had been deeply uncomfortable with Zimbabwe being raised as a major issue of debate at both the 2002 Brisbane and 2003 Abuja summits. As a matter of principle, it had been against the suspension of Zimbabwe from the Commonwealth at both summits. The Mbeki government had in fact pushed for the lifting of the suspension, despite the fact that Zimbabwe had ignored the corrective measures on governance and electoral reform recommended by the Commonwealth. The persistence of repression that came with the enactment of more sweeping legislation such as POSA and AIPPA underscored Zimbabwe's arrogance towards the calls for reforms from the Commonwealth and other international organisations. Nevertheless, it still came as a surprise that Zimbabwe's major defender at the Abuja summit was Thabo Mbeki.

The South African leader would have preferred a quiet diplomacy approach to ensure that Zimbabwe rejoined the Commonwealth rather than seeing its suspension extended. However, the length to which South Africa went to oppose the line orchestrated by most Commonwealth states stirred surprise in many quarters. By the end of 2003 there was not much to show for its quiet diplomacy. The political and economic crisis in Zimbabwe showed no signs of abating. The succession issue in ZANU-PF had been neutralised at its December 2003 annual conference and repression continued.

Perspectives on South Africa's quiet diplomacy ranged from the sceptical to the critical to those that were supportive and passionately defensive about this approach – very few held a neutral position on the issue. Those who were sceptical pointed to the fact that there had been no change in the political and economic situation in Zimbabwe since the inauguration of quiet diplomacy and that, in some instances, the situation had actually worsened. In South Africa, this position was articulated by a section of civil society and the press, typically along the lines of this critique:

As the battle lines have been drawn, one of the more puzzling realisations for democrats across the Southern Africa region has been that Mugabe does not fear the group of people with the power to bring him to his knees more quickly and peacefully than anyone else. This group is the South African government …. Is our government frozen by fear on the cusp of a difficult decision? Does Mugabe know that the ANC is so wedded to the former liberation movements that alone constitute legitimate governments in post-struggle states that it will not do anything it believes might endanger ZANU-PF's hegemony in Zimbabwe? (Mail and Guardian, 23 February 2001)

Such sentiments were apparently shared by much of the mainstream press, fuelled by the less than transparent communication of the government's policy on Zimbabwe. Individual ANC leaders including the former Defence Minister, Mosiuao Lakota, and the former Reserve Bank Governor, Tito Mboweni, expressed their exasperation with the policy. Mboweni remarked that Zimbabwe's lawlessness and collapsing economy were contributing to the depreciation of the South African Rand.

The independent Zimbabwean press, like that in South Africa, was also critical of Mbeki's 'quiet diplomacy'. In 2003, the *Daily News*, then the country's largest independent newspaper, observed that:

> *Mbeki has virtually endorsed the two elections (of 2000 and 2002) that others have condemned as grievously flawed .... He has pleaded for a chance to apply his quiet diplomacy, which many believe to be responsible for Mugabe's mounting arrogance. (Daily News, 26 September 2003)*

True, quiet diplomacy began to be associated with developments for which it was not directly responsible, such as the persistent repression that the Mbeki government itself condemned.

Nevertheless, the view spread in Zimbabwe that the policy was an alibi, if not an excuse, for inaction. For its part, the MDC was generally sceptical of quiet diplomacy; despite the fact that it was consulted by the Mbeki government, it showed little trust in the process. Its position, rightly or wrongly, was that the ANC government leaned towards the ZANU-PF government and that Mbeki's recognition and consultation of the MDC was grudgingly extended to it late in the day. The MDC thus urged South Africa to employ its economic muscle, including sanctions, to force a change in the policies of the Mugabe government.

On the whole, however, the critics of quiet diplomacy did not recommend a credible alternative, except that of coercive sanctions. This was often highlighted by those who defended the approach, for example, Foreign Minister Dhlamini-Zuma:

> *Our goal in foreign affairs is good neighbourliness, we build bridges across countries. Don't advocate war with Zimbabwe, we won't do it. (Ministry of Foreign Affairs briefing, Cape Town, 16 February 2001)*

This was echoed by Deputy Foreign Minister Aziz Pahad's comments on pressure from Western powers for South Africa to take a stronger line against the Mugabe government:

> *We don't believe that their megaphone diplomacy and screaming from the*

rooftops has helped .... If it is not diplomacy we pursue in Zimbabwe, then it is war. We will not go war with Zimbabwe. (Sunday Times, 29 September 2002)

Certainly, none of the critics of quiet diplomacy advocated military intervention. The colourful rhetoric about 'not going to war' was a device to pre-empt the basic criticism that the approach was not bearing fruit. In sum, the advocates of quiet diplomacy often appeared to overreact to criticism. Some commentators described this defensive reaction as a red herring:

Contrary to what Mbeki says, we are not called upon to invade Zimbabwe ... but we are called upon to speak for the values upon which our democracy is built. (John Kane-Berman, Business Day, 30 October 2002)

The Mugabe government itself was ambivalent towards quiet diplomacy. While the policy bought the Mugabe government time until 2008, it did not appear to fully trust the Mbeki government. Whenever the latter criticised Zimbabwe's policies or actions, there were sharp comments from Harare. In one such comment, it was remarked that South African government criticism:

neatly dovetails into Britain's grand plan for a global coalition against Zimbabwe .... A clear pattern is emerging of a build-up against Zimbabwe, and South Africa's complicity in a plot to overthrow ZANU-PF ... a betrayal difficult to stomach. (Herald, 3 December 2001)

Some of the more acerbic comments about South Africa's quiet diplomacy approach emanated from Jonathan Moyo, who was Minister of Information and Publicity from 2000 to 2004. His colourful rhetoric matched that of South African ministers when they talked of 'not going to war with Zimbabwe'. However, it did not disguise the fact that the Mugabe government would be concerned and feel betrayed if South Africa employed economic muscle against it.

It took victory by the MDC-T in the March 2008 election to lend greater urgency and enhanced prospects for quiet diplomacy, which culminated in the signing of a Global Political Agreement (GPA) that heralded the formation of a Government of National Unity (GNU). Even so, the GPA was tilted towards ZANU-PF, which amassed presidential powers and key ministries. The differences over quiet diplomacy were not smoothed out easily. A famous exchange of Notes between Mbeki and Tsvangirai in the aftermath of the GPA revealed ingrained mistrust between them.

It would be misleading to imply that Zimbabwe–South African relations were limited to the issue and process of quiet diplomacy. There were interactions over trade and role of the Organ of Politics and Security in SADC; there were differences over these issues during the Mandela presidency. Indeed, there was public South African criticism of Zimbabwe's intervention in the DRC during Mugabe's chairmanship of the SADC Organ (Campbell 2003).

With respect to wider African issues, Zimbabwe has an explicit position on the New Partnership for Africa's Development (NEPAD), for example. It endorsed the NEPAD process as an African-driven initiative in the belief that with proper management, the initiative would benefit the continent. However, it added a rider that it objected to what were described as 'attempts at hijacking NEPAD by donor nations and using it to divide the continent into "good" and "bad" Africans, with the former being rewarded and the latter punished' (Ministry of Foreign Affairs November 2010). Similarly, Zimbabwe has been less than enthusiastic about the African Political Review Mechanism (APRM) and has not conducted an APRM of its own, unlike countries such as South Africa, Ghana and Kenya.

Finally, an important component of Zimbabwe's foreign policy in the period from 2000 to 2008 has been international advocacy and lobbying for its land reform programme. As it spells out this issue:

> the land reform process which the West strongly criticised from its inception is an integral feature of Zimbabwe's foreign policy, and the reluctance by some countries to recognise its centrality to economic development and stability has continued to strain relations with some sections of the international community. (Ibid.:2)

To be more precise, the international community was not against the principle of land reform (UNDP 2002). It was the methods used to implement it, as described in Chapter 6, that were far from transparent and orderly that stimulated criticism against the process. Zimbabwe acknowledges the solidarity and support that it has received over the issue from SADC, AU, the Non-Aligned Movement and China (Ibid.). But the country's more expansive and populist hopes that its model of land reform would be adopted in Namibia and South Africa have proved far-fetched.

Zimbabwe's Relations with Western Powers

Zimbabwe's relations with Western powers were reasonably good up until the late 1990s. There was a coincidence between the degeneration into authoritarianism and estrangement with Western powers, especially Britain and the United States, and with some multilateral organisations. The political violence that was orchestrated by state institutions during the 2000 and 2002 election campaigns, together with a chaotic land reform process, deepened criticism of the Mugabe government by Western powers. It is not strictly true to say that the deterioration in relations commenced in 2000 with the start of land reform. The process had started earlier, around 1997–1998, with developments such as the aggressive campaign for gratuities by war veterans that led to devaluation of the Zimbabwe dollar; the bloody suppression of food riots in early 1998; Zimbabwe's intervention in the DRC and tightened censorship of the independent media. Domestic repression courted international criticism.

However, those analysts who have studied Anglo-Zimbabwean relations closely believe that relations soured significantly with the ascent of Labour's Tony Blair in 1997 (Chan 2003, 2006; Patel 2006). The comfort zone of relations with the Conservatives under Margaret Thatcher and John Major gave way to some chill. As one analyst put it:

> Blair cold-shouldered Mugabe at the Commonwealth Edinburgh summit in 1997 .... Perhaps the Foreign Office under Robin Cook and Tony Blair made their first mistake over Zimbabwe at that point – for Mugabe was certain that John Major had reassured him that Britain would indeed assist with funds for compensation. Blair was, of course, hurrying on from the Major era and thought that Britain was not committed to such previous understandings. (Chan 2003:111)

The breaching of an unwritten understanding, together with the famous letter by Clare Short, then Secretary of State for International Development, stoked anger on the part of the Zimbabwean government. This provided the context of vitriolic personal attacks and counter-attacks between Mugabe and Blair and sank Anglo-Zimbabwean relations to an unprecedented low, one from which they still have yet to recover. As it was observed:

> the exchange of strong words became surly in 2000, then insulting, then shrilly insulting. Mugabe labelled the British Government as one run by gays. Peter Hain, a junior Minister, called Zimbabwean repression of demonstrations 'thuggery, licensed from on high ... attacks encouraged, if not actually organised, by Mugabe'. It became an extraordinary exchange' (Ibid.: 152)

Box 9.1 – Highlights from a study on the Zimbabwe–EU dialogue under Articles 8 and 96

- *The Article 96 process was invoked very quickly while dialogue under Article 8 did not start properly .... Even though the EU had informed the Zimbabweans of their view, it seems that there were at least some misunderstandings or miscalculations on the part of the latter as they were surprised by the speed with which it was implemented.*
- *The government of Zimbabwe has constantly referred to the EU policy as having been dominated by the UK, even though a number of other EU Member States have the same views. There are also Member States whose bilateral relations with Zimbabwe are different from those of the EU.*
- *Zimbabwe has blamed EU sanctions for its economic crisis. Furthermore, it claims that Western donor agencies, the EU included, support the political opposition and affect the agenda of the opposition as well as NGOs' concentration on governance and human rights issues. The EU, and the UK in particular, are, it believes, pursuing a regime change in Zimbabwe.*
- *Because the appropriate measures are still applicable and the relations between Zimbabwe and the EU are not normalised, Zimbabwean authorities interpret and explain the situation to the public in a way that suits their own purposes. The difficult task of the Commission and Member States at local level is then to try to communicate to the public the actual content and purpose of their policy.*
- *The overall experience of the use of Article 96 in Zimbabwe has largely been negative, in the sense that various stakeholders are frustrated. Currently, however, there are interesting developments that might demonstrate that it is possible for the EU to translate its policy into positive measures.*
- *The preparatory discussion for the 10th European Development Fund was also intentionally used to enhance political dialogue. Considerable co-operation is taking place between Zimbabweans and Europeans, which is appreciated by the Zimbabwean partners.*

In summary, one could say that current weaknesses in coherence of the EU policy in Zimbabwe are due to the following:

1. *The aim to have a positive impact on a forthcoming election that was short-sighted with regard to the gradually developing situation.*
2. *The continuing crisis in Zimbabwe, in other words that the situation has yet to improve.*
3. *The difficulties for outsiders vis-à-vis influencing the Zimbabwean government.*
4. *The antagonistic attitude of some elements of the government of Zimbabwe towards donor countries.*
5. *The different opinions of the Member States as to the best way to improve the situation.*
6. *The fear that a policy change on the part of the EU means 'losing credibility'.*
7. *The inability to make alliances with Zimbabwe's neighbouring countries.*
8. *Zimbabwe having become a problem in EU–Africa relations.*
9. *The lack of an 'exit plan'.*

Source: CTS 2006:23-4

Zimbabwe's Ministry of Foreign Affairs acknowledged that this bilateral dispute was 'a very wasteful stand-off' which had turned attention away from the real priorities in existing frameworks for bilateral co-operation (Ministry of Foreign Affairs, 2010). In the last analysis, the standoff and shrill rhetoric between leaders of Zimbabwe and Britain benefited no one. In particular, Zimbabwe pursued a self-destructive path:

> *Blair did not get it right ... (but) was it then right to plunge one's own country into chaos, turmoil and precipitate decline for the sake of someone else mistake? To augment several times over his mistake with a catalogue of one's own? (Chan 2006:188)*

Mugabe bears responsibility for responding to the Blair government in such emotive terms that land reform was not, in the end, rationally planned and implemented. Once relations deteriorated, other casualties were arms exports to Zimbabwe that Blair had supported, and the shaping of tough EU policy towards Zimbabwe from 2002.

The relations between Zimbabwe and the EU deteriorated sharply in 2002, resulting in mutual recrimination rather than concerted dialogue. While the root cause of the deterioration can be traced to the slide into authoritarianism in Zimbabwe itself, particularly between 1999 and 2001, the mechanism for dialogue under the Cotonou Agreement was not systematically applied in that instance. The dialogue was supposed to have been pursued substantively under Article 8 of the Agreement before Article 96 could be invoked, but that was not the case. The concerns of the EU related to the deteriorating governance conditions in Zimbabwe, hence its call for:

- *An end to political violence, and in particular an end to all official encouragement or acceptance of such violence*
- *Concrete action to protect the freedom of mass media*
- *Independence of the judiciary and respect of its decisions*
- *An end of illegal occupation of properties and*
- *An invitation to the EU to support and observe the 2002 elections and full access to that end. (Mackie and Lehtimen, 2003:15)*

The dialogue over these governance issues was not exhaustive. Analysts have pointed out that there was an unusual haste in the progression from Article 8 to Article 96. This was one of the conclusions reached in study in which the present author participated in 2006 (see Box 9:1).

For its part, Zimbabwe made an uncompromising, if not bellicose, response to the EU's overtures. Stan Mudenge, the then Zimbabwean Foreign Minister, argued that the EU unilaterally decided to move the Zimbabwe–EU dialogue from Article 8 to Article 96 and stated that Zimbabwe had serious doubts as to the sincerity of the EU's intentions (Mudenge 2002). More pointedly, he remarked that:

> we have raised our concerns about what we view as a master–servant relationship in the manner that the EU imposed demands and ultimatums on us throughout the process of the so-called dialogue. In fact, we had no dialogue but a monologue. (Ibid.: 3)

The failure of the dialogue resulted in the imposition of targeted sanctions against the leading members of the Mugabe government. Insisting that there was nothing in the Cotonou Agreement that gave the EU the right to demand that it participate in election observation, the Mugabe government refused it permission to observe the 2002 election. Relations deteriorated sharply thereafter and have not improved since. Targeted sanctions have been renewed annually since 2002. Efforts by the Mugabe government to influence some EU states to revoke the sanctions failed. Until governance conditions improve substantially, there is little hope that these sanctions will be lifted. It must be added that in 2009–2010 the GNU failed to take advantage of the window of opportunity opened under the GPA to address the EU's concerns and so end the stalemate.

Similarly, relations between Zimbabwe and the United States since 2000 have been poor and constantly aggravated by flamboyant rhetoric from both sides. Like Britain and the EU, the US reacted sharply in 2000 to the spread of political violence that accompanied tightened authoritarianism in Zimbabwe. Its formal response was the invocation of targeted sanctions under the Zimbabwe Democracy and Economic Recovery Act (ZIDERA) of 2001. Through this legislation, Zimbabwe's access to finance and credit facilities from US and multilateral institutions was effectively blocked. ZIDERA empowered the US government to use its voting rights and influence as a major contributor to multilateral lending agencies such as the IMF, World Bank and the African Development Bank to veto applications for finance, credit facilities, loan rescheduling and international debt cancellation. Zimbabwe's relations with these agencies were immediately affected. The punitive sanctions embedded in ZIDERA also compounded the economic crisis of 2000 to 2008.

Indeed, until 2006, relations with the IMF were also frozen, further blocking Zimbabwe's access to international loans and investment and balance of payments support. At the same time, leading members of the Zimbabwean elite who were close to the Mugabe government had their assets frozen and personal business links with the US were adversely affected. On top of this, a travel ban was imposed on them. There is no doubt that although some pain was inflicted on Zimbabwe's elite it did not prompt the Mugabe government to change any of its policies. All that the elite has done has been to diversify their business operations to other parts of the globe, the Asia–Pacific region in particular.

To the extent that the UK, EU and the US and some members of the Commonwealth imposed targeted sanctions on members of Mugabe's ZANU-PF party, it is possible to speak of co-ordination of policy by these blocs. The content of the sanctions varied, but they sought to send a common message to Mugabe, namely, that he should allow a process of democratisation. Needless to say, Mugabe's stance has been uncompromising and he has gone on to mobilise international and regional support from organisations such as SADC, COMESA and the AU in his demand for the sanctions to be lifted. Much hair-splitting has occurred in the debate as to whether the sanctions are merely targeted smart measures in a context in which trade flows are unimpeded, or are more substantive than they appear. Had targeted sanctions and ZIDERA not come into play, it is likely that flows of credit and development assistance, including budgetary support, would have been more substantial during the decade 2000 to 2010. The persistence of authoritarianism under Mugabe has thus brought with it considerable cost. The stalemate in Zimbabwe–US relations was compounded by aggressive rhetoric on both sides, as the embassy dispatches published by WikiLeaks in December 2010 illustrated (see *Zimbabwe Independent*, 3 December 2010). This included former US Secretary of State Condoleezza Rice lumping Zimbabwe with 'rogue states' such as North Korea and Cuba and the demonising of successive US ambassadors to Harare. However, US Harare dispatches published in Wikileaks in September 2011 showed there was a great deal of secretive contact and dialogue between some senior ZANU-PF politicians and US diplomatic representatives.

The 'Look East' Policy

In response to sanctions and criticism from the West, Zimbabwe adopted a 'Look East' policy at the beginning of the new millennium. Mugabe famously remarked that 'we have turned east where the sun rises, and given our backs to the West where the sun sets' (Mugabe in Hilsum 2005:420). It was his gambit to seek partnership with a region of the world that was more sympathetic to his government, or at least did not make democracy a precondition of a partnership (Ministry of Foreign Affairs 2010). It was stated that 'the vision and strategies provide guidelines on the thrust of Zimbabwe's co-operation and prioritise projects in which Zimbabwe has comparative advantage' (Ibid). While Zimbabwe assiduously cultivated relations with such countries as Iran, Indonesia, India and Malaysia, the partnership with China dwarfed all other bilateral ties. Analysts such as Patel have interpreted this development a 'dispersal of dependence' by a small and poor state (Patel 2006:182). Arguing that China, as a rising world power, and Zimbabwe, as a developing country politically shunned by the West, have some compatibility in terms of their national interests, Patel asserted that there were reasonable prospects for mutual benefits. In fact, the 'Look East' policy had early foundations in a 1992 'economic thrust' to Zimbabwe's foreign policy; between 2002 and 2006 it had acquired a high profile because of the stalemate with the West (Ibid.).

However, even deeper foundations to those relations were laid three to four decades earlier. While relations between some African countries and China are of a recent vintage, that with Zimbabwe spans about 40 years, dating back to Chinese ideological and military support of ZANU, which would, as ZANU-PF, become the dominant ruling party at independence in 1980. If this can be interpreted as a long-term political investment it was one that bore fruit for the Chinese a generation later (Sachikonye 2007).

The economic and political dimensions of this relationship should be examined in the context of China's preoccupation with the extraction of natural resources, minerals especially, and its tolerance of authoritarian repression in Africa. The military dimension should be seen against the background of an arms embargo on Zimbabwe by the West, and the refurbishment of the state coercive apparatus against the opposition movement and civil society. In the case of Zimbabwe, it may be exception-

Box 9.2 – Examples of Chinese economic interests in Zimbabwe

- *The sectoral spread of economic co-operation between China and Zimbabwe cuts across most of the economic sectors. These include tourism, transport, energy, information technology, leather, textile, clothing and shoe industries*
- *Chinese operators are particularly dynamic in the construction sector, especially in housing. The Chinese firm, Sino-Zimbabwe Cement Company started cement production in September 2000 with a USD51 million investment*
- *In 2007, the Zimbabwe Government commissioned 424 tractors imported from China at more than USD25 million to be used in tobacco production. More tractors, combine harvesters and other farm equipment were imported in 2008. The Chinese state-owned firm, China International Water and Electric, was contracted to farm 250,000 acres in southern Zimbabwe. Chinese and Zimbabwean developers believed that the project would yield 2.1 million tonnes of maize every year. Payment would be in the form of tobacco.*

Source: Chakanya and Muchichwa 2009

al in terms of the country's consecutive ten-year economic contraction, but China's approach to resource extraction bears resemblance to that it has followed in other African countries. The same pattern is evident in China's export of manufactured items such as textiles, toys and buses to Zimbabwe, exports that have contributed to de-industrialisation in these sectors since the late 1990s. In addition, Zimbabwe's relationship with China also illustrates the latter's emphasis on personal ties with regimes and elites which are necessary for its economic and political advantage and manipulation. However, we are generally sceptical as to whether Zimbabwe is capable of extracting tangible benefits – beyond an immediate lifeline to buy time against the reform tide – from a seemingly one-sided relationship (See Box 9.2). As Karumbidza observed, whether the Zimbabwe–China relationship turns out to be 'a win-win one will depend much on how effectively Zimbabwe can build institutional and bureaucratic capacity to harness Chinese funds and investment for the benefit of the country' (Karumbidza 2007).

China has sought to project itself as a power that is disinterested in the domestic politics of the countries with which it has relations. It stresses the principle of non-interference, even where human rights violations are rampant. Where Western powers are reluctant to engage a country on account of its corruption and authoritarianism, China has no qualms about so doing. The Chinese stance in countries such as Sudan and Equatorial Guinea is thus cynical and self-serving.

In respect of Zimbabwe, China cannot claim to be adhering to the principle of non-interference. First, there are close party-to-party relations between ZANU-PF and the Chinese Communist Party, and these relations have been cemented by bilateral visits by high-ranking officials. The ruling elite in Zimbabwe have been the beneficiaries and accessories of Chinese investment in infrastructure projects and barter trade. Second, China has taken sides in the contest over media freedom between the Zimbabwean government and the opposition. It has exported equipment used to jam radio broadcasts aimed at giving 'voice' to the opposition, which is denied space on the state media. When the new law to monitor electronic mail, Internet traffic and other forms of communication was introduced, it was widely believed that Chinese expertise in this field would be drawn upon. Chinese proximity to the ruling elite might be an asset as long as the latter is in power, but it would lose its currency if political change did occur.

Third, the Chinese stance of 'non-interference' is undermined by its significant contribution to the process of militarisation in Africa. It has been observed that China has built several arms factories in Sudan; that it sold arms worth about USD1 billion to Ethiopia and Eritrea during their war in 1998–2000; and that it has supplied various armaments to countries such as Mali and Angola (Lee 2006). China has also become a significant military supplier to Zimbabwe. In recent years, it has exported 12 fighter jets, 100 army trucks and radio jamming devices with an estimated value of USD240 million to the country. Although precise details are difficult to obtain, Chinese military supplies have become more crucial because of the West's military embargo. In 2005, Zimbabwe's air force received six K8 jet aircraft for use in training jet fighter pilots and for 'low-intensity' military operations.

Although Zimbabwe's authoritarian mode and stand-off with the West has created economic and political windows of opportunity for Beijing, there are nevertheless some inherent risks in the relationship. One is Zimbabwe's economic stagnation; others are constant power cuts, fuel shortages, transport bottlenecks, and the breakdown of utilities and infrastructure, all of which represent a threat to commercial operations ranging from agriculture to mining and manufacturing to retailing.

Chinese operations in Zimbabwe cannot remain unscathed. Another risk is the insolvency of those interests that have borrowed Chinese capital. These include state institutions and parastatals. There have been reports of unpaid loans in the case of aircraft purchases and of construction projects, leading to suspension of work (Karumbidza 2007). The worry is that if Zimbabwe continues to borrowing heavily from China without making consistent repayments, it may be forced to mortgage yet more of its natural and national resources such as land and platinum and gold mines.

Their current relationship is not one of equals, despite all the rhetoric. The risk for Zimbabwe in its current position of weakness is becoming a dependent state in its relations with China, which would present both costs and opportunities for this emerging superpower. Indeed, during the second half of 2007, China appeared to be reviewing its relations with Zimbabwe. At that time, as the host of the forthcoming 2008 Olympics, this reflected some sensitivity to charges that it was consorting with African despots in Zimbabwe and Sudan. As one analyst observed:

> 2007 may mark a watershed in the relationship between the two countries. Whereas Mugabe may continue to 'look east' to survive, China does not seem to be willing to return the gaze directly. Rather China is becoming increasingly concerned about how it appears to the West. What is lost to Mugabe and other African leaders is that even the Chinese would admit that they would not be an emerging giant without Western technology and markets .... African leaders should be wary of simply looking East. They should heed Kwame Nkrumah's admonition that Africa needs to look forward rather than east or west for its development. (Matahwa 2007:5)

We broadly concur with this perceptive analysis.

Conclusion

In this chapter we have argued that Zimbabwe has consistently sought to punch above its weight in the realm of foreign policy. At the onset of independence, the country had a modest foreign policy that was largely focused on the southern African region, with special emphasis on the liberation process and regional co-operation. There was therefore sympathy for its military intervention to shore up the Frelimo government in Mozambique, and praise for its involvement in the subsequent peace process. With the drift towards authoritarianism in the 1990s, Zimbabwe's foreign policy became increasingly rhetorical and erratic. Even where the economic returns were minimal, there was a pronounced tendency to associate with maverick regimes in North Korea, Libya, Cuba, Iran and Venezuela, if only for ideological reasons. The leadership and anti-imperialist rhetoric in those countries had a certain appeal to the Mugabe government, which did not endear it to western powers.

The emphasis on principles of national sovereignty and territorial integrity was embedded in the country's foreign policy for both defensive and proactive reasons. Criticism of domestic authoritarianism was deflected on grounds of sovereignty, justifying non-interference, while the need to safeguard territorial integrity justified intervention in the DRC in 1998. Initial military successes were followed by reverses and stalemates that eventually resulted in a peace agreement. The domestic and external criticism of the intervention, not to mention the high cost of the expedition, showed a disconnection between the country's economic and diplomatic priorities and the readiness to project military power and exploit opportunities for accumulation by sections of the military and political elite. The overall result of the intervention demonstrated a medium-sized country's attempt to 'punch above its weight'.

We have also explored relations between Zimbabwe and South Africa, the West and the Asia-Pacific region, China especially. Zimbabwe's influence was shown to be relatively limited, despite its often flamboyant rhetoric about anti-imperialism, pan-Africanism and non-alignment. The Mugabe government's frustration with 'quiet diplomacy' reflected its authoritarian impulses, while poor relations with western powers underscored limitations in Zimbabwean diplomacy to positively project its domestic policies, including land reform. Although the objectives proved elusive, targeted sanctions were a symptom of the failure of this diplomacy. Although the 'Look East' policy initially gave some promise as a counterweight to being snubbed by the West, the weakness of its economic base made Zimbabwe less attractive as a destination for investment, even for China. By 2010, Zimbabwe's foreign policy continued to display signs of paranoia and introspection rather than project confidence and dynamism.

Conclusion: Towards a Renewal

This book is an ambitious attempt to ponder the key issues of politics, development and society in Zimbabwe. It has drawn on 25 years of research and publications on these issues. In reflecting on the 'Lost Decades', and especially the decade 1998–2008, a critical approach was consistently pursued. To that extent, this book is a critique of the politics of authoritarianism, of the economic paradigm pursued and of the lack of vision and strategy on transformation. This is not to say that these decades saw no positive achievements. For instance, growth in the social sector (especially education and health) was notable in the first decade of independence. Even so, such positive achievements experienced degrees of reversal in the third decade (2000 to 2010), thus proving that they had not been sustainable.

In this chapter, we highlight areas that could provide opportunities for Zimbabwe as it seeks recovery from decline and stagnation as well as from pessimism and angst. The first part of the chapter will recap the issues of the National Question and uneven development, the reform of the authoritarian state, the importance and re-orientation of political parties, and the renewed commitment to constitutionalism and democracy.

The National Question, Uneven Development and Healing

As Chapter 1 spelled out, the formation of the modern state of Zimbabwe is of relatively recent origin, spanning only about 120 years. Western and settler colonialism and African nationalism have been the major ideologies that have deeply affected our political system and behaviour. These ideologies also underpinned our politics before and after independence. The National Question has related to the process of creating national unity across ethnic, racial and social groups as well as the process of state-building. Although some stability and peace was created at independence following the integration of various armies, this proved temporary, as civil conflict in Matabeleland soon flared up. The Gukurahundi (1982–1987) and the repeated calls for a review of the killings, disappearances and other excesses of that era represent confirmation that the National Question still needs to be settled. While those events contributed to uneven development and meagre state support in Matabeleland, peripheral parts of other provinces such as Manicaland and Masvingo have also suffered state neglect. The perception that most development resources have been poured into Harare and Mashonaland provinces is, rightly or wrongly, further testimony to the fact that the National Question needs to be settled urgently and systematically.

Of this, the question of diversity in our national make-up is an inextricable part. Discrimination against some citizens is offensive to the values upon which our society and nation was founded. The National Question cannot be resolved if whites, Asians, Tonga, Venda and other groups have their rights trampled upon because they are in the minority. Authoritarian politics have evolved on the basis of such discrimination and disempowerment, and on the intolerance of diversity. There should be respect of diversity and striving for 'unity in diversity'. The legacy of original and reverse racism and discrimination should be urgently and systematically addressed, as should that of the violence of Gukurahundi. No true healing and reconciliation can be possible without a sincere 'owning up' to these legacies.

The Reconstruction of the State

Chapter 2 argued and showed that the inherited Zimbabwe state retained strong authoritarian and repressive features and functions. There were weak checks and balances between the key branches of the state. The autonomy of parliament and judiciary was weak, with real power centralised in the executive. The military–security–police complex has become increasingly influential as a major power centre in the state, hence the expression 'militarisation of politics'. These are unhealthy developments, especially for democratic politics. Reforming the present authoritarian state is imperative. In practice, this will entail reform of the security sector – the military, the police and the intelligence services – so that the extensive politicisation of these institutions is reversed. All three have become intimately associated with the ZANU-PF over the years, especially during elections, in which they have been viewed as playing an overtly partisan role. At the same time, their top echelons were involved in the accumulation of wealth during the military intervention in the DRC and in the land occupations and mining operations at home.

The capacity for policy design and implementation by the state bureaucracy has weakened over the years. Raising the quality of those recruited into the bureaucracy, and its capacity as a whole is equally important. The capacity for formulating and implementing a national development programme has two component parts. The first consists of a political leadership that is committed to national development goals and can motivate and guide the planning process. The second is a competent and professional bureaucracy that has the autonomy and power to implement the programme and respond to rapidly changing local and global conditions (ECA 2011:8). Zimbabwe's public bureaucracy will require significant revamping in order to significantly improve the capacity of the state.

Political Parties and the Political System

The role of political parties in Zimbabwean politics has not been given sufficient attention in most academic research, even though they are major players in shaping the discourse on national politics as well as power shifts in the country. Chapter 3 observed, for example, that monographs on political parties are rare. As institutions that provide basic representation, they aggregate the various interests in society, however imperfectly. Examining the ideologies and election platform of parties is crucial when scrutinising the latter's impact on the formulation of public policies. The wider context of party politics has, however, been one of authoritarianism and overwhelmingly repressive of opposition parties and CSOs. Any reform of the authoritarian state needs to redress this.

Historically, there is strong predilection towards factionalism in Zimbabwean political parties which often leads to intra-party conflict and violence. (The outbreak of intra-party violence is endemic at the stage of primary elections.) This applies as much to the ruling parties as it does to the opposition parties. Factionalism is not only partly a reflection of the lack of resolution of the National Question but also of party leaders' unbridled ambitions for power. It is also a reflection of a historically rooted political culture of violence that developed two generations ago. State activation of inter-party violence is a feature of Zimbabwean politics that needs to be tackled urgently. Measures should be taken against those who resort to violence as a method of mobilisation against other parties.

Constitutionalism and Democracy

Reform of the authoritarian state will require steadfast commitment to constitutionalism and democracy. As Chapter 4 spelled out, one of the litmus tests of constitutionalism has been the protracted process of constitutional reform from 1998 to the present. There has been a lukewarm commitment to constitutionalism by both ruling and opposition parties; they have tended to look at constitutions simply as a means to an end, namely attainment of state power.

Chapter 4 explored how the constitutional reform process has so far been a chequered one. There is clearly a need for greater commitment to constitutional reform that responds to the needs and aspirations of a wider and diverse society. A revised constitution should provide answers to some aspects of the National Question. It should, for example, encompass issues such as uneven development, devolution or decentralisation and diversity.

The Zimbabwe debate on democracy was recapped, highlighting an era when various schools of thought debated the question of democracy in a more civil manner. The debate should not have been closed prematurely by such assertions (as that of Robert Mugabe) that 'colonialism did not bring us democracy'. Nor should the discourse be viewed as primarily the agenda of CSOs, especially human rights organisations. The demands for democracy are in fact deeply rooted in Zimbabwean communities themselves. They should be answered. Political parties and governments should not take an equivocal and opportunistic position on the democracy question.

The electoral system and process was also explored in Chapter 4. The limitations of the system up to 2008 were highlighted. It was observed that they facilitated rigging and there was a debate on which was fairer, the first-past-the-post (FPTP) system or proportional representation (PR). The revised constitution should resolve the issue so as to address the problems associated with the FPTP system and also reflect citizens' views on this matter of electoral reform. In 2011, the credibility of the electoral system was still at stake – the ZEC had been deeply compromised during the 2008 election and there were many demands for its dismantling. Electoral reform and a reconstituted electoral commission are also imperative.

Towards Sustainable Development

Chapters 5 and 6 chronicled the formidable challenges to economic development and agrarian growth despite the country's early start in modernisation and infrastructural sophistication. During the decade 1998–2008, the key sectors of industry and agriculture experienced dramatic decline; indeed, the economy as a whole suffered a contraction of about 50 per cent in this period. An attempt was made to explain the decline, indicating that it was a combination of poor policy design, sequencing and implementation. There was often tardy implementation of various economic plans (some analysts counted up to ten aborted plans) during the three decades examined herein. The capacity of planning and execution of policy and programmes also registered a decline during this period, particularly between 1998 and 2008.

Long-term transformation of the economy will require a sustained assault on its structures of inherited dualism. Historically, dualism evolved as a consequence of the juxtaposition of a relatively well-developed and modern formal sector that employed about one million people (a fifth of the labour force) and an underdeveloped and backward rural economy, home to about 70 per cent of the Zimbabwe's indigenous population. The dualism that characterised the economy in the colonial era and still continues to do so today explains the perennial problem of the under-utilisation of resources, which ultimately lead to underdevelopment (Kanyenze *et al.* 2011). The structures of embedded dualism should be dismantled through systematic transformation.

As we observed above, the capacity level of the public bureaucracy is a vital ingredient for sustainable development, and for transformation in particular. Some scholars have highlighted 'bureaucratic capacity and "embeddedness"' as imperative for economic management that leads to transformation:

> to focus on East Asian states is to focus on the capacity of public bureaucracies. Nearly everyone agrees that when East Asian public bureaucracies are compared with those of developing countries in other regions, they were more closely approximate the ideal-type Weberian bureaucracy. Meritocratic recruitment to public service and public service careers offering long-term

> *rewards commensurate with those obtainable in the private sector were institutional cornerstones of the East Asian economic miracle. (Evans 2010:5)*

This position is reinforced by the opinion that reconstructing the administrative apparatus of the state is therefore a central task. The way forward:

> *does not lie in a wholesale neglect of existing capacities in the quest for 'new' wines, but rather in the utilisation, retooling and re-invigorating of existing capacities – including reversing the brain drain – and in rebuilding the educational and training institutions in the light of the long-term development needs rather than in the ad hoc manner encouraged by new 'capacity building' fads. (Mkandawire 2010:67)*

In addition to a competent and meritocratic public bureaucracy, another challenge has been how to establish 'social pacts' that would ensure the co-existence of what was termed 'patient capital' and 'patient labour', with the idea that labour would forego some of the gains in productivity on the grounds that profits would be reinvested to create further employment opportunities (Ibid.).

Substantive transformation will only be possible if a development-oriented state is in place. In Africa, economic transformation demands that the state play a central role – using a comprehensive development framework – in planning, articulating and implementing policies aimed at ensuring an efficient allocation of resources. However, the state must have the capacity to do this, and have the institutions to link the bureaucracy with key stakeholders. In other words, transformation in Africa, indeed in Zimbabwe, necessitates a developmental state and society.

Finally, corruption needs to be uprooted at various levels of the state, private institutions and society. Now at a worrying level, corruption makes the conduct of business more expensive than it should be. The propensity towards ostentatious expenditure on consumer goods and services such as luxury cars and frequent travel is common amongst leaders in government. More expenditure is directed to such consumerist items than to capital items with development dividends. A culture of business and probity as well as accountability, which is lacking among most of the political class, needs to be nurtured.

Towards Agrarian Recovery and Transition

Chapter 6 explained the principal motivation behind the accelerated land reform during *jambanja*. It also outlined the inconclusive debate between those who 'talk up' the reform and those who remain sceptical about its conduct and outcome. Political expediency played a major role in the timing and scaling up of land reform in a context in which ZANU-PF sought to diminish the chances of electoral victory for the MDC. The outcome of land reform has, broadly speaking, been agrarian decline. The factors behind this decline are multiple, ranging from inexperience, lack of skills and capital to frequent absence (by A2 farm owners) from farms, and so on. There is consensus between scholars who support and criticise land reform that 'overall agricultural output levels and productivity declined in the newly distributed areas' (Moyo *et al.* 2009:175). Furthermore, patterns suggest that the agrarian question of land and farm productivity, exploitative farm labour relations, the constrained public financing of agriculture and the market re-orientation toward cut-throat contract farming were among the critical weaknesses of land reform and its attendant (largely ad hoc) agrarian programme (Ibid.). Even the most optimistic review of the programme believes that 35 per cent of a sample of small-farmer households will be on an upward accumulation trajectory, with 21 per cent diversifying into off-farm activities, and 34 per cent being unsuccessful (Scoones *et al.* 2010:227-8). At the time of the review, ten per cent of the sample were already 'dropping out'.

What could be a path of recovery and transition, then? There would need to be a comprehensive review of land policy with a view to addressing mistakes and weaknesses. Such a review would need to be buttressed by a transparent land audit to identify patterns of land ownership, particularly the problem of multiple farm ownership. Issues of compensation to former owners, tenure security, tenancy arrangements, investment and credit arrangements, infrastructure development and the provision of skills training must also be addressed to ensure sustainable land reform.

Civil Society, State and Social Contract

In any annals on Zimbabwean politics and the development process in the post-independence period, the role of civil society would be prominent. CSOs tempered the growth and scale of authoritarianism, particularly during the decade 1998–2008. They proved a dynamic force in struggles for constitutional reform and human rights. Their power and influence much underestimated in the beginning, CSOs became a thorn in the flesh of an authoritarian state that sought untrammelled hegemony. Although numerically small and largely funded from outside, the role of CSOs in campaigning for good governance and human rights and in document-ing abuses and corruption was effective and kept Zimbabwe on the international radar and agenda.

This book has traced the various phases through which CSOs developed – from mainly humanitarian and development-oriented organisations to advocacy groups on such 'hard areas' as governance and human rights and to coalitions on specific issues such as electoral reform, media free-dom and women's rights. CSOs became effective watchdogs of the social contract between the Zimbabwean state and the wider society. But, as we observed, their advocacy role and critique of authoritarianism courted state repression, which reached a peak during the period 2000 to 2008. That this repression had a marked impact on the operational effective-ness, capability, funding and resilience on CSOs can be neither ignored nor underestimated.

Looking ahead, what then are the principal challenges and opportu-nities for CSOs in the democratic transition and development process? The challenges relate to continued authoritarian repression by a police state against activists, journalists, trade unionists and student leaders, amongst others. As we observed in Chapter 7, the wider environment has continued to have a deterrent effect on how CSOs organised their planning, operations and formulation of public statements. Second, the broader economic environment remains a challenge to CSOs. The envi-ronment of limited growth and investment affected CSOs to the extent that they also experienced a 'brain drain', resulting in the loss of skilled and experienced activists, and of institutional memory. Dependence on donor funding remains considerable and makes CSOs vulnerable to the allegation that they are pursuing external agendas. To avoid this, CSOs need to explore other funding paradigms that do not compromise their autonomy and sustainability; they should seek opportunities to diversify funding sources, and to negotiate more flexible funding arrangements. Third, there exists a threat of fragmentation as a multiplicity of CSOs sometimes leads to duplication and overlapping of operational areas, which can lead not only to wastage of much-needed resources but also the dissipation of energies. Fourth, the CSOs should carefully navigate their relationship with political parties. They should not compromise their autonomy for expediency if their credibility and non-partisan credentials are to remain above aboard. Difficult as it might be, their role as watch-dogs requires them to maintain political distance from both governing and opposition parties.

Despite this, there are considerable opportunities for CSOs in shaping the democratic transition and the development process. The formation of the Government of National Unity (GNU) in 2009, and the raft of reforms contained in the Global Political Agreement (GPA), confirmed the reform agenda of CSOs on a range of issues from human rights, justice and reconciliation to media and security sector reform. Although most reforms have not been fully implemented, the new environment allowed CSOs to push their advocacy and lobbying to a higher level.

A major opportunity for CSOs relates to the building of capacity, in particular in conducting training to raise competence levels and to develop leadership skills amongst their staff. This is imperative against the background of a high turnover induced by the above-mentioned 'brain drain'. Skills in risk management, strategic planning and scenario modelling would raise their capacity while competence in information and communications technology and the use of social media would strengthen inter-CSO communication and synergies and have broad impact on society. Regular publication of newsletters and bulletins would promote knowledge and understanding of the experiences, challenges and achievements of sister CSOs.

Society, Migration and Livelihoods

The lost decades witnessed profound changes in Zimbabwean society, changes whose depth and significance are still unfolding. The profundity and fluidity of those political and economic developments are difficult to measure, yet they are perceptible. The changes relate to deepening inequalities as the gap between the rich and poor widens while that between the privileged elite and the deprived majority grows. Amidst the increased levels of poverty, the minority affluent population has amassed considerable wealth, taking advantage of political power and their access to state resources and to land and minerals. Consequently, wealth distribution is now even more skewed than it was at independence in 1980.

Despite earlier gains in the education and health sectors, the decline during the period 2000 to 2008 was significant. By 2008, the economic crisis had gravely undermined the provision of basic schooling and health

209

services. Widespread school closures and a cholera outbreak in 2008 were the culmination of a decade-long decline. Combined with the HIV/AIDS epidemic, the inequalities and the collapse in social service provision affected the base and resilience of Zimbabwean society. Communities and families could not escape the ripple effects of these developments.

One major outcome of these developments was migration. Up to a quarter of the country's population left Zimbabwe, constituting one of the largest migration waves in Africa, if not in the world, in recent history. It has resulted in a significant 'brain drain', which negatively affected the capacity of public and private sectors yet also increased remittances which have positively boosted the livelihoods of those that remained at home. Some of the funds received have been invested in production, real estate, food, health and education, but most were spent on consumption items with little productive value.

The challenges and opportunities presented by the significant Zimbabwean diaspora are significant. How to encourage skilled and experienced Zimbabweans in the diaspora to return and work in the public and private sectors is a complicated process. It is partly dependent on the availability and quality of openings as well as levels of remuneration and promotion opportunities. There will be need for an innovative policy towards the diaspora so as to tap into its skills, resources and remittances. A forward-looking diaspora policy is an imperative.

Foreign Policy and External Relations

As a medium-sized power in the African context, Zimbabwe's options in foreign policy setting were limited. It had no strategic resources such as oil or an advantageous geopolitical location. Pragmatism during the early years of independence gave way to more ambitious interventions such as that in the DRC in 1998 and the bellicose stand-off with the West, especially Britain, the European Union and the United States from 2000. In particular, the period from 1998 to 2008 witnessed a belligerent but reactive foreign policy which was expressed in aggressive tones. While the emphasis on pan-Africanism and regional solidarity won friends for the Mugabe government in Africa and in the wider developing world, sanctions targeted at its leadership marked a low point in relations with the West and key multilateral institutions such as the IMF.

Chapter 9 spelled out the evolution of Zimbabwe's foreign policy and the rationale behind the initial focus on support for liberation movements in southern Africa and participation in the regional economic bloc of SADC. Military intervention in Mozambique to assist Frelimo in the civil war against Renamo was part of a successful thrust of this foreign policy. A foreign policy that was largely centred on liberation and development processes in southern Africa earned respect within regional bodies like the African Union and also in the Commonwealth, the United Nations and the Non-Aligned Movement.

However, when Zimbabwe sought to 'punch above its weight' through more ambitious military intervention, as in 1998 in the DRC, complications arose. The weak national economy could not sustain the intervention; indeed military expenditure precipitated an economic crisis. Accumulation by some senior politicians and military officers in mining and timber in the DRC did not compensate for the overall adverse effect of the intervention on the national fiscus. What the DRC intervention suggested was that there was a mismatch between Zimbabwe's foreign policy ambitions and its economic status. Throughout the decade of 1998 to 2008, the Mugabe government seemed to ignore the contradiction between aggressive rhetoric and weak economic power and influence. Despite flamboyant talk about anti-imperialism and neo-colonialism, the country's influence in bodies such as SADC and the UN weakened. Authoritarian repression at home stoked criticism of the government by these international organisations.

The frustrations arising from censure by the West and in regional organisations drove Zimbabwe to revive relations with China through the 'Look East' policy. While relations between ZANU-PF and the Chinese Communist Party dated back to the Cold War era, the accent in the new phase was on economic relations. Not only did trade expand between the two countries, but Chinese assistance was also crucial for the country's agricultural sector. Investment and grants came without such conditions as Western investors and donors specified. However, amidst speculation that land and minerals might have been mortgaged to the Chinese in return for loans, there are concerns that the relationship is one of dependence by the Zimbabwe state. On the whole, the amount of investment and aid received from China has been below expectations, a fact underscored by the renewed but tentative rapprochement with the West in the second half of 2011.

Finally, 'punching above one's weight' in foreign relations comes at a cost. Zimbabwe's experience during the period 1998 to 2008 demonstrated the limits of aggressive rhetoric in foreign policy. It also showed that without considerable economic weight, the means to project foreign policy are weak. A more modest, development-oriented and pragmatic foreign policy that focuses on regional economic growth and co-operation, and mutual relations with both the East and West, would yield more promising results for a medium-sized country like Zimbabwe. Ultimately, however, normalising relations with most countries, not least those in the West, hinges on Zimbabwe's progress in democratisation.

Select Bibliography

ActionAid, Combined Harare Residents Association, Counselling Services Unit and Zimbabwe Peace Project (2005) *An In-depth Study on the Impact of Operation Murambatsvina/Restore Order.* Harare: ActionAid, CHRA, CSU and ZPP.

African Community Publishing and Development Trust (1987) *Let us Build Zimbabwe Together.* Harare: Ministry of Community Development and Women's Affairs

— and ZHR NGO Forum (2009) *A People's Guide to Transitional Justice.* Harare: ACPDT and ZHR NGO Forum.

African Union (2008) *Report on the 2008 Zimbabwe Election.* Addis Ababa: African Union.

Alexander, J. (2006) *The Unsettled Land: State-making & the Politics of Land in Zimbabwe, 1893-2003.* Harare: Weaver Press; Oxford: James Currey.

Alexander, J., J. McGregor and T. Ranger (2000) *Violence and Memory: One Hundred Years in the 'Dark Forests' of Matabeleland.* Harare: Weaver Press; Oxford: James Currey.

Alexander, J. and B. Miles Tendi (2008) 'A Tale of Two Elections: Zimbabwe at the Polls in 2008'. *Bulletin of Concerned African Scholars,* no. 80.

Amanor-Wilks, D. (1995) *In Search of Hope for Zimbabwe's Farm Workers.* Harare: Panos Institute and Dateline Africa.

Amnesty International (2007) *Zimbabwe Human Rights in Crisis: A Shadow Report to the African Commission for Human and Peoples' Rights.* London: Amnesty International.

Auret, D. (1992) *Reaching for Justice.* Gweru: Mambo Press; Harare: CCJPZ.

Austin, R. (2009) 'The Zimbabwe Constitutional Reform Process', in NIMD, *Writing Autobiographies of Nations.* The Hague: NIMD.

Badza, S. (2005) 'Foreign Policy', in Centre for Peace Inititiatives in Africa, *Zimbabwe: the next 25 years.* Harare: Benaby.

Beckman, B. (2001) 'Civil Society and Alliance Politics', in B. Beckman, E. Hansson and A. Sjogren (eds), *Civil Society and Authoritarianism in the Third World.* Stockholm: PODSU.

Bhebe, N. (1990) 'The Nationalist Struggle 1957-62', in C. Banana (ed.), *Turmoil and Tenacity: Zimbabwe 1890-1990.* Harare: College Press.

Bloch, A. (2005) 'The Development Potential of Zimbabweans in the

Diaspora', *Migration Research Series no. 17,* Geneva: IOM.

Bond, P. and M. Manyanya (2003) *Zimbabwe's Plunge.* Harare: Weaver Press; Pietermaritzburg: University of Natal Press; London: The Merlin Press.

Booysen, S. and Toulou, L. (2009) 'Zimbabwe', in D. Kadima and S. Booysen (eds), *Compendium of Elections in Southern Africa 1989-2009.* Johannesburg: Electoral Institute of Southern Africa.

Bourdillon, M. (1997) *Where are the ancestors? Changing Culture in Zimbabwe.* Harare: University of Zimbabwe Publications.

Bracking, S. (2005) 'Development Denied: Autocratic Militarism in Post-election Zimbabwe'. *Review of African Political Economy,* vol. 32 no. 104-5.

Bratton, M. (1981) 'Development in Zimbabwe: strategy and tactics', *Journal of Modern African Studies,* vol. 19, no. 3.

Bratton, M. and D. Posner (1999) 'A First Look at Second Elections in Africa', in R. Joseph (ed.), *State, Conflict and Democracy.* Boulder: Lynne Rienner.

Bratton, M. and E. Masunungure (2011) 'The Anatomy of Political Predation: Leaders, Elites and Coalitions in Zimbabwe, 1980-2010', Development Leadership Programme Research Paper 09.

Bratton, M., R. Mattes and E. Gyimah-Boadi (2005) *Public Opinion, Democracy and Market Reform in Africa.* Cambridge: Cambridge University Press.

British Observer Group (BOG) (1980) *Report by the Group of Independent British Observers appointed by the UK Government.* London.

Campbell, H. (2003) *Reclaiming Zimbabwe: The Exhaustion of the Patriarchal Model of Liberation.* Trenton: Africa World Press; Cape Town: David Philip.

Carver, R. (1989) *Zimbabwe: A Break with the Past? Human Rights and Political Unity.* New York: Africa Watch.

Catholic Commission for Justice and Peace in Zimbabwe (CCJPZ) (2009) *Graveyard Governance.* Harare: CCJP.

CCJPZ and Legal Resources Foundation (LRF) (1997) *Breaking the Silence, Building True Peace: A Report into the Disturbances in Matabeleland and the Midlands, 1980 to 1988.* Harare: CCJPZ and LRF.

Centre for Democracy nd Development (CDD) (2000) *The Zimbabwe Constitutional Referendum.* London: CDD.

Centre for the Study of Violence and Reconciliation (CSVR) (2006) *Women on the Run: Women Survivors of Torture among Refugees in South Africa.* Johannesburg: CSVR.

— (2009) *Subliminal Terror? Human Rights Violations and Torture in Zimbabwe during 2008.* Johannesburg: CSVR.

Chakanya, N. and N. Muchichwa (2009) 'Chinese Investments in Zimbabwe', in A. Baah and H. Jauch (eds), *Chinese Investments on Africa: A Labour Perspective.*

Accra: African Labour Research Network.

Chan, S. (2003) *Robert Mugabe: A Life of Power and Violence*. London: I. B. Tauris.

— (2005) *Citizen of Africa: Conversations with Morgan Tsvangirai*. Cape Town: Fingerprint Cooperative.

— (2006) 'Zimbabwe's Foreign Policy: A Conversation', *The Round Table*, vol. 95.

Chetsanga, C. and T. Muchenje (2003) *An Analysis of the Cause and Effect of the Brain Drain in Zimbabwe*. Harare: SIRDC.

Chikanda, A. (2005) *Medical Leave: The Exodus of Health Professionals in Zimbabwe*. Kingston: SAMP.

Chitanana, T. (2010) 'Shouting to No One in a Vacuum', in D. Kaulemu (ed.), *Political Participation in Zimbabwe*. Harare: AFCAST.

Chitiyo, K. (2003) 'Harvest of Tongues: Zimbabwe's "Third Chimurenga" and the Making of an Agrarian Revolution', in M. Lee and K. Colvard (eds), *Unfinished Business: The Land Crisis in Southern Africa*.

Chiware, T. (2010) 'Obstacles to Political Participation in Zimbabwe', in D. Kaulemu (ed.), *Political Participation in Zimbabwe*. Harare: AFCAST

Chiwewe, W. (1989) 'Unity Negotiations', in C. Banana (ed.), *Turmoil and Tenacity*. Harare: College Press.

Chung, F. (2006) *Re-living the Second Chimurenga: Memories of Zimbabwe's Liberation War*. Uppsala: NAI; Harare: Weaver Press.

CIIR (1975) *The Man in the Middle: Torture, Resettlement and Eviction*. London: CIIR.

CIIR and CCJPR (1999) *The Man in the Middle* and *The Civil War in Rhodesia*. Two Reports compiled by the CCJPR and CIIR in 1975. Republished in 1999. Harare: CCJPZ.

Cliffe, L. and C. Stoneman (1989) *Zimbabwe: Politics, Economics and Society*. London: Pinter.

Commonwealth Observer Group (2000) *Report on the Parliamentary Elections in Zimbabwe*. London: Commonwealth Observer Group.

Conflict Transformation Service (CTS) (2006) 'Evaluation of the Consultative Processes under the Article 96 in the Cotonou Partnership Agreement'. Report prepared for MFA, The Netherlands.

Counselling Services Unit (CSU) (2010) Personal Communication. Harare.

Crisis in Zimbabwe Coalition (CZC) (2010) *Cries from Goromonzi: Inside Zimbabwe's Torture Chambers*. Harare: CZC.

Crush, J. and D. Tevera (eds) (2010) *Zimbabwe's Exodus: Crisis, Migration and Survival*. Kingston and Cape Town: SAMP.

Dabengwa, D. (1995) 'ZIPRA in the Zimbabwe War of National Liberation', in N. Bhebe and T. Ranger (eds), *Soldiers in Zimbabwe's Liberation War*. Harare:

University of Zimbabwe Publications.

Davies, R., (1988) 'The Transition to Socialism in Zimbabwe: Some Areas for Debate', in C. Stoneman (ed.), *Zimbabwe's Prospects: Issues of Race, Class, State and Capital in Southern Africa.* London: Macmillan.

— (2004) 'Memories of Underdevelopment: A Personal Interpretation of Zimbabwe's Economic Decline', in B. Raftopoulos and T. Savage (eds), *Zimbabwe: Injustice and Political Reconciliation.* Harare: Weaver Press.

Deininger, K. and L. Squire (1996). 'A New Data Set Measuring Income Inequality'. *The World Bank Economic Review,* vol. 10 no. 3.

Democratic Party (1991) *Party Constitution.* Harare: DP.

DFID and EU (1999) *Zimbabwe Land Reform and Resettlement Programme: Inception Phase.* London: DFID.

Dorman, S. (2001) 'NGOs and State in Zimbabwe: Implications for Civil Society Theory', in B. Beckman *et al., Civil Society and Authoritarianism in the Third World.*

Draft NGO Bill (2004). Harare: Government of Zimbabwe.

EISA (2008) *Report on 2008 Harmonised Zimbabwe Elections.* Johannesburg: EISA.

Ellert, H. (1989) *The Rhodesian Front War.* Gweru: Mambo Press.

ESC (1997) *Report of a Workshop on Electoral Reform.* Harare: ESC.

European Union Election Observation Mission (2000) *Report on Parliamentary Elections in Zimbabwe, June 2000.* Brussels: EU.

Evans, P. (2010) 'Constructing the 21st Century Developmental State: Potentialities and Pitfalls', in O. Edigheji (ed.), *Constructing a Democratic Developmental State in South Africa: Potentials and Challenges.* Pretoria: HSRC.

Fanon, F. (1965) *The Wretched of the Earth.* London: Penguin Books.

FAO and WFP (2008) *Zimbabwe: Crop and Food Security Assessment.* Rome: FAO.

FCTZ (2001) *Baseline study of Chihwiti and Gambuli Informal Settlements.* Harare: FCTZ.

_____(2002) *Assessment of the Impact of the Land Reform Programme on Farm Worker Livelihoods.* Harare: FCTZ.

Francis, D. (ed.) (2005) *Civil Militia: Africa's Intractable Security Menace?* Aldershot: Ashgate Publishing.

Gaidzanwa, R. (1999) *Voting with Their Feet: Migrant Zimbabwean Nurses and Doctors in the Era of Structural Adjustment.* Uppsala: NAI.

General Agricultural and Plantation Workers' Union (GAPWUZ) (2010) *If Something is Wrong.* Report for GAPWUZ by the Research and Advocacy Unit (RAU) and Justice for Agriculture (JAG). Harare.

GAPWUZ and JAG (2009) *Reckless Tragedy.* Harare: JAG.

Gibbon, P. (1995) *Structural Adjustment and the Working Poor in Zimbabwe.* Uppsala: NAI.

Global Political Agreement (GPA) (2008). Harare: Government Printer.

Gono, G. (2008) *Zimbabwe's Casino Economy*. Harare: Zimbabwe Publishing House.

Gordon, D. (2004) 'Development Strategy in Zimbabwe: Assessment and Prospects', in M. Schatzberg (ed.), *The Political Economy of Zimbabwe*. New York: Praeger.

Government of Zambia (1976) *Report of the Special International Commission on the Assassination of Herbert Wiltshire Chitepo*. Lusaka: Government of Zambia.

Government of Zimbabwe (1981) 'Growth with Equity: an economic policy statement'. Harare: Government Printer.

— (1991) 'Framework for Economic Reform 1991-95'. Harare: Government Printer.

— (1986) 'First Five-year National Development Plan, 1986-1990'. Harare: Government Printer.

— (1998) 'Zimbabwe: Programme for Economic and Social Transformation (ZIMPREST)'. Harare: Government Printer.

— (2005) 'Response to the UN Special Envoy's Report on Operation Murambatsvina'. Harare: Government Printer.

Government of Zimbabwe and United Nations (2004) *Zimbabwe Millennium Development Goals: 2004 Progress Report*. Harare: Government Printer.

Hamblet, W. (2009) '"Civilisation" and the Myth of African "Savagery"', *Pambazuka*, Issue 457.

Hamilton, K. (2003) 'Migration and Development: Blind Faith and Hard-to-Find Facts'. Washington: Migration Policy Institute.

Hammar, A. (2003) 'The Making and Unma(s)king of Local Government in Zimbabwe', in A. Hammar, B. Raftopoulos and S. Jensen (eds), *Zimbabwe's Unfinished Business: Rethinking Land, State and Nation in the Context of Crisis*. Harare: Weaver Press.

Hammar, A. and B. Raftopoulos (2003) 'Zimbabwe's Unfinished Business: Rethinking Land, State and Nation', in A. Hammar, B. Raftopoulos and S. Jensen (eds), *Zimbabwe's Unfinished Business: Rethinking Land, State and Nation in the Context of Crisis*. Harare: Weaver Press.

Helen Suzman Foundation (2000) *Political Opinion in Zimbabwe 2000*. Johannesburg: H.S. Foundation.

Herbst, J. (1990) *State Politics in Zimbabwe*. Harare: University of Zimbabwe Publications.

Hilsum, L. (2005) 'Re-enter the Dragon: China's mission to Africa', *Review of African Political Economy*, vol. 32.

Hlatshwayo, B. (1998) 'Making a Constitution: Background and Lessons from Uganda and Kenya', *Journal of Social Change,* no. 45.

Holderness, H. (1985) *Lost Chance: Southern Rhodesia, 1945-1958.* Harare: Zimbabwe Publishing House.

Human Rights Watch (HRW) (2008a) *All Over Again: Human Rights Abuses and Flawed Electoral Conditions in Zimbabwe's Coming General Elections.* New York: HRW.

— (2008b) *'Bullets For Each of You': State-sponsored Violence since Zimbabwe's March 29 Elections.* New York: HRW.

— (2009) *Diamonds in the Rough: Human Rights Abuses in the Marange Diamond Fields of Zimbabwe.* New York: HRW.

Ignatieff, M. (1994) *Blood and Belonging: Journeys into the New Nationalism.* Oxford: Blackwell.

International Bar Association (IBA) (2007) *Partisan Policing: an Obstacle to Human Rights and Democracy in Zimbabwe.* London: IBA.

International Crisis Group (ICG) (2005) *Zimbabwe's Operation Murambatsvina: The Tipping Point?* ICG Africa Report No. 97.

— (2004) *Blood and Soil: Land, Politics and Conflict Prevention in Zimbabwe and South Africa.* ICG Africa Report No. 85.

International Fund for Agricultural Development (IFAD) (2007) *Sending Money Home.* Rome: IFAD.

International Labour Organization (ILO) (2009) *Truth, Reconciliation and Justice in Zimbabwe: Report of a Commission of Enquiry.* Geneva: ILO.

International Monetary Fund (IMF) (2007) *Central Bank Quasi-fiscal Losses and High Inflation in Zimbabwe.* Washington: IMF.

— (2010) *Zimbabwe: Challenges and Policy Options after Hyper-inflation.* Washington: IMF.

Jones, J. (2010) '"Nothing is Straight in Zimbabwe": The Rise of the Kukiya-kiya Economy 2000-2008', *Journal of Southern African Studies,* vol. 36 no.2.

Kaarsholm, P. (2006) 'States of Failure, Societies in Collapse? Understandings of violent conflict in Africa', in P. Kaarsholm (ed.), *Violence, Political Culture and Development in Africa.* Oxford: James Currey.

Kadhani, X. (1986) 'The Economy: Issues, Problems and Prospects', in I. Mandaza (ed.), *Zimbabwe: The Political Economy of Transition.* Dakar: Codesria.

Kanyenze, G. (2004) 'The Zimbabwe Economy, 1980-2003: a ZCTU Perspective', in D. Harold-Barry (ed.), *Zimbabwe: The Past is the Future.* Harare: Weaver Press.

— (2009) *Labour Markets and the Rebuilding of Human Capital.* Working Paper Series no.3. Harare: UNDP.

Kanyenze G., P. Chitambara, T. Kondo and J. Martens (eds) (2011) *Beyond the Enclave.* Harare: Weaver Press.

Karumbidza, J. (2007) 'Win-Win Economic Cooperation: Can China save Zimbabwe's Economy?', in F. Manji and S. Marks (eds), *African Perspectives on China in Africa*. Oxford: Fahamu Books.

Keane, J. (1988) *Democracy and Civil Society*. London: Verso.

Kinsey, B., K. Deininger and J. Hoogeveen (2000) 'Productivity and Equity Impacts of Land Reform: The Case of Zimbabwe'. Unpublished paper.

Kriger, N. (1992) *Zimbabwe's Guerrilla War: Peasant Voices*. Cambridge: Cambridge University Press.

— (2003) *Guerrilla Veterans in Post-war Zimbabwe: Symbolic and Violent Politics, 1980-1897*. Cambridge: Cambridge University Press.

— (2005) 'Zanu PF Strategies in General Elections 1980-2000'. *African Affairs*, vol. 104/144.

LeBas, A. (2005) *Polarisation and Party Development: Capturing Constituencies in Democratizing Africa*. PhD thesis, Columbia University.

Lee, M. and K. Colvard (eds) (2003) *Unfinished Business: The Land Crisis in Southern Africa*. Pretoria: Africa Institute of South Africa.

Lodge, T. (2004) 'Quiet diplomacy in Zimbabwe: a case study of South Africa in Africa'. Paper delivered to the African Studies Centre, Leiden.

Luebker, M. (2008) *Employment, Unemployment and Informality in Zimbabwe*. Harare: ILO.

Mackie, J. and T. Lehtinen (2003) *Implementing the Political Dimensions of the Cotonou Agreement: EU Political Dialogue and Consultation with Zimbabwe*. Maastricht: ECDPM.

Magaisa, T. (2011) 'Constitutionality versus Constitutionalism: Lessons for Zimbabwe's Constitutional Reform Process', *Open Space*, Issue 1.

Magaramombe, G. and W. Chambati (2008) 'The Abandoned Question: Farm Workers', in S. Moyo, K. Helliker and T. Murisa (eds), *Contested Terrain: Land Reform and Civil Society in Contemporary Zimbabwe*. Pietermaritzburg: S and S Publishers.

Magunha, F., A. Bailey and L. Cliffe (2009) *Remittance Strategies of Zimbabweans in Northern England*. Policy Brief, School of Geography, University of Leeds.

Makina, D. (2007) *Survey of Profile of Migrant Zimbabweans in South Africa: A Pilot Study*. Johannesburg: IDASA.

— (2010) 'Zimbabwe in Johannesburg', in J. Crush and D. Tevera (eds), *Zimbabwe's Exodus*.

Makina, D. and G. Kanyenze (2010) *The Potential Contribution of the Zimbabwe Diaspora to Economic Recovery*. Harare: UNDP.

Makumbe, J. and D. Compagnon (2000) *Behind the Smokescreen: The Politics of Zimbabwe's 1995 General Elections*. Harare: University of Zimbabwe Publications.

Makumbe, J. and B. Raftopoulos (2000) *NGOs, the State and Politics in Zimbabwe*.

Harare: SAPES.

Mandaza, I. (ed.) (1986) *Zimbabwe: The Political Economy of Transition, 1980-1986.* Dakar: Codesria.

Mandaza, I. and L. Sachikonye (eds) (1991) *The One-Party State and Democracy: The Zimbabwe Debate.* Harare: SAPES.

Maphosa, F. (2010) 'Transnationalism and Undocumented Migration Between Rural Zimbabwe and South Africa', in J. Crush and D. Tevera (eds), *Zimbabwe's Exodus.*

Mass Public Opinion Institute (MPOI) and Afrobarometer (2006) 'Support for Democracy and Democratic Institutions', *Afrobarometer Briefing Paper,* no.27.

Mass Public Opinion Institute and Freedom House (2009) *Public Attitudes towards Transition in Zimbabwe.* Washington: Freedom House.

Masunungure, E. (2000) 'Political Culture and Democratic Governance in Zimbabwe'. Unpublished paper.

— (2004) 'Travails of Opposition Politics in Zimbabwe since Independence', in D. Harold-Barry (ed.), *Zimbabwe: The Past is the Future.* Harare: Weaver Press.

— (2009) 'A Militarised Election: The 27 June Presidential Run-off', in E. Masunungure (ed.), *Defying the Winds of Change: Zimbabwe's 2008 Elections.* Harare: Konrad Adenauer Foundation and Weaver Press.

Matahwa, O. (2007) 'China and Zimbabwe: Is there a Future?', *Africa Files,* vol. 6.

Mavhinga, D. (2011) 'The Inclusive Government: Milestones and Millstones', *Open Space,* Issue 1.

Mbetu R. and N. Musekiwa (2004) 'Farm Labour Conditions in the Post-land Reform Era'. Harare: FCTZ.

McCandless, E. and E. Pajibo (2003) 'Between Perception and Reality: Are NGOs Really making a Difference?' Harare: MWENGO.

McGregor, J. (2010) 'Between Obligation, Profit and Shame: Zimbabwean Migrants and the UK Care Industry', in J. Crush and D. Tevera (eds), *Zimbabwe's Exodus.*

McKinley, D. T. (2004) 'South African Foreign Policy towards Zimbabwe', *Review of African Political Economy,* vol. 31.

Meredith, M. (2002) *Robert Mugabe: Power, Plunder and Tyranny in Zimbabwe.* Johannesburg: Jonathan Ball.

Mhanda, W. (2011) *Dzino: Memories of a Freedom Fighter.* Harare: Weaver Press.

Ministry of Finance (2003) 'Budget Statement, 2003'. Harare: Government Printer.

Ministry of Foreign Affairs (2010) 'Zimbabwe's Foreign Policy'. Harare: Government Printer.

Ministry of Labour, Public Service and Social Welfare (1995) 'Poverty Assessment Study Survey'. Harare: Government Printer.

Mkandawire, T. (2010) 'From Maladjusted States to Democratic Developmental States in Africa', in E. Edigheji (ed.), *Constructing a Democratic Developmental State in South Africa*. Pretoria: HSRC.

Moore, D. (2010) 'Liberation Movements and Democracy in Africa: Beyond the Easy Answers', *Open Space*, Issue 2.

Moore, D. and S. Mawowa (2010) 'Mbimbos, Zvipamuzis and Primitive Accumulation in Zimbabwe's Violent Mineral Economy: Crisis, Chaos and the State', in V. Padayachee (ed.), *The Political Economy of Africa*. London: Routledge.

Movement for Democratic Change (MDC) (1999) *Constitution*. Harare: MDC.

Moyo, J. (1992) *Voting for Democracy: Electoral Politics in Zimbabwe*. Harare: University of Zimbabwe Publications.

Moyo, S. (1995) *The Land Question in Zimbabwe*. Harare: SAPES.

— (2001) 'The Land Occupation Movement and Democratisation in Zimbabwe: Contradictions of Neo-liberalism', *Millennium*, vol. 30 no. 2.

— (2007) 'Emerging Land Tenure Issues in Zimbabwe'. Harare: AIAS.

Moyo, S. et al. (2009) 'Fast Track Land Reform Baseline Survey in Zimbabwe: trends and tendencies 2005-06'. Harare: AIAS.

Muchena, D. (2011) 'Forgive us our debts: The Albatross around Zimbabwe's Neck', *Open Space*, Issue 1.

Mudenge, S. (2002) 'Statement to the SADC Task Force Ministers'. Harare.

Mugabe, R. (1989) 'The Unity Accord: Its Promise for the Future', in C. Banana (ed.), *Turmoil and Tenacity*. Harare: College Press.

Munando, E. (2011) 'Women's Participation in Politics', in D. Kaulemu (ed.), *Political Participation in Zimbabwe*. Harare: AFCAST.

Musekiwa, N. (2007) 'Local Governance', in L. Sachikonye *et al.*, *Consolidating Democratic Governance in Southern Africa: Zimbabwe*. Johannesburg: EISA.

NANGO (2002) 'NANGO Code of Conduct'. Mimeo.

National Alliance for Good Governance (NAGG) (2000) 'Constitution'. Harare: NAGG.

National Constitutional Assembly (NCA) (1998) *Newsletter*, vol. 1 no.1.

— (1999) *Agenda*, vol. 2 no. 1.

— (2009) 'Fighting for a New Constitution: Human Rights Violations experienced by Female Members of National Constitutional Assembly'.

Harare: Research and Advocacy Unit.

National Democratic Institute (NDI) (2000) 'Report of the International Pre-Election Observation Delegation to the Zimbabwean Parliamentary Elections'. Harare: NDI.

Ncube, W. (1991) 'Constitutionalism, Democracy and Political Practice in Zimbabwe', in I. Mandaza and L. Sachikonye (eds), *The One-Party State and Democracy: The Zimbabwe Debate.* Harare: SAPES.

Ndlela, D. (1986) 'Problems of Industrialisation, Structural and Policy Issues', in I. Mandaza (ed.), *Zimbabwe: the Political Economy of Transition, 1980-1986.* Dakar: Codesria.

Ndlovu-Gatsheni, S. (2010) *The Zimbabwean Nation-State Project: A Historical Diagnosis of Identity- and Power-Based Conflicts in a Postcolonial State.* Uppsala: NAI.

Ndlovu-Gatsheni, S. and W. Willem (2009) 'Making Sense of Cultural Nationalism and the Politics of Commemoration under the Third Chimurenga', *Journal of Southern African Studies,* vol. 35 no. 4.

Ndulo, B. (2000) 'Political Parties and Democracy in Zambia'. Paper prepared for the IDEA-SADC conference, *Towards Sustainable Democracy in Southern Africa.* Gaborone: IDEA.

Nkomo, J. (2001) *Nkomo: The Story of my Life.* Harare: SAPES.

Nugent, P. (2010) 'Mapping the African State', *New Left Review,* no. 63.

Nyagumbo, M. (1980) *With the People: An Autobiography from the Zimbabwe Struggle.* Harare: Graham Publishing.

Nyarota, G. (2005) *Against the Grain.* Cape Town: Zebra Press.

Overseas Development Administration (ODA) (1996) *Report of the ODA Land Appraisal Mission to Zimbabwe.* London: ODA.

Open Society Initiative for Southern Africa (OSISA), Open Society Institute (OSI), Bellevue/NYU Programme (2007) '"We have degrees in violence": A Report on Torture and Human Rights Abuses in Zimbabwe'. New York: OSISA, OSI and Bellevue/NY Programme.

Osaghae, E. (2004) 'Making Democracy Work in Africa: From the Institutional to the Substantive', *Journal of African Elections,* vol. 3, no. 1.

Palmer, R. (1977) *Land and Racial Domination in Rhodesia.* London: Heinemann.

Pan African Parliament (PAP) (2008) 'Report on the 2008 Zimbabwe Election'. Midrand: PAP.

Pasura, D. (2010) 'Regendering the Zimbabwean Diaspora in Britain', in J. Crush and D. Tevera (eds), *Zimbabwe's Exodus.*

Patel, H. (1985) 'No Master, No Mortgage, No Sale: The Foreign Policy of Zimbabwe'. Nairobi: Centre for Research, Documentation and University

Exchanges.

— (2006) 'Zimbabwe's Foreign Policy: a conversation', *The Round Table*, vol. 95.

Paxton, R. (2004) *The Anatomy of Fascism*. London: Penguin Books.

Raftopoulos, B. (1999) 'Problematising Nationalism in Zimbabwe: A Historiographical Review', *Zambezia*, vol. 26 no. 2.

— (2000) 'Civil Society, Governance and Human Development in Zimbabwe'. Paper prepared for the Poverty Reduction Forum, Harare.

— (2006) 'Reflections on Opposition Politics in Zimbabwe: The Politics of the Movement for Democratic Change', in B. Raftopoulos and K. Alexander (eds), *Reflections on Democratic Politics in Zimbabwe*. Cape Town: Institute for Justice and Reconciliation.

— (2006) 'The Zimbabwean Crisis and the Challenges of the Left', *Journal of Southern African Studies*, vol. 32 no. 2.

Ranger, T. (1995) *Are We Not Also Men? The Samkange Family and African Politics in Zimbabwe*. Harare: Baobab Books; London: James Currey.

— (ed.) (2003) *The Historical Dimensions of Democracy and Human Rights in Zimbabwe*. Harare: University of Zimbabwe Publications.

Reeler. T. (2004) 'Sticks and Stones, Skeletons and Ghosts', in D. Harold-Barry (ed.), *Zimbabwe: The Past is the Future*. Harare: Weaver Press.

— (2008) 'Subliminal Terror? Human Rights and Torture in Zimbabwe in 2008'. Report prepared for Centre for the Study of Violence and Reconciliation, Johannesburg.

Rukobo, A. (1991) 'Misplaced Emphasis in the Democracy Debate', in I. Mandaza and L. Sachikonye (eds), *The One-Party State and Democracy*.

Rupiya, M. (2004) 'Contextualising the Military in Zimbabwe between 1999 and 2004 and Beyond', in B. Raftopoulos and T. Savage (eds), *Zimbabwe: Injustice and Political Reconciliation*. Harare: Weaver Press.

Rutherford, B. (2001) *Working on the Margins: Black Workers, White Farmers in Postcolonial Zimbabwe*, Harare: Weaver Press.

Sachikonye, L. (1993) 'Structural Adjustment, State and Organized Labour in Zimbabwe', in P. Gibbon (ed.), *Social Change and Economic Reform in Africa*. Uppsala: NAI.

— (1996) 'The Nation-State Project and Conflict in Zimbabwe', in A. Olukoshi and L. Laakso (eds), *Challenges to the Nation-State in Africa*. Uppsala: NAI.

— (2000) 'An Audit of the Zimbabwe Electoral System', in H. Kotze and B. Rasch (eds), *Elections and Democracy in Southern Africa*. Oslo: Norwegian Institute of Human Rights.

— (2001) 'The Institutional Development of Unions in Zimbabwe', in B.

Raftopoulos and L. Sachikonye (eds), *Striking Back*. Harare: Weaver Press.

— (2003) 'The Situation of Commercial Farm Workers after Land Reform in Zimbabwe'. Report prepared for the Farm Community Trust of Zimbabwe (FCTZ), Harare.

— (2004) 'Land Reform and Farm Workers', in D. Harold-Barry (ed.), *Zimbabwe: the Past is the Future*. Harare: Weaver Press.

— (2005) 'The Land is the Economy: Revisiting Zimbabwe's Land Question', *African Security Review*, vol. 14 no. 3.

— (2007) *Diamonds in Zimbabwe: A Situational Analysis*. Johannesburg: OSISA.

— (2010) 'Remittances, Informalisation and Dispossession in Urban Zimbabwe', in J. Crush and D. Tevera (eds), *Zimbabwe's Exodus*.

— (2011) *When a State turns on its Citizens*. Johannesburg: Jacana Media.

Sachikonye, L. and S. Bracking (2006) 'Remittances, Poverty Reduction and the Informalisation of Household Wellbeing in Zimbabwe'. Global Poverty Research Group Working Paper no. 45.

— (2009) *Development Finance, Private and Public Sectors in Zimbabwe: Sustainability or Odious Debt?* Brooks World Poverty Institute Working Paper no. 84.

Sachikonye, L., S. Chawatama, C. Mangongera, N. Musekiwa and C. Ndoro (2007) *Consolidating Democratic Governance in Southern Africa: Zimbabwe*. Johannesburg: EISA.

Sachikonye, L. and O. Zishiri (1999) 'Tenure Security for Farm Workers in Zimbabwe'. Friedrich-Ebert-Stiftung Working Paper no. 27.

Saki, O. (2010) 'Linking Political Participation, Democracy and Human Rights', in D. Kaulemu (ed.), *Political Participation in Zimbabwe*. Harare: AFCAST.

Salih, M. (2003) *African Political Parties: Evolution, Institutionalisation and Governance*. London: Pluto Press.

SALO (2009) 'Country Focus Paper: South Africa's Relations with Zimbabwe'. Cape Town: SALO.

Scarnecchia, T. (2008) *The Urban Roots of Democracy and Political Violence in Zimbabwe*. Rochester, NY: University of Rochester Press.

Scoones, I., N. Marongwe, B. Mavedzenge, J. Mahenehene, F. Murimbarimba, and C. Sukume (2010) *Zimbabwe's Land Reform: Myths and Realities*. Oxford: James Currey; Harare: Weaver Press; Johannesburg: Jacana Media.

Sibanda, E. (2007) *The Zimbabwe African People's Union 1961-1987: A Political History of Insurgency in Southern Rhodesia*. Trenton: Africa World Press.

Sithole, M. (1986) 'The General Elections 1979-1985', in I. Mandaza (ed.), *Zimbabwe: the Political Economy of Transition*.

(1999) *Zimbabwe: Struggles within the Struggle*. Salisbury: Rujeko Publishers.

Sithole, N. (1958) *African Nationalism*. Oxford: Oxford University Press.

Smith, I. (1997) *The Great Betrayal*. London: Blake Publishing.

Solidarity Peace Trust (SPT) (2003) 'National Youth Service Training – "shaping youths in a truly Zimbabwean manner"'. Durban: SPT.

— (2007) 'Destructive Engagement: Violence, Mediation and Politics in Zimbabwe'. Durban: SPT.

— (2008) 'Desperately Seeking Sanity: What Prospects for a New Beginning in Zimbabwe?' Durban: SPT.

Southern African Development Community (SADC) (1998) *Regional Human Development Report*. Harare: UNDP.

— (2004) 'Principles and Guidelines governing Democratic Elections'. Port Louis: SADC.

Stoneman, C. (1988) *Zimbabwe's Prospects: Issues of Race, Class, State and Capital in Zimbabwe*. London: Macmillan.

Stoneman, C. (1989) 'The World Bank and the IMF in Zimbabwe', in B. Campbell and J. Loxley (eds), *Structural Adjustment in Africa*. London: Macmillan.

Suttner. R. (2010) 'Violence: necessity or virtue?' *Mail and Guardian*. 14 May 2010.

Tekere, E. (2007) *A Lifetime of Struggle*. Harare: SAPES.

Tendi, B. (2008) 'Patriotic History and Public Intellectuals Critical of Power', *Journal of Southern African Studies*, vol 34 no. 2.

Tengende, N. (1994) *Workers, Students and the Struggles for Democracy: State-Civil Society Relations in Zimbabwe*. PhD thesis, Roskilde University.

Tibaijuka, A. (2005) 'Report of the Fact-Finding Mission to Zimbabwe to assess the Scope and Impact of Operation Murambatsvina'. New York: United Nations.

Transparency International (2010) *Corruption Perceptions Index*. Berlin: TI.

UNDP (2002) *Land Reform and Resettlement: assessment and suggested framework for the future* Harare: UNDP.

— (2008) *Comprehensive Economic Recovery in Zimbabwe*. Harare: UNDP.

United Nations Economic Commission for Africa (UNECA) (2010) *Elections and the Management of Diversity in Africa*. Addis Ababa: UNECA.

UNICEF (2009) 'Zimbabwe's education crisis worsens'. Harare: UNICEF.

— 'Reviving health services could close gaps in Zimbabwe'. Harare: UNICEF.

Utete, C. (2003) 'Presidential Land Review Committee (Utete Report)'. Harare: Government Printer.

Verba, S. (1965) 'Comparative Culture', in L. Pye and S. Verba (eds), *Political Culture and Political Development*. Princeton: Princeton University Press.

Weitzer, R. (1984) 'Continuities in the Politics of State Security in Zimbabwe', in M. Schatzberg (ed.), *The Political Economy of Zimbabwe*. New York: Praeger.

Werbner, R. (1995) 'In Memory: A Heritage of War in Southwestern Zimbabwe', in N. Bhebe and T. Ranger (eds), *Society in Zimbabwe's Liberation War*. Harare: University of Zimbabwe Publications.

Women of Zimbabwe Arise (WOZA) (2007) *Women of Zimbabwe Arise*. Bulawayo: WOZA.

— (2008) *The Traumatic Consequences of Gross Human Rights Violations suffered by WOZA Women*. Bulawayo: WOZA.

World Bank (1995a) *Zimbabwe: achieving shared growth*. Washington: World Bank.

— (1995b) *Zimbabwe: performance audit report*. Washington: World Bank.

Zanu-Ndonga (1979) *Constitution*. Harare: Zanu Ndonga.

Zanu-PF (1999) *Constitution*. Harare: Zanu PF.

Zimbabwe Congress of Trade Unions (ZCTU) (1996) *Beyond ESAP*. Harare: ZCTU.

Zimbabwe Electoral Support Network (ZESN) (2002) 'The Zimbabwe Presidential Election, March 2002'. Harare: ZESN.

— (2008) 'Report on the Zimbabwe March 29 2008 Harmonized and June Runoff Elections'. Harare: ZESN.

Zimbabwe Human Development Reports (ZHDR) (1998, 1999, 2000, 2003) Harare: Poverty Reduction Forum.

Zimbabwe Human Rights NGO Forum (1999) 'A Consolidated Report on Food Riots 19-23 January 1998'. Harare: ZHR NGO Forum.

— (2000a) 'Who is Responsible? A preliminary analysis of pre-election violence in Zimbabwe'. Harare: ZHR NGO Forum.

— (2000b) 'A Report on Post-election Violence'. Harare: ZHR NGO Forum.

— (2000c) 'Organized Violence and Torture in Zimbabwe in 2000.' Harare: ZHR NGO Forum.

— (2001) 'Who was Responsible? Alleged Perpetrators and their Crimes during the 2000 Parliamentary Election Period'. Harare: ZHR NGO Forum.

— (2006a) 'Exploring Transitional Justice Options in Contemporary Zimbabwe'. Harare: ZHR NGO Forum.

— (2006b) 'Who Guards the Guards? Violations by Law Enforcement Agencies'. Harare: ZHR NGO Forum.

— (2007) 'Their Words Condemn Them: The language of Violence, Intolerance and Despotism in Zimbabwe'. Harare: ZHR NGO Forum.

— (2009a) 'Only Bruises on the Soles of their Feet: Torture and Falanga in Zimbabwe'. Harare: ZHR NGO Forum.

— (2009b) 'Taking Transitional Justice to the People: Outreach Report'. Harare: ZHR NGO Forum.

Zimbabwe Institute (ZI) (2004) *Playing with Fire*. Cape Town: ZI.

— (2008) *The Security-Military Business Complex and the Transition in Zimbabwe*. Cape Town: ZI.

Zimbabwe Peace Project (ZPP) (2008) 'Post-March 29th 2008 Elections Violence, Report 1'. Harare: ZPP.

Zinyama, L. and D. Tevera (2002) 'Zimbabweans Who Move: Perspectives on International Migration in Zimbabwe'. SAMP Migration Policy Series no. 25.